At Home and in the Field

At Home and in the Field

ETHNOGRAPHIC ENCOUNTERS
IN ASIA AND THE PACIFIC ISLANDS

Edited by
Suzanne S. Finney
Mary Mostafanezhad
Guido Carlo Pigliasco
Forrest Wade Young

University of Hawai'i Press
Honolulu

20 19 18 17 16   6 5 4 3 2

Library of Congress Cataloging-in-Publication Data

At home and in the field : ethnographic encounters in Asia and the Pacific islands /
[edited by] Suzanne S. Finney, Mary Mostafanezhad, Guido Carlo Pigliasco,
Forrest Wade Young.
     pages cm
  Includes bibliographical references and index.
   ISBN 978-0-8248-4759-3 (cloth) — ISBN 978-0-8248-5379-2 (alk. paper)
1. Ethnology—Fieldwork—Asia. 2. Ethnology—Fieldwork—Oceania. I. Finney,
Suzanne S., editor. II. Mostafanezhad, Mary, editor. III. Pigliasco, Guido Carlo,
editor. IV. Young, Forrest Wade, editor.
  GN346.A8 2015
  305.80072'3—dc23

             2014045427

Printed by Maple Press

Contents

PART 9. DEEP ENCOUNTERS: WORLDVIEW, RELIGION, SPIRITUAL PRACTICES

Preface

Mulling the Intimacies of Dislocation

Christine R. Yano

Reading through these various ethnographic encounters presents a surfeit of riches. One gets a strongly visceral sense of the field experience—the wafting aromas of meals cooking, the adrenalin of literally running for one's life, the overheard sounds of a neighborhood without walls. One also gets an appreciation for the toll of insights derived through the challenges of the unfamiliar at its many stages and forms of knowing. These musings from the field make every effort not to romanticize, but to give readers substantive reality checks from those who have been there and done that. In short, the chapters in this volume instruct us that fieldwork is always challenging and sometimes arduous in ways that are unexpected. But it is in the unexpected that the rewards lie.

In fact, this is why we, as scholars, do fieldwork. We are part traveler, part bookworm, part misfit (sometimes in our home cultures, more so than in our host cultures). We share the faith of our disciplines—here primarily anthropology, but also ethnic studies, geography, linguistics, Pacific Islands studies, political science, and even history and philosophy—that something might be gained by being there, challenging our preconceptions, taking us out of our comfort zones into the unknown and presumed rewards of discomfiture. Fieldwork typically reveals as much about ourselves as individuals as it reveals something about the group of people or place we are studying. But "reveal" may be too loaded a term. This suggests that there is a body of knowledge waiting to be uncovered by the researcher through the process of fieldwork. This picture does not give enough credit to the interaction itself—one that is shaped as much by the fieldworker as by the field. Both the fieldworker and the field transform each other in the process.

At times as researchers we may count things, measure distances, and make charts. These efforts are important, but may reveal more about our assumptions than about the places we study. Indeed, just as often as not, we ponder the uncountable, the immeasurable, the unchartable. We work to dream in others' languages, move our bodies the way they do, don the mask that lets us believe we may be able to pass as native to some small degree. And we have faith that the dreaming may disrupt our lives in ways that we can begin to understand. We go to the field armed with high hopes and fears for our dislocation. We trust the encounters, revel in the anecdotes, and sometimes remember to write them down. These constitute data, even if they arrive on our doorstep unformed and unprocessed. Call them gifts of fieldwork, the small and large insights that may come to us unawares. Of course we strive to be as aware as possible. But as so many of these field-workers recount, awareness may be a conceit of post-fieldwork reflec-tions, rather than a research strategy that guides the encounter. Would the National Science Foundation fund a research methodology based in "serendipity"? Probably not. But any fieldworker understands the limits of our best-laid plans. We proffer humility at the doorstep of the encounter.

Importantly, these chapters reveal other kinds of fieldworkers than the ones I describe above. They are conducting fieldwork at home, fully realizing that different degrees of home-ness may yet beg dislocation. "Indigenous," "insider" research, "homework"—what they add to our discus-sion of fieldwork lies in the complex relationships of familiarity that they bring to research. Their ready-made, deep-seated obligations and affilia-tions are ones that other fieldworkers may accrue over time. Thus, the continuum stretches across boundaries of insider–outsider, particularly as the outsider becomes more and more an insider, or is allowed particu-lar access to where few insiders may be allowed. Doing ethnography at home may be no more or less discomfiting, only differently so, from doing fieldwork elsewhere. Further, even amid what looks like familiarity lurks the unfamiliar—the insider language of a subculture, the hidden club-house within an urban setting, the coded visual cues of membership. Add to this mix the confusion when a fieldworker looks like a local, but is not. This situation points up the significance and implications of identities—perceived, performed, and accrued over time. The hallmark of fieldwork lies not so much on which side of the fence one takes up temporary residence, but in the continual and deliberate attentiveness of dislocation that may yield insights.

The relations of fieldwork incur deep obligations. And these obligations are well expressed in these various chapters. The obligations are not only to those individuals who have shared their lives but also to the field itself, held more broadly, as a site of lasting engagement and even advocacy. Here the morality of fieldwork, the ethics of asking people to give—frequently and deeply—brings research to its knees. These are not cut-and-dried things, but delicate negotiations that tug hard at our consciences.

Finally, one must ask, what of this might be particular to the Asia and Pacific Islands regions from which this volume emanates? Certainly, there is much shared with the processes of fieldwork in any number of sites. But consider these as regions that have held long relationships with fieldworkers (and colonists and corporations), developing in the process particular attitudes toward being studied (and ruled). In many cases, these are regions imagined by outsiders as sites of plenty. Their cultures (particularly gendered as women) have often been romanticized as paradisical and alluring, and thus the destination of tourists. Fieldworkers in some of these areas may have to define themselves and their purposes in contradistinction to journalists and travel writers. Furthermore, these are regions that have yielded their own share of researchers—often trained abroad—actively decolonizing first- and third-world relations. Many of these regions possess their own universities that are in extended conversation with other institutions of higher learning globally. The result is a complex mix of power relations (the researched and the researchers, as well as the researched researcher) filled with ambiguities and ambivalences.

In fact, these ambiguities and ambivalences provide the critical texture of field encounters in Asia and the Pacific Islands. Each encounter meshes with a long history of encounters—imagined and otherwise, symbolic and literal—that provide a significant backdrop to the chapters in this volume. Led by a new generation of scholars in the field, this collection has its value in the tapestry of multiple disclosures of dislocation in the Asia-Pacific encounter. These disclosures weave a multidimensional portrait of intimacies that lead to insight. The profundity of the anecdote beckons. Awash in bodies, sentiment, responsibilities, and reciprocity, these stories beg our close and critical attention.

Introduction

Suzanne S. Finney, Mary Mostafanezhad,
Guido Carlo Pigliasco, and Forrest Wade Young

Thought provoking, sometimes humorous, the ethnographic encounters described in this anthology should resonate with many readers and provide valuable talking points for students and scholars to explore the human diversity that makes the study of ourselves and each other simultaneously rewarding and challenging. These stories will be of particular value to anyone with an interest in the cultural and social worlds, as well as global conditions of peoples of the Asia and Pacific Islands region.

Ethnography is a research method used by social scientists to examine how everyday and local practices are reflective of broader cultural, economic, environmental, and political trends. Contemporary fieldwork and ethnographic writing, as noted by leading anthropologists George Marcus and James D. Faubion (2009), "is not what it used to be." The ethnographic updates (post-2000) featured here highlight new forms of writing and research prevalent in twenty-first-century ethnography. Ethnographers now investigate subjects such as the laboratories of scientific communities and the "virtual worlds" of cyberspace that challenge previous norms of what constitutes appropriate topics of ethnographic research. This anthology includes writings on digital social networks in Papua New Guinea and robotics communities in Japan that show ethnography adapting to twenty-first-century human lives.

Emerging trends in ethnographic writing now highlight autoethnography, narrative, and politically engaged participant observation. Moreover, ethnographers today no longer always conduct remote fieldwork, writing about peoples and issues far from their home worlds and social identities;

they conduct "homework" (Visweswaran 1994, 101; Teaiwa 2004). Homework is ethnography that directly engages with issues and identities in which the ethnographer finds political solidarity and belonging in fields at home. While twentieth-century ethnography often involved a quest for self discovery, through "the detour of the other" (see Rabinow 2007, 5), writings based in homework involve no detour. In this anthology, homework is highlighted by the work of scholars such as Hokulani K. Aikau, Lynette Hiʻilani Cruz, and Ty P. Kāwika Tengan. Their teachings about Hawaiian culture, social predicaments, and worldview derive from direct inquiries into their own genealogies and political concerns as Kānaka Maoli people indigenous to Hawaiʻi. These case studies of homework demonstrate that ethnography is a flexible methodology that can be expanded to engage in subjects and fields of inquiry of interest to scholars with postcolonial, indigenous, and minority identities that often have been excluded or marginalzed by "classic" definitions of fieldwork and ethnographic writing.

The ethnographic writings and reflections featured in this anthology illustrate that many people of the region are responding to new developments and predicaments associated with globalization. Interestingly, these stories are less often tales of transnational identity than they are narratives of cultural belonging and struggle for place. Written from a variety of academic disciplines (ethnic studies, geography, anthropology, history, linguistics, media studies, Pacific Islands studies, philosophy, political science, sociology, and tourism), the stories are organized into nine sections defined by themes commonly addressed by ethnographers. Thus, while the stories are geographically situated, the issues represented are global in scope.

This anthology is designed as an educational resource for introductory courses in Asian and Pacific Islands studies, human geography, cultural anthropology, and ethnic studies, among others. All of the authors published in this volume are affiliated with the University of Hawaiʻi, and many of the stories are written by scholars with indigenous or national identity in the region. It was inspired by our students and colleagues in the Asia and Pacific Islands region who sought geographically relevant ethnographies. We hope that the book represents a thoughtful contribution to the realization of this endeavor through the stories of ethnographic encounter that follow.

PART 1

Real Encounters

Predicaments of Ethnographic Fieldwork

(overleaf photo) The Mekong Delta region, known as Song Cuu Luong (Nine Dragons), is rich in agriculture, and abundant in tropical fruits such as papayas, milk fruit (or milk apples), mangoes, durians, longans, dragon fruit, and water coconuts. Enhancing the area, the surrounding environment is also full of beautiful tropical flowers, and is excellent for farming and fishing. Tourism and tour guides can be seen everyday in the narrow waterways that can be traversed by small boats, in an area where the mighty Mekong finally drains into the South China Sea. Photo by Carl Hefner.

Introduction

SUZANNE S. FINNEY

THE STORIES OF THIS SECTION introduce prosaic kinds of predicaments of ethnographic research: problems of various sorts that ethnographers encounter and strive to learn from, while conducting field research. As you read the stories, you will start to gain an understanding of what it means to be "in the field," and how challenging and rewarding fieldwork can be despite all its obstacles. Ethnographic fieldwork should begin to emerge from these stories as a method that can be applied not only to learn about one's research topics and fields of inquiry but also to learn, reflexively, about oneself, one's own sociocultural worlds, and the global condition.

Carl J. Hefner, Jaida Kim Samudra, and Suzanne S. Finney introduce some of the more serious problems ethnographers may encounter. In "Tempting the Nāga: Local Knowledge and Mysteries of the Mekong," Hefner reflects upon a journey along the Mekong River that he undertook to introduce students to ethnic groups and sociocultural worlds from China and Cambodia, to Laos and Vietnam. His story discusses encounters in the field that could have led to death—the most serious predicament an ethnographer can confront. Hefner highlights the ways an appreciation and respect of local cultural knowledge—a major topic of ethnography—was fundamental to surviving and thriving within the worlds of the Mekong. Samudra, while conducting multisited fieldwork on a transnational martial art in Indonesia, reflects upon actually becoming embroiled in street violence in her story, "Attacked in the Field: Encountering a Street Gang While Studying Peace in Java." Though initially traumatized, she ultimately conceives the experience as fundamental to becoming an insider within the White Crane

Silat martial-art community. In "A Question of Permission in Pohnpei" Finney reflects upon her struggles to gain local permission to conduct research from a paramount chief, *nahnmwarki,* of the island of Pohnpei, Federated States of Micronesia, despite official permission from the state government. Beyond revealing the complexities of actually carrying out research, the story illuminates some of the nuances of traditional chiefly power and cultural protocols in Pohnpei.

Lisa Humphrey and Alexander Mawyer introduce more humorous predicaments in the field. Humphrey's "An Anthropologist Behaving Badly: The Case of the Missing Watch on Waya Island, Fiji" recounts how she learned sociocultural principles of Fijian reciprocity while, ironically, lying to the community hosting her research in Waya Island, Fiji. Mawyer's "Grandmothers, Sharks, and Other Dangerous Things: Persistent Crises in Mangareva, French Polynesia," in addition to returning readers to the serious dangers of fieldwork introduced by Hefner and Samudra, reflects on the funny predicament of being perceived as a viable husband for local women in Mangareva. Mawyer, importantly, also elaborates some of the general nuanced knowledge that can be gleaned from attending to the everyday predicaments of fieldwork. His, as well as all of the other stories of this section, provide an important narrative introduction to the practice of contemporary ethnographic inquiry.

Tempting the Nāga

Local Knowledge and Mysteries of the Mekong

CARL J. HEFNER

THE MIGHTY MEKONG RIVER is one of the largest rivers of the world, and one with increasing ecological, economic, and political regional significance in Southeast Asia as local, regional, and international agents fight for its future development or conservation (Campbell 2009, 1–12). As an anthropologist specializing in Southeast Asia, it was my good fortune to be asked to teach a course in Asian Studies at the University of Hawai'i-Mānoa that would focus on the numerous ethnic groups and geography of the Mekong River—the focus of my ethnographic field research for many years. Particularly exciting was the fact that the semester-long course was to be followed by a field study that would take students enrolled in the course, several Thai professors from collaborating institutions, and me along a monthlong journey down the Mekong. Beginning our journey in Kunming, China, we would follow the mighty Mekong River as it flows through six countries all the way through to the Vietnam delta region where the river drains to the South China Sea. As professor for the course, I knew that this was to be a journey that would both enlighten and challenge the students who took the course, most of whom had never traveled through Southeast Asia.

With an array of aquatic creatures that include the world's largest freshwater fish—the giant Mekong catfish—that can weigh up to 670 pounds (Mansfield and Koh 2008, 15), and the increasingly endangered Irrawaddy dolphin (see Beasley et al. 2010), it is not hard to imagine how stories of the river abound. Powerful Nāga spirits, for example, which are said to take the bodily form of a great snake with either a single head or multiple heads (Holt 2009, 17–19), are said to dwell within and near the river depending on the

season (Hashimoto 2008, 221). In Laos, to ensure protection from malevo-
lent Nāga, sometimes water buffalo, pigs, and chickens are sacrificed (Hashimoto 2008, 228), and local festivals of increasing interest to global tourism (see Cohen 2007) continue to honor Nāga with offerings of alcohol,
cake, fruit, and rice (Hatsadong et al. 2006, 73). According to Khmer traditions, the survival of peoples of the river depends upon the goodwill of the
Nāga (Gaudes 1993, 352–353). As we began our journey we could only hope
that the Nāga would extend their goodwill to protect us as well.

Our travel, leaving from the port in Kunming, China, was orderly and
smooth, as the Chinese "fast" boats had modern instruments, and were
manned by professional boat captains who were quite capable of navigating
the fast-moving river. The river, coming out of the mountains and originating in the high mountains of Tibet, is elegant and relatively fast moving until it reaches Laos. As a group, we were all taken aback by the beauty
of the mountain slopes that surround the river, as the sights along the river
through Laos are breathtaking. As the sun rises and sets on the river, there
is a mystique and awe that seems to evoke a spiritual feeling among some
of us, reminding us that geography, culture, and the human spirit have a
connection, a kind of "power of place" (see Harm de Blij 2009). A person
traveling through Laos on the Mekong could just sense the thousands of
years of history of the region, intuitively knowing that each area was different and special. On at least one occasion, as the boat navigated the river, the
students were able to see shifting cultivation in action, as swidden farmers
were using elephants to clear trees that had been slashed from the forested
mountainside.

In the craggy mountainous regions of Laos, the Mekong is wide, in
places quite muddy, and to the casual observer, the water placid and slow
moving. However, it was obvious that there was more to this river than meets
the eye, as we could all witness swirling riverside eddies and whirlpools,
indicating that there were unpredictable currents, which through our observations proved to be treacherous to the houseboats that navigate the mighty
Mekong waters in this region. Each time we rounded a bend, we could plainly
see the splintered remains of various boat crackups, found scattered along
the rocky sides of the Mekong serving as silent reminders of the power of the
current and the inherent dangers. We all knew that there must be a tremendous amount of local cultural knowledge (see Geertz 1983) surrounding
various sites along the river, and that these wrecks were silent reminders
of the power of the currents and the force of the water.

As if we had not seen enough reminders of the forces of nature in this
area, there was another moment in time when the power of the Mekong

River was definitely shown. Jenny, an avid swimmer, personally experienced the treacherous river currents that compose the winding Mekong River as it makes its way through the mountains. In the late afternoon, as we arrived at an area known as Pakbeng in Laos, most of us made our way up the hill into our bungalows for the evening. However, now in my bungalow on the hillside, I just happened to be looking out the window, and as I glanced toward the river, Jenny had spontaneously jumped into the Mekong from a pier for a swim. Frightened for her, I began to yell to a group of our students who were walking a ways upstream along the shore. However, at first no one could hear my warning calls. Soon, Jenny was definitely in over her head, and quickly overtaken by the fast-moving Mekong currents.

Luckily, local Lao fishermen, floating in their boats near the edge of the river, had witnessed the event. As we called out in vain, Jenny was soon saved by the fishermen who floated their hand-carved wooden boats over to pick her up out of the water. Following the rescue, the fishermen began to impart local knowledge of this particular part of the river. Stunningly, the Lao fishermen began to relate that this area is known to all who live here as one of the many places of the Nāga. The locals all felt that without this knowledge you are taking huge chances, and putting your life at risk. Just around the bend, they said, there was a very dangerous current and a drop in the river toward the rocks that surely would have caused injury. That evening we all felt fortunate that all was well, and everyone had a new appreciation for the power of local knowledge that enables one to survive.

Continuing our journey, we knew one thing for sure: it would take years to acquire even a partial understanding of the regions of the river we were moving through, and in our short time there, we would only be able to grab a fleeting glimpse of local wisdom. As we proceeded in a southerly direction on the Mekong River, we had new geography to encounter, and could only hope that our journey would continue in a safe manner.

Once into Cambodia, the plan was to visit Khmer sites, then to travel by land until we got to a subsidiary of the Mekong, a river known as the Tonlé Sap that connects to Tonlé Sap Lake—the largest freshwater lake in Southeast Asia. In a great act of nature during the wet season, the Tonlé Sap River actually reverses its flow, and the lake expands from approximately one meter deep and 2,500 square kilometers to nearly ten meters deep and 15,000 square kilometers (Kummu et al. 2006, 502). For thousands of years, there has been a wealth of local knowledge of the hydrodynamics that make up the timing, duration, and volume of the seasonal flow reversal into and out of the Tonlé Sap Lake. Annual celebrations such as the Bon Om Tok (Water Festival) mark the end of the season as lake waters flow back into the river (Keskinen 2006, 466). Houseboats, which are year-round habitation for the Cambodians who make their living on this river, are seasonally towed from one area to another, based on the level of the river. As we entered the region of Lake Tonlé Sap, we were able to witness scores of fish that were kept in wells in the Cambodian houseboats. Fish were still actually living within the general confines of the lake, but captive in a wire cage within the houseboat, illustrating the ingenuity of the boat design and the people.

As we woke to a beautiful radiant sunrise on the lake, no one really knew the extent of the adventure we were about to experience. We needed to get down to two small boats that would take us for the next seven hours down the Tonlé Sap River to Phnom Penh. To get to the boats we first had to climb aboard large flatbed stake trucks that would now transfer us through the extremely muddy flats adjacent to the river. As we stood in the back of the large trucks, they shook, rattled, and rolled, at times sliding sideways through the mud, as we traveled approximately one kilometer to the river. Several of the students nearly became sick from the shaking of the trucks, and once or twice the trucks almost lost control, as if they were going to turn over. Finally arriving at the boats, we were amazed that the boats that would take us traveling on the Tonlé Sap River were so small, consisting of an outboard gasoline engine connected to a long driveshaft, and balanced on a fulcrum in the middle of the boat such that the operator could lift the propeller completely out of the water. We soon found out why this was important.

As we boarded the boats with our backpacks and bottles of water, we then embarked on a very precarious journey down the Tonlé Sap River on the way to the intersection of the Mekong and the city of Phnom Penh. We knew that there was a great deal of discussion among the drivers of the trucks and the boat operators, but since it was in Khmer, we sincerely trusted that all was going to be fine. However, we later realized that the discussion had to be about the fall of water and the lowering of the water levels in the river, as we encountered our first snag only about one and a half hours into the journey along the waterway. The small boat came abruptly to a stop, stalled on a sandbar, and with confidence the boat operator, cigarette in mouth, lifted the prop, cleared the seaweed and debris, and then rocked the boat and fully gunned the engine to shoot the boat and all of us flying off the sandbar. The boat plunged back into the water, and with a nonchalant countenance, the boat operator resumed his duties navigating the river. Within our travel group, many were beginning to ask, "will we survive hitting sandbars and debris for the next six and a half hours and arrive safely at our destination?"

When this happened a second time and we were motionless in the river, some became very worried, and the predicament became more intense. The small boat rocked in the river, as water lapped against the sides of the boat. The hot sun had been beating on us for several hours, and a few of the students were now seriously worried, as we sat baking in the hot midday sun. The question arose from one of the students, "Professor, are we gonna die here?" "No," I said with a good deal of trust and confidence, knowing in my mind that these waters had been traversed for centuries by intrepid boatmen, and with the assuredness that the locals knew their business on this river. Confident in the idea that local knowledge would pull us through, I answered, "I think you have to trust the boatmen, and their knowledge and understanding of the fluctuations in water levels of this river. We will survive with their help, as their experience and instincts about this river will be invaluable to successful navigation during this rough period."

As the afternoon was waning, the Cambodian boatmen's skill in negotiating the dangers of the river guided us to a safe landing along the shoreline of Phnom Penh. As the day ended, and the rays of the setting sun began to cast beautiful patterns over the city, I could not help but think about our journey along the mighty Mekong and the tributary, the Tonlé Sap River. Our predicaments of this eventful day were now as the shadows across the city, faded and seemingly in the distant past. I reflected on the great movement of water, the rise and fall of the great Tonlé Sap Lake and river. I pondered the greatness of the Khmer civilization, water, and the incredible knowledge of hydraulics that supported a vast civilization.

Our study tour now prepared for the next destination in our journey, the Mekong as it enters Vietnam, and we were excited to continue our quest to better understand the ethnic groups and geography of the Mekong River. Somehow, we knew that the spirit of the Nāga was protecting us and keeping us out of harm's way. Among ourselves, we began to understand how the spirits and the power of place are inextricably intertwined in local knowledge. The rich diversity of the area, the beauty of the geographical landscape, the massive movement of water, and the incredible practical, spiritual, and mystical knowledge of the people of this region were really more than any of us could take in, and we knew that the journey was, for all of us, only the beginning of a long association with this magnificent river.

An Anthropologist Behaving Badly

The Case of the Missing Watch on Waya Island, Fiji

LISA HUMPHREY

FOR AN ANTHROPOLOGIST, FEELING DISCOMFORT in the field is normal. It does not matter how eager you are to be there. You are often in a foreign (to you) place, far from your usual support networks. This is the whole point—the discomfort you feel is in fact fundamental to your fieldwork. Your task in your new surroundings is to transcend the limitations of your comfort zone and gain anthropological insights by making "the strange familiar and the familiar strange." You undertake this challenge as a privileged guest of the people among whom you are living. So you try to always be on your best behavior, responding to discomfort with grace. Sometimes you fail.

In June 2000, I began my doctoral fieldwork on Waya, a small island in the Yasawa Group, Fiji's westernmost archipelago.[1] Waya is forty kilometers (and two to four hours by boat) from Viti Levu, Fiji's largest and most populous island. About one thousand people, all ethnic Fijians, live in Waya's four coastal villages, which are connected by mountain and coastal footpaths. In 2000, there were few of the amenities that I was used to in the United States: no (nongenerator) electricity, no hot water, no regular phone service, no Internet, no cars, and no stores (except for village cooperatives selling staples like tea and flour). Waya's people and happenings were so interesting that I rarely missed those things.

I was researching how Wayans use traditional clan histories to support, and challenge, claims to chiefly titles and landownership. These are delicate matters and I was anxious not to offend. So I spent my first six months on Waya soaking up as much of the language and codes of proper behavior as I could before posing difficult questions about history, chiefs, and land. I settled in with a wonderful extended family of about ten people near the village of Nalauwaki on Waya's northern coast. This family embraced me as a member: I dined with them on Fijian staples such as fish and cassava, slept in their beautiful thatched *bure* (house), and partook in family weddings and funerals. Over time, other Wayans began to treat me as an honorary member of the island's wider network of clan-based kinship and social relationships. I knew I had passed a happy milestone when people around the island began to affectionately tease me using the names of my Fijian family's totem tree and fish. Even better, I knew how to appropriately tease back.

Still, six months into my stay on Waya, I desperately wanted a break. It was almost Christmas and I missed my family and friends back home. I was tired from the constant strain of decoding and balancing my growing number of Wayan relationships, each of which carried elaborate—and sometimes bewildering—reciprocal obligations and benefits. To make matters worse, December is summer in Fiji and the heat was suffocating. And so I lost my cool over, of all things, the loss of a beat-up old watch.

It all began one afternoon when I went with a few Nalauwaki village women to take a refreshing dip at Rurugu, a stream just outside the village. After we returned to Nalauwaki, I discovered that a watch I had taken off and stowed before my swim was missing. The items that had been with the watch—backpack, money, and camera—were all still there. I felt like I had been punched in the gut. But why? The watch was old, inexpensive, and had recently started to get on my nerves. The wristband stank from months of dried sweat. Worse, the alarm function had become resolutely stuck on 10:17. Every morning and evening at that hour, no matter how hard I tried to make it stop, the watch screeched loudly, annoying everyone within hearing distance.

Yet I was not okay with the watch's disappearance. Loud and smelly though it was, the watch had been with me for years. I had worn it through many previous adventures in the Pacific and beyond. It was a tangible memento of my pre-Waya existence and self, and I was yearning for both. I needed the watch back—urgently. I retraced my steps between Nalauwaki and Rurugu without success, carrying on a frantic inner dialogue: How could the watch have simply disappeared? Someone must have taken it, right? Who? There had been so many people around. How could I get the watch back? Where to even begin?

As my Australian friends in Fiji would say, I was "losing the plot." I was unraveling, becoming a little weird. Publicly, I managed to keep a poker face. I may have "lost the plot" but I knew that it would be terrible behavior to show public upset over an old watch. It would be even worse if I appeared to accuse anyone of theft. So I kept quiet. That night I listened hard for the screeching alarm, but 10:17 came and went in silence. I fell asleep tormented, not knowing what I was going to do.

I woke up the next morning with a plan. To get my watch back, I was going to work the *kerekere* system. In Fijian, the word *kerekere* literally means, "please." It also refers to an important system of reciprocity among Fijians. If you have a close relationship with someone, you can *kerekere* a favor or an item from them. In return, you are obliged to help them out when they *kerekere* something from you. The closer the relationship, the more you can ask for and the more you are expected to give. Ideally, in this system everyone's needs are looked after.[2]

I had seen *kerekere* operate in ways large and small. One small example: I had brought a baseball cap with me to Waya as a gift for a teenaged boy I knew from earlier research visits. He happily accepted the cap on the morning that he agreed to accompany me for a long walk around the island. Half an hour into our journey, his cousin ran down to the beach exclaiming how much he loved the cap—how very, very much he loved it. The message was clear. My teenaged friend cheerfully handed the cap over. Weeks later, I saw the cap on yet another person's head in a different village. Through *kerekere,* objects are circulated and bonds are strengthened.

Not everyone on Waya loves the *kerekere* system all the time. Friends confided in me that they sometimes hid things they did not want others to *kerekere*. Sometimes they fibbed about what they had or did not have, to work the system to their advantage or to bypass the system altogether. The key was to be subtle so that you did not offend anyone and disrupt the wider balance of reciprocity.

My plan to work the *kerekere* system was this: I would give my watch a story that transformed it from a seemingly insignificant object into something so special that only people closest to me could justify having it. I went for maximum effect. My watch would be a special gift to me from my deceased grandmother, of whom I thought whenever I wore it. I knew how compelling it would be to have the watch reflect loving bonds of kinship. Once the story was known, wherever the watch was, *kerekere* principles would generate social pressure to return it to me.

My story was a lie from start to finish. It was a lie that has shamed me to this day, and for which my grandmother would have been ashamed for me, too. Regrettably, shame did not stop me from my crazy pursuit of the missing watch, and I plotted my next maneuver: I would release my story into the "coconut wireless," local slang for the lightning-fast pathways of oral communication that connect Wayan kinship and social networks. Through the "coconut wireless," information can speed from one end of the island to another in less than an hour, despite a lack of phones.

I unveiled my grandmother story that day over lunch. While dining on fresh fish with my host family and assorted Nalauwaki villagers, I chose a conversational pause to lament in a low-key tone how I had carelessly mislaid the watch my grandmother had given me. "*Kerekere*," I said, "if you come upon the watch, please tell me. I would be so happy to see it again and think of my grandmother." Everyone nodded in sympathy and I said no more. Now I had to be patient and let the "coconut wireless" do its thing. Like a mantra, I repeated to myself, "*Mālua*, Lisa, *mālua*." Slowly, Lisa, slowly. Slowly and carefully, I had learned, was the best way to accomplish things on Waya.

I did not have to be patient for long. There was an unexpected development in the case of the missing watch the very next evening. I was sitting on the large *rārā* (village green) in Nalauwaki, relaxing with a group of about fifty villagers after a daylong wedding feast. The clans of the bride and groom had exchanged elaborate speeches and made mutual presentations of food, bundles of cloth, dried *yaqona* (kava) root, and woven mats. Now these formalities were over and all was quiet on the *rārā* except for periodic calls by the chief's *matanivanua* (spokesman) for another round of *yaqona* drinking.

Then, suddenly, the *rārā*'s evening air was pierced by a familiar sound— SCREECH! SCREECH! SCREECH! SCREECH! SCREECH! SCREECH! Aha, I said to myself, it must be 10:17. Every head, mine included, swiveled to find the source of the disruption. A young woman whom I barely knew sheepishly took the watch off her wrist and shoved it deep into the grass until the alarm stopped. I was within ten feet of my watch! But how was I going to get it back without embarrassing this young woman or her family? I kept my poker face. I needed to reassess my strategy. "*Mālua, Lisa, mālua.*"

The next morning, I took action. I sought out a group of Nalauwaki women belonging to the clan of the girl's mother and joined them for breakfast. They were having fun gossiping about the wedding the day before. Perfect! Adopting a smile tinged with sadness, I chimed in with, "*Ei lei!* (Alas!) Did anyone hear the noise on the *rārā* last night? I was so stupid to have misplaced that watch a few days ago! I should have at least turned off the alarm before losing it!" Everyone laughed. Then one of the ladies said, "THAT watch! That is your grandmother's?" Hiding my glee that the coconut wireless had worked so fast, I replied with a sad smile and a mild joking inflection, "Yes . . . I think of her whenever I see it—or hear it!" There was more laughter and an exchange of meaningful looks. I knew that the case of the missing watch would soon be solved.

Sure enough, that afternoon, a young man whom I knew well approached me as I relaxed in the shade near the beach. I'll call him "Jone." Jone sat down and gently placed my watch on the ground between us. My heart swelled with absurd joy. I waited for him to speak. "I found your watch a few days ago, lying forgotten in the sand near the village," Jone said. "My cousin asked to wear it and she took it to the *rārā* last night. But here it is again." He looked down solemnly at the smelly, screechy old watch—the supposed special gift from my grandmother. I assumed a matching expression and, following Fijian custom, clapped several times to formally accept the watch back. "Thank you so much," I said. "Thank you and your cousin for saving the watch from being lost forever in the sand!" And then I put the watch back on my wrist.

The second I felt that smelly wristband touch my skin, I was flooded with shame and regret. I felt like a complete jerk—the most deceitful jerk of all time. Jone had found that watch somewhere (did it really matter where or how?) and he had put it on. If he liked it, why should he not have it? I wanted more than anything to give the watch back to Jone. But now I was locked into my shameless grandmother story. Jone and I were not close enough for him to comfortably accept the watch back now.

Every night for weeks thereafter, I tossed and turned in the summer heat, agonizing over my bad behavior. How could I have been so petty and conniving? How could I have lied to people with whom I had worked and lived, and who had been so kind to me, over an old watch? I told myself that the culprit was fieldwork fatigue. At a time when I yearned for home and family, my watch had felt like a comforting old friend I could not bear to lose. When I lost the watch, I "lost the plot." That was understandable, right? I reassured myself that, even in my craziness, I had worked hard to play by the Wayan rules of good behavior—at least outwardly. I had bent but not broken the rules of *kerekere,* a skill I had learned from my Wayan friends. To the best of my knowledge, nobody had gotten hurt or lost face. In the end, it was just an old, beat-up watch that smelled bad and had a stuck alarm. For Jone and his cousin, it was easy come, easy go. Right?

Maybe. But years later I remain troubled by the case of the missing watch and the questions it provokes about the ethical predicaments of fieldwork. We anthropologists go into the field determined to do our best. We often fail in small, and sometimes big, ways. (I will not spill any confidences here, but I know that I am far from the only anthropologist who has behaved badly in the field.) In behaving badly, had I been a bad anthropologist?

Or, despite my bad behavior, had I still managed to be a good anthropologist? This embarrassing episode demonstrated that I had learned a lot during my first six months on Waya, even if I had not used that knowledge nobly in my pursuit of the watch. I also like to think that I came away from the case of the missing watch with a more nuanced comparative understanding of Wayan and American social interactions and obligations, and what it means to "own" an object. Most important, I vowed afterward to never again behave so badly on Waya—and I kept that vow. Was all this enough to balance my anthropological ethics sheet? I can argue different answers but am satisfied by none.

When I left Waya at the end of eighteen months, I gave away most of the possessions I had brought with me. I gave my "grandmother's" watch back to Jone. I told him that I wanted to leave the watch with him because he had saved it from being lost forever. He appeared moved; I certainly was. (He also seemed happy that I had replaced the smelly wristband and had finally figured out how to silence the alarm.)

I do not know what has happened to the watch since then. If it has not already died and gone the way of broken watches everywhere, I hope that it is traveling happily through the Wayan *kerekere* network, helping to underscore bonds of kinship and friendship. Now *that* would make my grandmother proud.

Notes

1. For more information on Fiji's geography and history, see Chandra and Mason (1998) and Lal (2002).
2. See Ravuvu (1983) and Nayacakalou (1978) for more on *kerekere* and the complexities of kin and social relationships in Fiji.

Attacked in the Field

Encountering a Street Gang While Studying Peace in Java

Jaida Kim Samudra

One morning in Central Java, Indonesia, Teguh (my research assistant) and I were walking to a community center where I planned to record a focus-group discussion among students of White Crane Silat (WCS), the martial art that was the focus of my research.[1] We stopped to buy water and snacks. Leaving the store, we saw a man standing with his arms folded, straddling the sidewalk. As we passed him, the man grabbed Teguh's shoulder and then started throwing punches. Teguh, a high-ranking WCS trainer, easily parried his punches. His attacker gestured, and a dozen more men ran out from nearby alleys. One man behind me held my arms as the others surrounded Teguh and began kicking and punching him.

I was dumbfounded by the unprovoked attack. Had they confused Teguh with a member of a rival gang? I screamed in Indonesian: "*Kenapa?!*" (Why?!) hoping to alert them to their mistake. I did not know there had been reports of street gangs killing people in that town, but Teguh knew our lives were threatened. He yelled at me to run, but in the adrenaline surge of the attack reverted to his native tongue, Javanese, which I did not speak.[2] I could not understand him, but the bystanders did and quickly fled.

I saw Teguh bending over under the assault. I thought, "No one will help him. I'm the only one who can try." I twisted out of the grasp of the man behind me, cocked my right fist, and punched one of Teguh's attackers in his left temple. I felt no fear, only the conviction that I must reach Teguh.

The hazards of fieldwork have changed since anthropology became a scholarly discipline. A century ago, most anthropologists hailed from

European or North American countries. They undertook fieldwork in remote, technologically undeveloped regions of the world. Reaching field
sites required traveling for weeks or months by boat, horse, or foot. Once
settled in some tiny village, they survived without access to medical clin-
ics, potable water, electricity, or telephones. Anthropology students expected
to get sick from water- or insect-borne diseases or have small scratches
fester into septic ulcers. Professors told them such discomforts were part of
the rite of passage toward becoming anthropologists.

Physical hazards were compounded by psychological ones. Anthropologists seldom worked in teams, so often felt isolated. They might spend
six to eighteen months learning the local language before being able to converse with the people they were studying. They were expected to establish
rapport with people who often viewed them as strangely ignorant, nosy in-
truders. No wonder anthropologists often succumbed to culture shock. Culture shock does not mean being surprised by cultural differences or shocked
by different values; it is a psychological disorder resulting from immersion
in unfamiliar social interactions and worldviews. Anxiety, depression, ago-
raphobia, even hatred of the people who surround you can be triggered by
misreading their social signals, not sharing their fundamental beliefs, and
not knowing survival basics such as how and what to eat, where to defe-
cate, urinate, and bathe, and what animals, people, places, or activities are
dangerous or taboo. Sometimes anthropologists' paranoia was warranted;
they have been chased away by people who misunderstood their presence
or were offended by their faux pas. Ethnographers have been beaten, raped,
or killed in the field when they did not have enough cultural and political
information to gauge the danger of their circumstances or whom to trust.

I had read about such risks in my methodology courses, but did not
worry because I expected my twenty-first-century field experience to be quite
different. Now that over half the world's population lives in cities, more anthropological fieldwork is being conducted in urban settings. I knew I would
be staying in technologically developed areas from which I could e-mail or
telephone family and friends back home whenever I liked. Furthermore,
I was no stranger to the community I was studying. I had trained WCS
in California for nearly two decades and visited the Pusat (WCS headquar-
ters) in West Java in the mid-1980s. During my fieldwork in 2000, I rarely
had difficulty establishing rapport. As soon as I joined the training sessions, *pesilat* (martial artists) recognized I was part of their community.
I developed close friendships in the field, especially with Teguh. Consequently, I never experienced the culture shock so often reported in classic
anthropology.

Also unlike earlier ethnographers, I was not stuck in one place. My fieldwork was multisited, meaning I traveled wherever necessary to observe and interview people doing *silat* (Marcus 1995). I joked in e-mail to colleagues that the deadliest risk I faced was asphyxiation from diesel exhaust inhaled on Java's congested roads. Sometimes I sported bruises or muscle aches from *silat* practice, but overall I felt safe in Indonesia. I chafed at my protective *silat* brothers who insisted on chaperoning me as they would their own Indonesian sisters or girlfriends.

It never crossed my mind that I might be attacked by a street gang or get into a fight unrestrained by sparring etiquette.

I do not remember what happened after that first punch. My memory remains stroboscopic—flashes of color, movement, noise. But Teguh's attackers must have been surprised by my incursion. Some turned on me. I blocked most of their blows and distracted them enough for Teguh to break free. As soon as I saw he was out of the melee, I ran after him.

We sprinted down alleyways to lose the gang. When I could run no farther, Teguh flagged a *becak* (three-wheeled pedicab) and directed the driver toward the community center. When some of the gang members caught up with us on motorcycles, the frightened *becak* driver ordered us off and pedaled away. We started to run again, but one of the men grabbed me as two others chased Teguh. I saw one man pick up a large rock to use as a weapon. I screamed. Teguh turned and saw blood trailing down my face from where my sunglasses had been driven into my skin by an unblocked punch. He suddenly looked so ferocious that our assailants backed away.

Teguh and I ran again until we reached a small outpost where military personnel served as civilian police. Safe, I thought. I collapsed on a couch inside, my stomach cramping from shock. The police questioned Teguh aggressively, then began propelling him toward the door. Teguh later told me they accused me of being a prostitute and him of starting the fight. The police said they would take him to the gang leader to clear up the matter, but Teguh believed they planned to allow him to be beaten to death. I did not understand anything they said, but terrified of being separated, I clung to Teguh and began sobbing. Having an overwrought foreign woman on their hands apparently discomfited the police enough that they let us go, though only after Teguh bribed them.

I originally became an anthropologist because I was troubled by public depictions of human nature as inherently aggressive, of humanity fragmented into competing factions. Evidence of people building peaceable relationships that crosscut ethnic and religious categories is often neglected by the media and academia. Yet in the early twentieth century, Robert Lowie, one of the founders of modern American anthropology, noted "that individuals associate irrespective of whether they belong to the same family, clan, or territorial group; and that such associations play a dominant part in the social life of many peoples rivaling and sporadically even overshadowing other ties" (Lowie 1947, 309). Lowie called such voluntary associations "sodalities" and considered them universal social phenomena. I wanted to study how international, multiethnic, and nonsectarian sodalities develop even within divisive political contexts. The Republic of Indonesia seemed an appropriate setting since it was infamous for violent outbreaks between rival groups. Pundits liked to predict that this nation, founded in late 1949 after winning independence from Dutch colonizers, was doomed to disintegrate. One of its military leaders even claimed Indonesia had a "culture of violence" that encouraged "fighting between families, fighting between villages, fighting between tribes, fighting between ethnic groups, and finally fighting between religions" (quoted in Collins 2002, 582).

The friendly, cooperative relationships among diverse WCS students seemed to contradict such statements. Thus, although my field site was a school where people practiced interpersonal combat, my research agenda focused on peace, not violence. Indeed, a martial art school can be an appropriate site for investigating peaceful community because martial artists practice controlling aggressiveness and martial art teachers often inculcate ethics against violence (Samudra 2003).[3]

We finally reached the community center where the *silat* group I had planned to interview still awaited us. After Teguh told them what had happened, they began planning to find and beat up our attackers. I argued against retaliation because it could lead to a scandal that would diminish the reputation of the WCS school.[4] And what if someone got killed? Teguh agreed to accompany me back to West Java on condition that I never again speak about the incident.

It was not easy to behave normally after we returned to the Pusat. I told myself my injuries did not look worse than those following a rough sparring session, but I was upset that no one noticed my distress. I knew that Indonesians show respect by not asking a lot of personal questions. Letting people handle their own problems is also part of the martial art ethos. Usually I found such attitudes restful, but traumatized by the attack, I interpreted silence as lack of compassion.

The first time someone threw a hit toward my face during *silat* class, I burst into tears and fled the room. Then I quit training. When I walked down a crowded street, I had auditory hallucinations of people screaming, so I stopped going out. I withdrew to my dorm room, where I brooded over the gaps in my memory of the fight. I asked Teguh what he recalled, but he said that if I insisted on discussing it, he would have to return to Central Java to kill our assailant.

I did not understand his reaction, but tried to abide by his request. I now understand him better. Javanese men are normally quite reserved, but my reminding him of the incident threatened his emotional self-control. He was ashamed he had not been able to protect me and angry I had endangered myself by joining the fight. He was also ashamed that I, a foreigner, had been attacked in his country. I never blamed Indonesian society, however. I knew that street gangs existed in every nation-state characterized by extreme economic inequalities and mass unemployment, including the United States.

My symptoms worsened over the next month. Finally, I explained my problem to Teguh in cultural terms: "Maybe Indonesians don't talk about these things, but I'm an American. Americans talk about everything. I'm going to go crazy if I don't talk to someone." He then permitted me to tell the WCS Grandmaster about the attack.

The Grandmaster explained the physiological mechanisms of memory loss following a chaotic, violent episode. He provided me with a new interpretation of the experience by saying: "You are a fighter! You never threw up [after the fight]. You didn't get a fever that night. And you didn't get very bruised or feel any pain. That's because you do *silat*. Your body has learned to control normal physical reactions such as vomiting, fever, and bruising." My symptoms disappeared after that conversation, and I was able to complete my ethnographic research.

I did not write about the attack until now because of Teguh's stipulation that I not broadcast the incident.[5] It was also too difficult to make sense of the violence at close range. Even "ethnographers who study violence have experienced bewilderment on first seeing it" and find it difficult to remain analytically detached (Robben and Nordstrom 1995, 13). An anthropologist who was raped while in the field writes that she "was in no position to record, understand, or utilize" the information about gender and sexuality that came her way afterward; putting her "situation to anthropological use felt blasphemic" at the time (Moreno 1995, 243–244). Like her, I could not turn my intimate trauma into a professional narrative.

Nor could I brush it off as just a hazard of fieldwork. Yet now I feel that it was indeed a rite of passage—not as an anthropologist, but as a martial artist. By reframing my actions and physiological responses into proof that I was a fighter who could protect herself and help a friend escape a dozen (albeit untrained and disorganized) attackers, the Grandmaster showed me I was truly an insider in the White Crane Silat community.

Notes

1. With over three hundred ethnic groups spread over more than seventeen thousand islands, the Republic of Indonesia has one of the most diverse and largest populations in the world. Each school of *silat* (self-defense) is usually associated with a specific village, ethnic group, religious organization, or political party. WCS is taught in the second largest *silat* school in the nation; it is the only *silat* school in which gender, ethnicity, nationality, religion, and class are not barriers to membership.
2. I conducted research in Bahasa Indonesia, the official language used in education, business, and government. It is not the first language of most Indonesians. Javanese is the most widespread native tongue because the Javanese are the largest ethnic group and the political capital of Indonesia is on Java.
3. The counterintuitive notion that martial arts foster peaceful community has been supported by psychological studies suggesting that aggressive behavior diminishes over time among children taking self-defense classes (Twemlow and Sacco 1998; Zivin et al. 2001).
4. A primary ethical responsibility of anthropologists is not to bring harm to the people or communities they study (AAA 2012).
5. Over a decade later, Teguh's emotions, like mine, have subsided. He gave me permission to write about the attack as long as his real name was not included.

A Question of Permission in Pohnpei

Suzanne S. Finney

NEGOTIATING WITHIN TRADITIONAL leadership in a place where one has no cultural standing can be frustrating at best and paralyzing at worst. The history of foreigners in the Pacific Islands is filled with stories of these outsiders being used for political or social gain either with or without the foreigners' direct knowledge.

My personal experience with these situations resulted from fieldwork conducted in 2000 in Pohnpei (see Finney and Graves 2002 for report). Pohnpei is part of the Federated States of Micronesia (FSM), which consists of four states (Kosrae, Pohnpei, Chuuk, and Yap) across three thousand miles of the tropical northern Pacific. It is also an island with a long and strong tradition of traditional authority within each of the five districts (*wehi*) that compose the island. The people respect the paramount chiefs of each *wehi*, who hold the title *nahnmwarki*. But their traditional authority is undermined by the Western-style political system that "runs" the country, with local, state, and national agencies operating largely outside the sphere of influence of the traditional leadership. This political system has been in place in various forms since the Spanish established an administrative center in what is now the state capital of Kolonia more than 125 years ago.

In 2000, funded by a grant from the American Battlefield Protection Program of the U.S. National Park Service, our team of five archaeologists and graduate students arrived in Pohnpei to investigate the remains of several shipwrecks thought to be the whalers sunk by the Confederate raider CSS *Shenandoah* as part of its activities at the end of the Civil War in America (April 1865). The story and the wrecks are known to the Pohnpeians, but there is not much interest in them since they represent events from outside the local culture. There was interest in what we were doing, but the investigation itself did not generate any concern because we were looking at a site of Western activity.

Still, I wanted to be sure that all possible vested parties were contacted and I asked several people, both within the government and the community, if I should contact the local *nahnmwarki* to let him know what we were doing. This was my second time at the site; my first trip was in 1999 and on both occasions I asked this question. Everyone told me this would not be necessary, stating one of two reasons. First, the site was in the water and we were accessing it by water, which meant there would be no land access to the site, and therefore no permission to access the site by land. *Nahnmwarki* used to have authority over the waters in their provinces, but all water rights that the traditional leadership may have had were removed by the German colonial administration in the early twentieth century.

The second reason was that the project we were working on was small and no one I spoke with thought the *nahnmwarki* should be bothered or would be interested in such a small project; that is, there was no need to disturb him for something like this. To approach the *nahnmwarki* meant that I needed a Pohnpeian to make the introduction and act as escort. Without anyone willing to do this, and based on the advice I received not to bother the *nahnmwarki* with something so small, we began the project.

The harbor we were working in is part of the *wehi* named Madolenihmw, which is also the location of the famous and contested site of Nan Madol. I say contested because there is persistent debate in Pohnpei over who owns the site. The Pohnpei state and FSM national governments contend it is state property and want to manage it as public land. The *nahnmwarki* views it as private property, belonging to his family. This conflict continues to the present. At the time of my research the state government was in the habit of authorizing research and projects involving Nan Madol without permission from the *nahnmwarki*.

Even if I had known that, I am not sure I could have anticipated the events that unfolded one day when we were getting ready to go out to the site. A man came up to us and said he was a representative from the *nahnmwarki* and that he was there to stop us from conducting our research since we did not have proper permission. We were told if we went to the site we would be arrested. We were expected to stop work on the project until we could get approval from the *nahnmwarki*.

Never mind that the *nahnmwarki* had no authority to arrest people, or that Madolenihmw had no official boat with which to go and arrest us on the site. When he left I spoke with our boat driver, who was the one who told us they had no boat to carry out their threat. He was still willing to take us to the research site if we wanted to go. He was also from another *wehi*. I suspected his answer might be different if it was the *nahnmwarki* from his *wehi* issuing the command. I spoke with the members of the team, all of whom came from the United States like me. They were all willing to go. But it was my decision. I was the only one actually planning to focus my career in the the Pacific Islands; the other team members had their own interests and projects elsewhere, so if continuing the project without permission from the *nahnmwarki* resulted in some future problems working in Pohnpei, it would not affect them.

I was not sure if I was going to continue my research in Pohnpei, but I had already made friends there from my previous visits, and I was an anthropologist, trained and committed to working within cultural boundaries and constraints rather than against them. We had permission to conduct the research from the proper state authorities, and the rights of *nahnmwarki* over the waters around the island had long been removed, but it just did not feel right to go against his express instructions not to continue. Besides, I had no idea at the time what had prompted this completely unexpected intrusion into our work. So I called off the research for the day and we ended up exploring a few of the tourist dive sites instead, observing coral reefs and manta rays instead of mapping shipwrecks.

The following day started what was to become a weeklong struggle to obtain permission from the *nahnmwarki* by going to visit him. For those of us conducting field research in seasons measured in weeks rather than months or years, the loss of a week to pursue this was huge. But I was committed to getting permission, so I continued to work within the Pohnpeian traditional and government systems, slowly inching my way toward a meeting.

I contacted the Historic Preservation Office (HPO) right away. It is through this office that permission to conduct archaeological research is obtained from the state, and I knew the head of the office needed to be involved if anything was going to be settled. It was from him I learned that this really had nothing to do with our project; we were being used as the only available resource at hand to let the HPO know that the *nahnmwarki* was not happy with being excluded from decisions regarding research in Madolenihmw, specifically Nan Madol. This was a common response I got from others as word spread through the community, as it does on small islands, that there was a problem. We became known as "the archaeologists," and everywhere we went in town people already knew who we were.

Several different people came up to me and told me they sympathized and that they did not believe the *nahnmwarki* was right to do this. It had nothing to do with me personally, they all said, this was his way of sending a message to the government. But no one, true to tradition, would publicly speak out against the *nahnmwarki* and no one would have gone to him to speak about this. The only way to continue the research was to get his permission.

At the end of the week, working with the HPO, we were finally able to schedule a meeting with the *nahnmwarki* and his advisers. During that time we had been unable to conduct any research. When we were able to go see the *nahnmwarki* to ask for permission, we had to bring a small offering of food or drink, so we went and bought a case of grape soda. Soda in hand, the Historic Preservation Officer, a friend who lived on Pohnpei and who would act as translator for me, and I went to visit the *nahnmwarki* in a small house in Kolonia.

I do not speak Pohnpeian, but even if I did, I do not think it would have been easy to be at the meeting without a translator. Pohnpeian has a special form of the language that is used only for speaking with the *nahnmwarki*, so even if one were to learn everyday spoken Pohnpeian, one would still need to learn this special form for our meeting. I was not aware how much English the *nahnmwarki* might know, so I expected the entire meeting to be in Pohnpeian. I also did not expect to participate, but to sit there dutifully contrite and quiet while the advisers and the Historic Preservation Officer dealt with the real reasons for the delay in the project.

I sat on the floor with everyone else, never looking directly at the *nahnmwarki*, out of respect for the Pohnpeian belief that a spirit sits on each of his shoulders and one should never make direct eye contact, and listened politely while issues were discussed, apologies were made, and the matter was sufficiently resolved for me to complete the work. The *nahnmwarki* gave his permission, and after that there were no problems continuing the project.

Three years later, in 2003, I went back for further fieldwork. At that time I did not have to meet with the *nahnmwarki*, nor did I have any problems accessing the site, so whatever issues had been between the two groups, the traditional leadership and the state government, seemed to be no longer a concern.

As I mentioned, I do not see how this incident could have been prevented. Even the Pohnpeians involved with the project were caught off guard, and no one gave me any warning or indication that there was a problem with the *nahnmwarki* that could result in a temporary halt to our work. But once the matter arose, the only two options available were to proceed without his permission, or stop our project and wait for permission. I am satisfied that the response I chose, to wait until we could get his permission, was the best option, and I believe the sympathetic response from the community was proof that this was the right choice.

Did I feel used by the *nahnmwarki*? He did take advantage of our being there to make his frustration known to the state government. Issues of water rights and permission and land ownership are still being contested today, so this is not a problem that has gone away. But while I suspect that this one incident did not serve to strengthen the traditional leaders' authority versus the newer Western-style state and national governments, I understand the desire to take advantage of an opportunity to voice displeasure with the current system. By threatening our project the *nahnmwarki* was able to bring attention to an ongoing concern he had about who has authority over cultural and historic sites in his *wehi*. In this case the *nahnmwarki* found a way to make his frustration known to the state government without affecting the local population. This incident was just one of many such examples of local leaders who seize an opportunity to solve a separate issue. It seems that my experience was but one in a long line of negotiations during changing times.

Grandmothers, Sharks, and Other Dangerous Things

Persistent Crises in Mangareva, French Polynesia

Alexander Mawyer

Moments characterized by some personal danger, whether conceptual, practical, or social, are an important genre of ethnographic storytelling. Since they draw attention to the fact of fieldwork, such anecdotes contribute to its enduring romance. In contemporary work, anecdotes often deploy an ironic self-regard that simultaneously critiques the putative romance of fieldwork while confoundedly maintaining it. At their best, such stories provide a useful contrast to the more lasting and sometimes profound crises and challenges confronting local communities. Scratch one of your anthropology professors and it may well turn out that she or he is reminded of a moment in the field when something startling and memorable happened. I too have anecdotes that speak to such moments. I trot them out in appropriate venues and put them to work.

My fieldwork has been in French Polynesia, a partially autonomous French dependency in the southeastern Pacific. Like Oceania in general, this region is vast and complex. Five island groups distinct in geography, language, culture, and history are notable for the density of their lines of connection as well as potent aspects of disconnection. Two of these groups, the Society and Marquesas Islands, are well known in scholarly writings, art, literature, and film. Giants cast long shadows. Such well-known islands can obscure even basic facts or knowledge of their neighbors, including the Gambier Islands in the far southeast of the region.

Rising from the oceanic deeps about 1,700 kilometers from the Societies, the Gambier are eight high islands amounting to 27 square kilometers of land and numerous *motu* or islets encircling a 90-kilometer barrier reef and vibrant coral lagoon. Terrains including high grassed peaks, up-land pine forests, traditional and neotraditional down-slope woods, and highly varied near-shore house gardens and plantations of taro, manioc, and varieties of sweet potato characterize all of the high islands, of which Man-gareva is the largest. Prior to the arrival of Europeans, the islands of the chain were densely occupied. However, the sixty years following first contacts with European outlanders saw a tragic demographic apocalypse resulting in the emptying of the bays, the silencing of many villages, the dissolution of the traditional competing chiefdoms, and the loss of an immense legacy of local language and culture. By the 1880s, the archipelago's population had reached a low point of fewer than five hundred people, and the vast majority of its inhabited bays were rapidly turning into wilds.

Today, however, the Gambier's population is burgeoning and push-ing back out into these formerly inhabited spaces, yielding encounters that can be both surprising and disconcerting in their historical inflections, as families—whether youthful or mature couples—clear land off for the first time in many decades or even in a century. New technologies, particularly satellite-supported radio, television, and Internet, as well as increased flights and cargo-ship arrivals have made the islands more attractive homes for the current generations of youths and working-age adults who might other-wise have sought life elsewhere in Tahiti or France, the United States or New Zealand.

Most Mangarevan families support themselves directly or indirectly by farming pearls. After a lustrous twenty years in the 1980s and 1990s pro-duced a great deal of wealth from the sea, a collapse in pearl revenues and governmental attempts to restructure the industry by excluding small-time farms from participation, beginning around 2000, yielded talk of a "per-sistent crisis." Fears about the industry of cultured pearls thus joined ranks with a number of other local crises perceived as imminent, from contem-porary ecological problems of trash and diminishing fresh water on small islands to profound questions of personhood and identity—for instance, how to avoid cultural erosions, including the ongoing loss of language, and renew important traditions.

A sense of crisis has thus been an important feature of the contem-porary moment for Mangarevans. Confounding and enduring issues of de-velopment, modernity, globalization, and cultural preservation are perceived and regularly discussed over dinner, while repairing nets on the platforms of pearl farms during the working day, in front of the island's trade stores, and in living rooms after the evening TV news broadcasts. A pervasive sense of crisis also resonates with the kinds of profound issues that motivate anthropological research, justify its funding, and energize our passions as scholars. But such topics of heightened importance sometimes obscure or overshadow aspects of the everyday lives and experiences of real people that are just as important if not as easily recognized. On a number of occasions, everyday happenings that I initially experienced as personal crises, in some opposition to the kinds of collective crises discussed above, taught me something meaningful about anthropology, about doing anthropology, and about life in the Gambier. These stories initially seemed to me merely personal before I came to understand them as anthropological moments that helped me move beyond abstract concerns and into the fabric of daily life, where the fundamental issues confronting local communities often find their actual expression.

During the years of planning my fieldwork, evening TV news broadcasts seemed to play a huge role in local conversations, considering that there were only a few radio stations, biweekly flights, and only a single television channel dating to the end of the 1980s to funnel external news into the island. Here was a chance to carefully study broadcast reception and the social significance of news in circulation in a tightly news-bounded setting, and an opportunity to identify and enter fluidly into concerns of broad public interest, the stuff of news. With the anticipatory romance of fieldwork in mind, I imagined a number of happy surprises, the regular accidents of everyday life bubbling along, but I did not imagine the cable guy.

My fieldwork began in earnest a few days after New Year's 2002 when I began the complex, multistage, and nearly full-day journey from Tahiti, across the Tuamotu atolls, to Mangareva. I traveled by small plane from Papeete, Tahiti, to the Tuamotu atoll Hao. Another plane took me from Hao to the long *motu* Totegeigei, and finally to Mangareva by municipal ferry. All the challenges of transit, the distance in a small plane over the deep ocean, the stops and boat ride, lived up to my anticipations. Imagine my surprise on learning that the same plane dropping me off was coincidentally picking up technicians from the Office of Posts and Telecommunications (OPT), who had in the previous weeks upgraded the island's technoinfrastructure. Indeed, they had just made it possible to receive a broad array of television signals from the decommissioned and newly repurposed Intelsat satellite previously used by the United States to monitor French nuclear testing over nearby Moruroa and Fangataufa.[1] So much for the dependability of research plans; Mangareva had gone the full cable-box route. With the availability of many channels of film, cartoon, music video, and sports, few folks were talking about the news. Years of coursework and prefield study, my nearly yearlong proposal preparation and defense, the methodologies

submitted to granting agencies, long conversations with my dissertation committee members, all turned to ash in my mouth within minutes
of arrival.

Moments of some danger take other forms as well. Over the course
of my first six months, before my wife joined me, and as I reconfigured my
project, I often had a period of unscheduled time in the mid-afternoon. Several times a week, I was invited to take Nescafé with a group of senior women,
all mothers and grandmothers who no longer worked outside the domestic
sphere but whose labors should be understood as the foundational glue of
a great deal of contemporary social order. Such afternoon *varaga,* or conversation, seemed to play an important role in establishing a shared,
community-wide sense of the issues of the day and the broad concerns of
the island. Our talk ranged over numerous topics, from the little things of
village life, shows playing on the newly available channels, tides and currents in the pearl industry, successes of children and grandchildren at school,
to more profound issues including the actions of the Gambier's leading men
and women, the future of Mangarevan language and culture, and regional
and national politics. On a number of occasions, these otherwise kind and
generous ladies would turn the talk in a rather scandalous direction. Mock-
ing my status as a supposedly married person before my wife had physically joined me on the island, on several occasions one or another of them
posed a rather indelicate proposal: You know, my granddaughter thinks
you are rather handsome . . . Oh, what handsome babies you would have
(cough) . . . You know, she's just inside (pointing). Silence. My somewhat ca-
gey response could be depended upon to generate howls of laughter. Um,
maro'i, thank you, I would respond, *ei mate 'ia vau . . . ki toku ipo e* (but my
wife would kill me). On the first occasion, I assumed this was mere pleas-
antry, the humor of the senior generation. Later, several similar incidents
left me rather shocked and not at all certain about the codes of humor involved, particularly when, one day, I couldn't help but overhear several men
at the post office laughing gently at me as I was leaving with stamps in hand,
"his wife would kill him." Were the uncomfortable if amusing ribbings I
received rather more serious than I understood?

Throughout my time on Mangareva, when English-speaking outlanders arrived for reasons other than official, and at least twice for official
reasons, I was sometimes asked by the mayor or others to serve as an inter-
preter and facilitator. Several of these occasions proved once-in-a-lifetime
opportunities. One time, after she had joined me in the field, my wife and
I arranged a boat to travel to Temoe Atoll about forty kilometers southeast
of Mangareva to accompany a visiting archaeologist who hoped to take scaled

photos of the precontact stone works. Visiting Temoe requires a swim from the deep ocean over the breaking reef into the lagoon in low tide. When first entering the water to start the swim, I was shocked to hear the captain start yelling in extreme consternation, *mago, mago, requin, requin,* having spotted a large tiger shark swimming in feeding agitation just ahead of us, along the drop-off of the reef's ocean edge. Usually nonplussed by *mago,* the captain's friends Niko and Pano, who were swimming onto the atoll with us to do a spot of lagoon net fishing, were equally intense, directing us all together into a still circle until the shark was out of sight. After the photographic excursion and successful net fishing amid yet more encircling sharks (these were small reef sharks well over twenty in number visible by fin-count), our swim back out to the boat against the rising tide, over the breaking reef, pulling three man-sized bags of more-or-less-bloody fish behind us, produced an evident anxiety in Pano and Niko. Meanwhile, my wife had cut her leg badly coming over the reef. Niko, raised in the Tuamotu islands, suggested that no one put masks on or look underwater and instead focus on swimming out to the boat. A quick glimpse under the surface revealed the sensibility of this suggestion—I saw a very large number of dangerous animals swimming in a fearsome geometry just under and around us in all directions, a scene that chills me to this day. Happily we all pulled up onto the deck of the boat without incident. I have never seen two swimmers more relieved to come up out of the ocean.

This story asks you to consider such anecdotes by way of pointing to the at times challenging personal dimension of fieldwork, and of course fieldwork can quite literally be dangerous. However, it does so not merely to highlight the fact of the fieldworker as an embodied, practically situated, socially embedded person with respect to the individualized pragmatic or psychological challenges of being there. Rather, it does so in order to set up a broader tension between the kinds of personal crises that characterize the predicaments of fieldwork with the sorts of persistent crises that draw many anthropologists to the field in the first place.

Looking back at the place of these fleeting moments in my own fieldwork has fostered a sense of the long-running relationship between the romance of anthropology and danger. Research is expensive and the human condition fraught. The intersection of fundable issues, disciplinarily hot topics, and long-running human concerns has perforce, and for good reason, oriented so much of the best anthropology to forms or aspects of crisis from the conceptual and slow running, such as language loss or other forms of cultural erosions, to the dynamics of economic life on the fringe of a global order that cannot always be depended upon to desire one's pearls, to changes in the statutes governing autonomy and the constitution of politics, to the intimate and visceral in the legacies of French Pacific nuclear testing.

This then is another sort of predicament, that one is drawn too far into the study of persistent crises, and misses what is there to be learned from the risks and challenges latent in the quotidian, the everyday. Or, that as outsiders, we impose an anthropological sense of persistent collective (or social, or global) crises on the local, at the risk of missing critical dimensions of local significance. The possibility of being eaten, devoured by sharks, injured while swimming over breaking reefs, almost crushed by a yacht coming off of Pitcairn (another story), deliciously mocked by grandmothers, foiled by everyday contingencies, draws attention to the problem of one's entanglements in a small place, the everyday and not-so-everyday risks of life in the world.

Stories such as mine about the fragility of research plans, the uncertainty of social relationships and the goodwill of others, and the fragility of the human body are all more than merely piquant. They point to the sorts of everyday issues with development, modernity, and globalization that rest at the heart of real human engagements with the world, with others, and with others in the world. Here they point toward fundamental issues with technosocial shifts and the ways that emerging technologies are hinged to many facets of life and may complicate research plans that do not take change into account; they point to demographic legacies and the social histories of westerners in these islands, for instance, how men coming onto and off of these lands have acted and interacted with local women, and how many seemingly humorous sentiments may be layered in uncomfortable histories of encounter; and they point to everyday qualities of emergency and palliative health care, issues of everyday risk and safety and health, that should *also* be at the heart of contemporary anthropological projects—not in place of, but complementing concerns about tectonically vast persistent crises.

We are writers of limited comments, of parenthetical and explanatory statements that provide context about something in a certain number of characters. In the case of the anthropological statement, that something is *culture*—that affordance, at once individual and collective, that provides a shared response to, and accommodation with, the fact of being in the world. Moreover, anthropological notes should have an essential modesty, acknowledging the limits of observation and interpretation. Anthropology is writing about culture, and anthropological writings are themselves a potent form of culture. However, anthropological writing is a note, and not the thing itself. Writings about the lives of cultural others are necessarily fragments: parenthetical if explanatory, bounded if illuminating, partial if revelatory.[2]

Certainly, the idea of anthropology as note-like, as offering a narrow glimpse of the lives of others, had a definite resonance for me in the lead-up to my own fieldwork in French Polynesia. Even so, I still had to learn how to take note, how to acknowledge and value the potential insights made possible by otherwise seemingly minor events and everyday moments. Between differences in language and the legacies of the imposition of colonial states, even in an age of renewed, powerful linkages between Oceanic peoples and places, the contemporary French Pacific, including the Gambier Islands, too often appears visible as if from a distance, through a mist. I recommend that if one would pass through this mist, attention be paid to the modest crises and dangers, bumps and laughs, and toothy things of the everyday in addition to the persistent concerns with the global, the nuclear, the modern, and the economic that dominate so many of our best disciplinary intentions. Attention to the everyday taught me that while the profound concerns of anthropological theory are never entirely visible, aspects of them do emerge and become surprisingly intelligible in easily overlooked, passing moments.

Notes

I wish to thank the editors for extremely useful comments on an early draft, as well as several of my students, particularly Marie Soderbergh, for useful feedback.

1. The French state moved its nuclear testing establishment to French Polynesia in the mid-1960s. The individual, social, and cultural legacies of the nuclear experience—testing finally ceased in 1996—are still unfolding to this day.
2. Student readers interested in these points may wish to pursue them further with Clifford Geertz in his inimitable *The Interpretation of Cultures* as well as the stimulating *Writing Culture: The Poetics and Politics of Ethnography*, edited by James Clifford and George Marcus.

PART 2

Meaningful Encounters

Learning, Representing, Engaging the Field

Introduction

FORREST WADE YOUNG

ETHNOGRAPHERS HAVE CLASSICALLY STUDIED the ways human realities and practices are "culturally constructed" or acquire symbolic meaning in relation to worlds of social relations and institutions. In other words, how "people act in relation, not to brute reality, but to culture-specific modes of perceiving and organizing the world" (Rosaldo 1988, 78). Analysis of culture-specific modes of human life examines the normative behavior and thoughts people acquire and learn as members of a social group. Today, ethnographers often see themselves less concerned with describing "whole" cultures, as was the classic goal, than with analyzing the significance of particular cultural practices (Rabinow et al. 2008, 35). Moreover, contemporary ethnographers now often study human lives beyond the ways they are culturally constructed; they are interested in the ways human realities and practices are meaningful in light of global developments, problems, and processes.

This section consists of stories that illustrate how contemporary ethnographers begin to encounter cultural meaning in their fieldwork. It is critical to note how they develop new "roots" and alternative "routes" (Clifford 1996, 216) for ethnography, while at the same time finding important research value in classic techniques of ethnographic fieldwork: *participant observation* (learning about cultural practices by actively engaging in the normative ways of life in a society) and *ethnographic interviews* (learning about cultural worlds by asking members what various aspects of their society mean to them).

Serge A. Marek, Hirofumi Katsuno, and Margaret Barnhill Bodemer all locate their research in urban areas—rooting fieldwork in a location that was generally discouraged in classic studies that stressed research in communities at the periphery of global trade and development. Marek's "Fieldwork as Transformative Experience: Learning to See Positive Māori Urban Identities" reflects upon how ethnographic research enabled him to challenge stereotypical views of urban Māori that he had assumed valid. Katsuno's "The Cultural Power of Robots in Japan" addresses an increasingly popular new topic for "rerouting" ethnographic inquiry: science and technology studies (STS) that examine how scientific knowledge is culturally produced. Conducting fieldwork "at home" in Japan, Katsuno shows that by deep participant observation in the daily lives of robot builders—through the construction of his own robot—he is able to understand and identify with the sociocultural world of Japanese robotics. Bodemer's "Fieldwork on Two Wheels in Hanoi, Vietnam, or How I Learned to Stop Worrying and Enjoy the Ride" also adumbrates a new topic of ethnography: museums. Interestingly, using standard methodological techniques, she shows how "the field" is often not transparent in contemporary ethnography, but is actively constructed by the ethnographer.

Hong Jiang and Jonathan Y. Okamura foreground some of the ways that representation and engagement in contemporary fieldwork can be embroiled in complex local politics. Jiang's "Encountering Maoist Propaganda in Pastoral Inner Mongolia" introduces readers to some of the politics of representing development in the traditionally pastoral Mongol community of Uxin Ju in the Ordos region of northern China. Given the historical effects of Maoist political programs in this region, she finds that, at best, only "partial truths" (Clifford 1986) can be gleaned from ethnography. Okamura's "When the Field Is Your Home: Doing Advocacy Work and Academic Work in Hawai'i" is a story of homework in political solidarity with Filipino communities in Hawai'i struggling against racism and social inequality.

Fieldwork as Transformative Experience
Learning to See Positive Māori Urban Identities

SERGE A. MAREK

AT THE BEST OF TIMES and in the most ideal conditions, doing social science fieldwork in a foreign place and culture is challenging. No level of preparation can fully prepare a researcher for what lies ahead. Certainly, with the perspective of hindsight accrued most recently from working with Māori in Auckland, Aotearoa,[1] I could give a person venturing into the field for the first time some very utilitarian advice. For example, make as many connections as possible before going into the field; know which interview style works best for you and check your equipment obsessively; find a fieldwork book to peruse throughout the fieldwork experience; and stay in touch with your contacts as much as possible after leaving the field.[2] But perhaps more important than careful preparation designed to deal with pitfalls, unexpected occurrences, and faulty equipment is to be open to the possibility that fieldwork itself will profoundly influence the very nature and focus of your research. The fieldwork experience has the potential to be a transformative experience both in terms of your research focus and your growth as a researcher and human being.

In light of my research in urban Aotearoa, I would argue that perhaps the most important skill that a researcher can bring into the field is the ability to learn from that experience *as it is happening*. Researchers must be open to the possibility that their interactions with individuals and groups can, and often do, profoundly change the research that they are doing. This skill—what I refer to as *flexible fieldwork*—can lead to research that is more productive (both theoretically and practically), and to outcomes that are more meaningful both for the researcher and the people or organizations that are the focus of the research. While one can find several definitions of the word "flexible," my favorite, and the one that best fits what I mean by "flexible fieldwork," comes from the Merriam-Webster online dictionary: "characterized by a ready capability to adapt to new, different, or changing requirements." The words "new," "different," and "changing" are an inherent part of most people's fieldwork experiences, and, I argue, the level of success and productivity that comes out of fieldwork will be based to a significant extent on how much the researcher embraces these challenges rather than viewing them as burdens or barriers.

I went into the field with the intention of researching the relationship between Māori identity and urbanization in Aotearoa, and my experiences there illustrate well the importance of being flexible (as defined above) when doing research in a foreign place and culture. Most of the literature I had read prior to going to Aotearoa led me to think of the relationships between Māori and cities as predominantly negative—as resulting, for example, in the loss of cultural traditions and community; the onset of profound urban poverty; and higher rates of negative social and health statistics than the majority white population. However, through the process of meeting with Māori from a wide range of backgrounds I began to realize that there was much more to the story of Māori urbanization than just negative effects or cultural resistance.[3] More specifically, I began to realize that part of this lack of understanding stemmed from a gross misrepresentation of this relationship that I developed from a literature that focused on the city primarily as a place of crisis or difficult challenge for Māori. In other words, I began the process of shedding the perception that the city was for Māori exclusively a site of oppression, repression, and assimilation.

At some point when undertaking empirical data collection, you must be prepared for the possibility that your basic research assumptions and questions are inherently flawed. And when this happens it is critical that you do not "flee from the scene" completely discouraged and disheartened (an easy thing to do when you are alone in a foreign place). When I first began interviewing Māori from all walks of life, it quickly became obvious to me that my questions pertaining to the city-as-problem discourse made many of them uncomfortable. For example, early on I generally introduced my research to people I wanted to interview by talking about the influence on me of the movie *Once Were Warriors* (Tamahori 1994). I quickly figured out, however, that Māori in general found this portrayal of their culture embarrassing, shameful, and grossly stereotyped. As one Māori music DJ put it to me when discussing this movie's connection to Māori urban life, "that was just a slice of life . . . it's like saying the whole world's a ghetto . . . it's not . . . that's just that corner of the road." Through my conversations with Māori, I came to realize that this discomfort stemmed from a feeling on the part of many of the Māori I spoke with that I, as an outsider, was bringing to the table a host of preconceived negative notions about Māori urban experiences. From this realization I was forced to reassess these preconceived notions and begin, instead, to really listen to the stories that were being told to me; and these stories were just as often about positive urban identities as they were about negative ones. This was a critical step because it forced me to transform myself (or at least attempt to do so) from a person of authority to one of humility. And, as it turns out, a stance of humility was the starting point toward a greater understanding of the complexity of Māori urban experiences and, especially, the many positive identities stemming from these experiences.

As I met with Māori in Auckland and elsewhere, I was repeatedly confronted with Māori that seemed anything but marginalized by their urban experience. I can draw on many examples of Māori who are interacting with the urban context in ways that go beyond crisis or resistance. However, one of the best examples occurred early in my research when I had the opportunity to informally interview Lyonel Grant, a master carver and accomplished artist of Ngāti Pikiao and Te Arawa descent.[4] As is often the case with fieldwork, this was not a planned meeting. I only came to know of Lyonel through several other people I spoke with who suggested that he was doing work related to my research focus. At that time Lyonel was overseeing the design and construction of a *marae* being built on a university campus in Auckland.[5] Only the most senior Māori master carvers and builders are tasked with such an undertaking, so I knew I would be meeting someone important. When I first met Lyonel I was still operating within a discourse that viewed the dominant Māori urban experience as one of crisis and resistance. When I left my meeting with Lyonel I was on the path to deconstructing this discourse and rebuilding it to encompass a world where some Māori are developing positive urban identities.

On this first visit to Ngakau Mahaki (the name of the elaborately carved main meeting house), construction of this *whare nui* (big house) was still very much under way. I was taken into the carving shed and introduced to Lyonel. Meeting a Polynesian master carver is like meeting a Polynesian master navigator. There is just something in their eyes that tells you of a deeper connection to the spirit world and a deeper set of knowledges than most other people you meet. I knew immediately that this was a time to put away the recorder and notepad and just listen and learn. After introductions were made, I was given a tour of the main carvings that were still in the process of being created for the *marae,* and as Lyonel's story began to unfold, a whole new way of understanding the relationship Māori have with cities exploded in my mind. Lyonel told me that coming to Auckland was always a challenging experience for him because he was not used to the overwhelming intensity of buildings, people, and traffic (he is from a smaller city called Rotorua). He told me this to relate how difficult it was for him, at first, to imagine a *marae* within this type of urban context. And yet, as he allowed himself to experience the space and place where this *marae* was going to be built, and as he adjusted to his life in Auckland, he began to understand that no matter how much concrete and steel overlay the land, there were still Māori spirits and landscapes present. This understanding of Māori landscapes persevering within the context of the urban was inspired, interestingly enough, by time Lyonel had spent in Honolulu. He told me that once, while looking at Honolulu from the highpoint of Tantalus, he had a vision of peeling back the "urban fabric" and seeing the Hawaiian spirits and landscapes emerging from underneath all the concrete and steel—buried perhaps, but not gone.

From this vision one of the main carvings he was working on emerged, and it is one that became a metaphor for how I began to understand my research. This carving depicted a stylized map of Auckland, complete with roads organized on a grid and little cul de sacs. But dramatically bursting out of various parts of the map were Māori spirits and images. These images represented, according to Lyonel, the power and resilience of Māori landscapes and spirits regardless of the weight of a Western-built environment that had been imposed since the coming of Europeans. Moreover, these images represented the power and resilience of a people, despite seemingly impenetrable material and social forces, to assert their human geographies through their physical presence. Māori empowerment is grounded in their reinterpretation of the urban-built environment, and their active social engagement within this urban context.

A second carving shown to me by Lyonel was envisioned while he was walking down a railroad track in Auckland. He came upon a graffiti burn that struck him as both beautiful and meaningful. He decided to incorporate this image into one of his carvings and, in so doing, managed to demonstrate the ability of even the most traditional forms of Māori cultural production—*marae* carvings—to appropriate images and symbols from the urban context and turn them into powerful components of a Māori cultural landscape. This is a critical point because it demonstrates one of the most important characteristics of positive Māori urban identities: the ability to incorporate non-Māori sociocultural and sociospatial elements and transform them into profoundly Māori ones. By doing so, Māori incorporating these identities are not only able to withstand the influence of negative outside forces but also are able to absorb them and reinterpret them in ways that acknowledge and further Māori worldviews and values for progressive growth.

Meeting Lyonel had a profound influence on my research focus. I began to conceive of ways to research and discuss Māori urban identities and experiences not as a problem to be identified and solved, but rather as a way to celebrate the power of cultural adaptability and innovative responses to the urbanization process. It was this realization that consolidated a major thesis of my ongoing research: Māori are often developing urban identities and creating urban geographies that are grounded in empowerment rather than only in crisis, assimilation, and resistance. And it was—and here is the critical point—my experiences *in the field* that played a crucial role in enabling me to question the dominant discourse of urban Māori as a problem and begin to investigate Māori senses of urban possibilities.

I would argue that the best qualitative social science research does not begin with a clear structure or outline, or with fully explicated theory and methodology, but rather that these develop through the process of the research itself. In many ways this runs counter to the research process as it is taught, yet this may come closer to what actually happens for many researchers, especially when they venture out into the exciting but messy world we call "the field." Allowing this process to unfold, and allowing oneself as researcher to develop and modify theory, methodology, and structure creates a research context within which the researcher is far more open to the stories, activities, phenomena, and forces that one is attempting to understand and analyze. This openness is critical because it honors those individuals and groups that are the focus of the research by allowing them to critically influence the direction, content, and spirit of the research being done. It is also important because it forces the researcher to remain deeply aware that it is never truly possible to objectively approach the study of human processes and phenomena. Any claim to do this is an act of appropriation and artificial division that will not only seriously compromise researchers' conclusions but also mark researchers as positioning themselves in a superior position vis-à-vis the people or organizations that are the focus of the study. Ultimately, being flexible in the field—being capable of adapting to new, different, or changing requirements—will allow your research focus to grow and blossom, and will lead to experiences that will transform you as a researcher and as a human being.

Notes

1. Aotearoa is the Māori place name for the country more commonly referred to as New Zealand; Māori is the collective name for the people of Polynesian origin who first discovered Aotearoa eight hundred to one thousand years ago.

2. The research discussed here is based on fieldwork undertaken in 2001, 2007, and 2008 in Aotearoa over a collective period of roughly six months (Marek 2010). This research consisted primarily of interviewing, both formally and informally, Māori living in cities, as well as participating in the everyday life of several Māori organizations with which I became associated, and documenting the cultural landscapes of Māori urbanisms through photographs, models, maps, and writing. The goal of my research was, and continues to be, to better understand and elucidate the relationship between contemporary Māori culture and cities in Aotearoa.

3. Throughout the course of this fieldwork I met many Māori, both formally and informally. My goal was to meet Māori from various socioeconomic, professional, and place backgrounds so as to get as broad a cross-section of Māori living in urban areas as possible. I did twenty intensive semistructured interviews with Māori living in Auckland, and more informal interviews and "talk-story" sessions with Māori and non-Māori in Hamilton, Rotorua, Gisborne, and Wellington. The Māori I spoke with included a DJ, cafe manager, several architects, a graphic designer, several professors, a PhD student, artists, a master carver, a master weaver, a filmographer, and several musicians. Their ages ranged from young adult to elderly, with an even mix of men and women.

4. Māori who have ancestral knowledge can, more often than not, identify their *whānau* (extended family), *hapū* (clan), and *iwi* (tribe). In Lyonel's case Ngāti Pikiao and Te Arawa are the *iwi* from which he is descended.

5. *Marae* are among the most profound and visible cultural landscapes found within Māori society. They are most noted for their elaborately carved meeting houses, but also consist of other buildings that together are enclosed by some sort of wall or fence. *Marae* are intensely revered sacred spaces, but also spaces that are used constantly in Māori society as places of teaching, places to solve community issues, places to bid farewell to the dead, and places to celebrate, honor, and welcome visitors. Arguably, one cannot truly understand Māori culture and society without understanding the *marae*.

Fieldwork on Two Wheels in Hanoi, Vietnam, or How I Learned to Stop Worrying and Enjoy the Ride

MARGARET BARNHILL BODEMER

LOOKING BACK ON MY INITIAL FIELDWORK experience in Hanoi, Vietnam, I realize now several things. First, I was terrified about "getting it right." Second, I was terribly anxious about meeting new people and making good impressions. Third, I basically was completely unsuited to participant observation, being very shy and "not much of a joiner" by nature. At the time though, I was mainly concerned with actually getting myself to my field site as I imagined it: the Vietnam Museum of Ethnology. My project aimed to contribute an ethnography of the museum as a site of intersections between domestic and foreign visitors, and between "official knowledge" and "popular knowledge" about Vietnam and its "national identity." I envisioned spending the majority of my funded year in the museum itself: interviewing and observing people, participating in events, getting to know the people behind the scenes, and so on. Sounds like a pretty typical anthropological fieldwork plan, doesn't it?—albeit, set in a museum instead of a village or other bounded site. Unfortunately, the closest place I found to live was a twenty-minute drive across town. Here is where my trouble began, or so I thought, because what I came to realize was that my "field site" was quite literally all around me.

Motorbikes are the primary means of transportation for most people in Hanoi. The capital city is a growing metropolitan area with traffic jams that are becoming more and more infamous. With a total national population estimated at ninety-one million, Vietnam's cities are not yet mega-cities on the scale of Bangkok or Jakarta or Los Angeles, but the population density of its two major cities, Hanoi and Ho Chi Minh City (HCMC), is astounding: 1,962 people per square kilometer for Hanoi and 3,530 for HCMC.[1] Motorbikes recently replaced bicycles, and although cars and buses are starting to become more common, Hanoi's many narrow roads make them impractical, and their high cost makes them unattainable for most people. Motorbikes thus reign. Unfortunately for me, I have always been completely terrified of any two-wheeled motorized transport. In order to get across town to the museum, I had the following choices: take a public bus and make several connections squeezed armpit to eyeball with others, take a motorbike taxi (*xe ôm*), ride a bicycle, or learn to drive a motorbike.

Being an independent person, I decided to get a bicycle and power my own commute. I geared up with a nice one-gear made-in-China pink bicycle and even managed to find a helmet. It turns out that December is pretty cold, and half a decade of graduate school in sunny Honolulu hardly prepared me for Hanoi's bone-chillingly wet winters. My bicycle commute took forty minutes each way and meant being stuck in air-clogging traffic amid the thousands of other commuters, most of them on motorbikes or on city buses belching black exhaust. After six weeks of recurring bronchial infections, I decided to learn how to drive a motorbike. Surprisingly, driving a motorbike was not that challenging, but the rules of the road and the seeming chaos of being jammed together with thousands of other motorists on the Hanoi roads were too challenging for my nerves.

On the other end of my commute, I faced similar difficulties. Each day that I arrived at the museum via some means of transportation besides my bicycle, at the end of the day I needed to find a way back. Outside the museum was a motley crew of motorbike taxis and car taxis parked and waiting for visitors leaving the museum in need of transport. After a series of misadventures with several of these guys, I realized it was all a scam. Each charged exorbitant fares, whether it was the taxicabs with their rigged meters, or the *xe ôm* asking rates that even a foreigner would reject. Furthermore, in the late afternoon, these guys were either sleeping off a long lunch at the pub (*bia hơi*) or still getting drunk on bad wine or, worse, causing erratic and outright dangerous driving. Because of the relatively far distance from the city center, these guys cornered the market and drove away legitimate competition.

Having sworn off these particular *xe ôms*, I went back to my bicycle commute. When I parked my bike each day in the museum employee lot and checked in with Mr. Cường, the parking lot guard, we chatted about the little things. One day I explained my problem and asked him, "How do I find a good *xe ôm?*" The next day, he told me he had found someone to help, and called over Mr. Anh, a museum employee in green coveralls . . .

one of the gardening staff! Well, it turned out he would not mind giving me a ride home each day, and a bit of extra income could help. Aha, I thought, this is the perfect arrangement, at least for returning home. At last, salvation! However, after two glorious weeks of stress-free rides home, Mr. Anh injured his arm and could not drive. Embarrassed, Mr. Cường volunteered to take over ferrying me on his own motorbike, but leaving his job at the museum for a half hour seemed like too much to ask of him, and I realized this would not work for the rest of the year.

Consequently I realized that I needed to find a motorbike taxi or *xe ôm* (literally, to sit behind the driver and hang on). The problem was, how would I find someone reliable and trustworthy in my new neighborhood? Previous summers spent doing language study in Hanoi had provided me with plenty of experience hiring taxis on the streets, and I was proud of my self-proclaimed *"xe ôm radar"* that helped me assess the potential merits of a driver quickly: he should be clear-eyed, not reek of alcohol, look steady, and convey a sense of calm, or at least, indifference toward a Vietnamese-speaking foreigner. In fact, some of my favorite conversations in the past had been with these drivers. However, in my neighborhood, I had not seen any motorbike taxis, or else I did not know how to recognize them. Here, outside the city center and tourist district, *xe ôm* drivers with their calls of "moto moto" and their penetrating stares seemed nowhere to be found.

I should pause and describe my neighborhood, Hanoi's Đống Đá district, and its very busy thoroughfare, Cát Linh Street. We rented a house, found through a real estate agent specializing in foreigners, that was located about halfway down one of the warren-like alleys off the main street. Like all the surrounding houses, ours was a narrow house, opening onto the alley, and surrounded on both sides by other houses. Known as "tube-houses," these long and low houses typify premodern Hanoi house architecture and are traced back to the eleventh century when houses surrounding the imperial citadel were taxed based on how much of the dwelling faced the street. Thus, Hanoians built their houses with the smallest face possible, to avoid high taxes. These houses were also often connected to markets and shop-houses, with stalls in front, which would close at night (Hoang and Nishimura 2000, 36). Furthermore, feudal regulations prohibited common-ers from building homes higher than the residences of kings (Hoang and Nishimura 2000, 46). Our house was originally one of these typical tube-houses, but its owner had recently reinvested the money made by renting to foreigners, to build several additional levels, until ending up with a six-story, three-bedroom, four-bathroom building with a rooftop terrace. Most of our neighbors had three- and four-story homes, so ours was somewhat conspicuous. We were the only foreigners in the area, at least as far as we knew.

Initially I asked our landlord (who did not live onsite) if she would introduce us to the neighbors, but she refused my request. Eventually I did manage to introduce myself to the immediate neighbors but for the most part I did not have a good way to describe what I was doing, other than working at the museum, which I discovered few of them had visited. Although they were cordial, I felt extremely awkward in these interactions after the first few weeks and I began to focus again on getting to work at the museum. Unwittingly, I began to ignore my neighborhood and surroundings.

After deciding to hire a driver, I could not easily observe whether or how my neighbors hired *xe ôm* or not. Every time I left my home and ventured out into the alley and out onto the street, I wondered how to find a good *xe ôm*. I knew that local people, in particular, those who did not drive themselves, often hired these reasonably priced and convenient motorbike taxis. For example, older women who did not drive but occasionally needed a ride to buy meat at a farther away market. How did they find them? As I strolled past the woman who sold noodle soup (*phở*) every morning in our alley from 6:00 to 9:00 with benches full of children and adults happily slurping away, I wondered whom to ask. The same as I passed by the woman who sold tea, sweets, and tobacco at the end of the alley from 7:00 in the morning until 2:00 in the afternoon. These features of local life began to be invisible to me, as I became increasingly anxious about attracting attention and just wanting to blend in. In my anxieties I began psychologically and physically isolating myself on my rooftop veranda, afraid of interacting with the people in my neighborhood. Somehow I began to forget about participant observation, what some argue is still the key feature of ethnographic fieldwork: being among people, participating in and observing what they are doing and so on. I began to forget about the broader context of my museum study: the larger sociocultural world of Hanoi and Vietnam itself.

Finally, one afternoon upon returning home, as I turned off the main street and into our alley, and I passed as usual the woman selling tea, it hit me: I needed to ask for help and advice! It had worked at the museum with Mr. Cường—why not in my neighborhood? The next morning, amid the usual chaos of people crowding through the alley going to work and school, I nervously and shyly approached the woman selling tea at the end of the alley. I figured at least there, if it turned out badly, I could slip away into the madness of the street and pretend it never happened. I primly addressed her, "Elder sister, can you help me?" And lo and behold, she gestured for me to sit down on one of her benches. Perching there I suddenly realized a completely untapped aspect of my fieldwork: my neighborhood. After two months, I had never spoken to anyone sitting there drinking tea, slurping noodles, or smoking tobacco out of their tall bamboo water pipes. Shyly, I asked her whether she knew a good *xe ôm* in the neighborhood who could take me to work. Without blinking an eye, she replied, "of course, just wait while I call him over." She stood up and waved to someone across the street with its six lanes of heavy traffic. Elated, I settled on the pencil-thin bench and concentrated on not toppling over out of sheer excitement. I could hardly concentrate on speaking correctly enough to have a chat with the tea lady, whose name turned out to be Mrs. Chi.

Literally within three minutes, a largely unremarkable-looking, middle-aged man in a worn T-shirt, jeans, plastic sandals, and faded cap pulled up on a worn but sturdy-looking, late-model Honda Wave. He popped the kickstand down and asked the central question: "Where are you going?" A brief exchange occurred, introductions were made, and the museum's address explained. And just like that I was on my way—not only to the museum that day—but also to the rest of my fieldwork. Over the next ten months of my fieldwork, Mr. Hùng,[2] or one of his colleagues, provided me with a safe and worry-free commute. Not only was he courteous, but I soon discovered he was one of the calmest and most skilled drivers I had ever encountered in Hanoi. Gradually, Mr. Hùng and I developed a kind of rapport, or a comfortable working relationship based on personal contact, that is so key to the ethnographic endeavor.

My search for a *xe ôm* and my interactions with Mr. Hùng and others in the neighborhood ultimately helped me realize that, beyond my fancy research proposal and well-laid plans, what I also needed was to learn as much about how people lived as possible. To understand why people did and thought the way they did, I needed to learn how to behave and how things worked. I needed to ask people for help. Finding transportation became the ability to find the hidden sources of everyday knowledge, hidden in plain sight. In asking for help, I had to become more honest and humble about my activities and I finally began to become a participant observer, an ethnographer. Inadvertently, in my personal and professional anxieties, I had become ensconced on my own "veranda," like the "armchair anthropologists" of old, regarding whom Bronislaw Malinowski had written:

> The anthropologist must relinquish his comfortable position in the long chair on the veranda of the missionary compound, government station, or planter's bungalow, where, armed with pencil

and notebook and at times with a whisky and soda, he has been
accustomed to collect statements from informants, write down
stories, and fill out sheets of paper with savage texts. He must go
out into the villages, and see the natives at work in gardens, on the
beach, in the jungle; he must sail with them to distant sandbanks
and to foreign tribes, and observe them in fishing, trading, and
ceremonial overseas expeditions. (1948, 146)

His reference to "savage texts" notwithstanding, Malinowski helps clarify
the kernel of truth that I had been ignoring. My interactions with Mr. Hùng
and my neighbors offered windows into the lives of ordinary people and
into the "imponderabilia of native life and typical behavior" (Malinowski
1961, 20)—features that people take for granted, but from which the ethnographer can learn. For example, one morning during our ride to the museum,
we saw a procession of colorfully dressed people, bearing large trays
and bundles walking along a dike. "An engagement party," commented
Mr. Hùng. He proceeded to discuss all the aspects of a traditional Vietnamese wedding, and then made comparisons with contemporary Hanoi weddings and those in his home province of Nam Định.[3] The more I talked with
Mrs. Chi, who ran the tea stand, the more I learned about the lives of these
so-called petty traders (người bán hàng rong) who subsisted on such enter-
prises that served the neighborhood, but occupied a somewhat marginalized social position. A widow, Mrs. Chi had also suffered disfigurement that
prevented her from keeping "a real job," her son told me one slow afternoon
at the tea stand. Here is where I began to realize the need for participant
observation to better understand the broader context of people's lives for
my study of the museum.

Each morning at 8:30 Mr. Hùng would stop outside the rented house
I shared with my husband. Each afternoon at 4:30 he would be outside the
gate of the museum. After about three months he told me one day: "I bought
a cell phone; here is the number; call me when you are ready." By the time
my fieldwork was ending and it was time for me to return home, he had
made preparations to purchase his own motorbike, in part helped by the
extra income from my commute. Owning a motorbike meant he would be
able to make a better living and, presumably, greater financial independence and stability. After all, he not only supported his wife and young
son, but also other relatives back in Nam Định province.

Being ferried on the motorbike allowed me twenty minutes each way
of freedom, to go unnoticed, since I adopted the coverings that most women
and some men wear in traffic: long-sleeved shirt with built-in bandanna and

hand-coverings, a hat, and sunglasses. The shirt was one that I bought along-side the road, sold especially for women on motorbikes to cover themselves from the dust of the road and the burning rays of the sun. Women wear these to keep their skin from getting dark, and even some men wear dust-masks, as everyone complains about respiratory ailments caused by the dust of the road. When a photo of my outfit circulated, one friend back home teased me: "This looks like a lady who keeps a thousand cats at home, scary." As I tell my students when I describe these adventures, at least I did not carry an umbrella as some do. In the larger context of Hanoi traffic, my outfit blended in and I became unnoticeable. This also granted me the only time of anonymity in my fieldwork, where I felt that everywhere I went people stared at me as a foreigner in their midst, albeit one who spoke the language. As many fieldworkers have discussed, the lack of privacy in the field is often a typical experience. This had contributed to my experience of culture shock, of that alienation and discomfort often experienced in a new setting that can cause emotional distress and even physical illness.

Asking for help and stepping out of my comfort zones helped me to overcome this culture shock and led to new discoveries, almost like cross-ing a barrier. Anthropologists often say that participant observation teaches us as much about ourselves as about the peoples and cultural practices we study—I found this to be true. I never realized how little I like to be the center of attention. In our neighborhood, with its warren of alleys, every-one knows what is going on. Everyone knows what everyone else is doing. There is a total lack of privacy. Even when you draw your curtains and go to sleep at 4:00 in the morning you still hear the woman open the alleyway storage shed to pull out her benches and soup-making operation. Every Saturday morning the neighborhood work party convened at 6:00 outside our door, and marked the occasion with a wake-up call of someone banging on a metal pie pan with a wooden spoon. When we first moved in, I put out a bag of recyclables and within minutes it was scavenged by collectors. Want to know why Mr. Dao left his wife? Ask the woman selling fruit from baskets two doors down. Want to know why Mrs. Chi's daughter is not married yet? Ask at the tea stand. And so on. Ultimately I had to learn how to tap into these local networks.

It turns out that Malinowski complained—secretly, he thought—about this stuff too. How could he know his wife would one day publish his diary with these thoughts (Malinowski 1989)! But of course in the end, this is the start of making good ethnography—this is how we gain those insights into the basic norms and expectations in our host communities. As anthro-pologists, again and again, we find that we end up having to ask for help, put ourselves out there, and be fools. Looking back, I can see that the personal and professional anxieties I experienced during my fieldwork were not uncommon. The initial few months especially were characterized by culture shock, lack of self-confidence, and an uncertainty about the whole enterprise. I felt the need to "get it right" but in a sense did not know where to start. As Paul Rabinow candidly reflected, "[Having arrived I] had little to do but to start 'my' fieldwork. Actually it was not exactly clear to me what that meant. . . . After all, now that I was in the field, everything was fieldwork" (2007, 11). In my case, I realized not only "everything was fieldwork," but that participant observation also sometimes meant "to put aside camera, note book and pencil and to join himself in what is going on" (Malinowski 1961, 21).

In ethnographic fieldwork, experiencing the everyday lives of people in your fieldwork site is essential. Ideally, the anthropologist should be involved in the world around themselves as much as possible, observing what people do, and establishing a means to analyze everyday life in addition to their specific topic of study. This creates a basis for your understanding of the problem you are exploring. So much of existing in a new environment is learning how to behave. The routine elements of daily life itself can present many challenges, which as a researcher, you may not realize you have to face. Learning and living everyday life is both complex and simple, provided you can ask for help. After all, as Malinowski can still remind us: "Open-air anthropology, as opposed to hearsay note-taking, is hard work, but it is also great fun" (1948, 147).

Notes

1. Figures drawn from the 2009 census and reported on the General Office of Statistics Web site, http://www.gso.gov.vn. The population is categorized into fifty-four ethnic groups, including the ethnic Vietnamese who account for 85 percent of the population. The national language is Vietnamese and religions include Buddhism and Catholicism. National politics and history include the dominant narrative of "resistance to foreign aggression" against the Mongols, Chinese, French, and Americans, among others. Geographically, Vietnam is often described as having the shape of a dragon, with a long coastline and fifty kilometers across at its narrowest. The length of the country roughly corresponds to the geographic area of California, Oregon, and Washington combined.
2. Rather than Mr. or Mrs., Vietnamese employs personal pronouns in addressing others. In local terms, I would use "anh" with Mr. Hùng, or, "older brother" for someone slightly older than me, in a relatively formal setting

with someone whom you do not know well. In this essay, I use "Mr." so as not to alienate the reader.

3. One of Vietnam's fifty-eight provinces, Nam Định is located ninety kilometers south of Hanoi and is unusual in its large numbers of Catholics, many of whom trace their genealogies to seventeenth-century conversions. Many taxi drivers, laborers, and petty traders are what might be considered "migrant workers" who come to the city for work, while their families stay in the village, relying on remittances from their city-dwelling kin. They are not recognized as Hanoi residents by the authorities, since they are without identification cards, so many live somewhat marginally.

The Cultural Power of Robots in Japan

HIROFUMI KATSUNO

THE SENSATIONAL 1996 DEBUT of Honda's P2, a bipedal robot capable of walking with unprecedented fluidity in motion, represented a technological breakthrough in humanoid projects within the field of Japanese robotics. P2's successor, ASIMO, released in 2000, further accelerated the boom in humanoid research in Japan. While most human-shaped robots outside Japan are relegated to university laboratories, in Japan the humanoid robot has become a site of intense political economic, sociocultural, and emotional investment. The motivations and desires to develop humanoid robot technology emanate from various sources, including the government, big industry, academic and scientific institutions, and amateur technologists. These diverse players and interests are united by a strong hope that the developing field of humanoid robotics will become a major industry and a globally recognized cultural icon of twenty-first-century Japan.

As an anthropologist who studies Japan, I have been concerned with the cultural expression of humanoid robots and their social impact in society. How does this emergent technology set a dramatic stage for shaping a broad array of imagination, obsession, and desire in the world's preeminent technological society? What kinds of meanings and concerns are attributed to humanoid robots? Why is Japan so deeply fascinated with this particular technology that it has devoted more to the development of humanoid robotics than any other country? What is the relationship between the development of this technology and the fact that Japanese popular culture contains many robotic stories and images?

With these questions in mind, I conducted fieldwork from September 2005 through June 2007 among a community of technological visionaries who engage in the nascent technoculture of humanoid robots. I entered this community as a native Japanese anthropologist, but this community has its own culture, history, and literature. It was new to me. In September 2005, I started fieldwork in Fukuoka city. The primary reason for this choice was its designation as a special unregulated district that encourages experimentation with robotics in public space. The city government operates an interactive robotics museum called Robosquare that links the general public with industrial, governmental, and academic institutions. The museum has more than fifty kinds of robots on display and attracts more than 100,000 visitors annually. It also holds various kinds of events such as robot contests and academic and business conferences, as well as robotics classes for adults and children. I started my pilot project at Robosquare in September 2005, in order to research robotics policies, expand my research network, and gather background information on robotics-related events in Japan. In the first two months at Robosquare, I spent most of my time interviewing museum visitors and researchers who engaged with the projects at Robosquare.

At the same time, I was seeking a "real" field site—a particular group or community setting—where I could conduct intensive participant observation for an extended period of time. Since my intention was to analyze people's subjective experiences with robots, my own commitment to the first-hand experience of robotics was necessary. The research reached the first turning point in November 2005, when I had a chance to attend a robot-building workshop for the general public at Robosquare. Using a KHR robot kit,[1] and with extensive help from graduate students who were affiliated with Robosquare, I attempted to build a one-foot-long human-shaped robot. The completion of this robot—although it was barely able to walk in its early stage—brought about a drastic change in my fieldwork. In March 2006, I was invited to participate in a robot battle competition at the museum. The performance of my robot was woefully insufficient in competition with other robots. But though I lost, I was greatly rewarded in my fieldwork. Along with other local robot builders, including some from the same workshop, I met highly skilled robotics hobbyists from all over Japan, most of whom regularly participated in an event that is among the most popular and frequently held humanoid robot spectacles: Robo-One.[2] The vast majority of these technological enthusiasts were male corporate engineers who have professional levels of engineering expertise and knowledge. Relying on their technological competence, early adopters of this new technology designed and built their own personal humanoids as leisure activity. Yet even for these professionals, what lies behind their passion for robot building is the romantic potential to realize a common boyhood dream—the creation and possession of a real robot.

Based on our common experience at the competition, seven of us from Fukuoka formed a group to develop our robots collaboratively and started to meet at Robosquare on a weekly basis. This group became the main community of my fieldwork. We met almost every weekend at Robosquare from 10:00 in the morning to 6:00 in the evening to develop our robots together. We also met several times a week after work, sharing an obsessive passion for robot building and deep interests in engineering. In most of these meetings, even in the most casual one in a small pub, we did not talk about anything except topics related to robotics, or technology in general. Besides these regular meetings, we also met to demonstrate our personal humanoids in public spaces, such as museums and department stores, as well as traveling to other cities, such as Tokyo and Osaka, to participate in Robo-One–related events. In this process, my fieldwork network had expanded to several other cities. Thus, my own participation in creating a robot as a neophyte robot builder led to deeper involvement in the community of engineers.

My involvement as a core member of the Fukuoka group required a great deal of reflexivity because it forced me to consider how my participation as practitioner influenced the formation of this community as well as the ways by which I observed it as researcher. In other words, I had to reconcile tensions between my dual identities of inside practitioner and outside observer. The boundary of these identities became increasingly blurred, particularly through my own extensive exposure (along with my robot) upon the front stage of robot culture. In the robocentric climate of mid-2000s Japan, I was invited to participate in more than ten public events in Fukuoka and Tokyo. Venues included a hospital, a science museum, an industrial exposition, and a festival at a subway station. Within the space of a single year I was interviewed as a robot builder by a number of mass media companies and institutions: national television stations such as NHK and TV Asahi; local news stations in Tokyo and Fukuoka; a local newspaper; a German national broadcast company; one robotics-related print magazine; and two Web-based magazines.

In this situation, I attempted to create and maintain my point of view as an outside observer by keeping a reflexive description of my subjective, lived experiences in the form of a field journal. In this practice, I not only documented observational, descriptive information (for example, settings, actions, and conversations), but I also actively recorded my own insights, impressions, speculations, thoughts, questions, and criticisms. The following quote from my field journal vividly portrays my self-reflection (with some sense of confusion) on the very processes by which I became deeply involved as a participant as well as observer in the robotics community:

> It was a splendid mid-November day when I went to a large robot exposition held at the gigantic complex called Akihabara Crossfield—the central institute of information technology in Tokyo. Despite the clarity of light outside on that sunny day, stepping into the exposition venue, I felt as if I had come out from the shade into the sun. This space seemed to have nothing to do with the "recession ripple" or "sense of stagnation" which had dominated Japan's public mentality for over a decade. The space was filled with real laughter and a sense of wonder. Above all else, it was full of dreams, individual and collective, shaping an integrated worldview and story. A crowd already surrounded Honda's Asimo, the world's most advanced bipedal humanoid robot, surrounded by signs reading "The Power of Dreams." Asimo's movements were so fluid and lifelike that they stirred the public imagination for the robotic future, as if the long-anticipated and dreamt-of age of science fiction lay tantalizingly around the corner.
>
> After the first round of the Asimo show, I went on to the waiting room for exposition participants. My robot was to compete in the martial arts tournament. Other participants—mostly corporate engineers, who made their own humanoid robots in their leisure time—had already made the final adjustments to their robots. The tables had been crammed with various kinds of industrial tools. I found a clean table at the edge of the room, where I opened my carrying case and put my robot on it. I checked the remaining battery level, as well as the condition of the radio transmitter. I had started making this radio-operated robot over a year ago, but I had recently made major changes to the design. I called it Wilder 01. Modeled upon an American football player, it was designed to replicate a variety of human movements. The robot was probably a reflection of my nostalgia for a former identity, because I played college football myself, but who knows?
>
> Moving to the wings, I saw a huge crowd surrounding the stage, most of whom had probably come there directly after Asimo's first round. Media queues took up positions in the front row, waiting to start shooting the next robotic martial arts competition that would start in a minute or so. My name and the name of my robot were called. I stepped

up on the stage, holding Wilder 01. My opponents' robot was called A-Do and had a huge head of distinctive hair. Sugawara Yusuke, one of "her" creators, is a robotic engineer who often appears in various media outlets and major robotic events as a master robot builder.

With the referee's call, "Fight!" the two robots quickly took side-steps in time and kept their proper distance. Soon after, both of them landed their first attacks simultaneously. My robot gave a quick jab while A-Do did a "forward handspring kick." A-Do's attack, with the force of its whole weight behind the two-footed kick, not only drowned out Wilder 01's light punch but also knocked off "his" body casing. In a moment, the referee started to call "One, two, three . . ." It echoed in the venue with the roar of the crowd. Wilder 01 slowly but steadily bent his legs, twisted his torso, squared his elbows, and finally stood up like a real human just as the referee called out "Seven." Again, the audience pulsed with excitement. Meanwhile, A-Do had already stood up, proudly raising her hands to receive waves of applause from the audience. As the roar got louder, I felt an intimate connection with the audience through my robot's performance. . . .

In the convivial, informal setting of an izakaya (a Japanese-style restaurant) after the event, Sugawara and I sat next to each other and looked back on when we first met at a robot competition in Fukuoka in March 2006. When I was just starting my fieldwork with this community, I spoke with Suguwara as an outside researcher. He explained his obsession with robot building: "I believe that human beings are programmed to form special emotional attachments to human-shaped objects, and we, the robot builders, are those who grew up under the strong effect of this particular gene. Otherwise, I can't explain even to myself why I am so into this, almost as if I were possessed!" Unable to fully verbalize his love of robot-building, he finally told me, "You should just make a robot to fully understand it!" This conversation motivated me to actually create my own robot, although I thought at first that this was a totally quixotic challenge.

Since then, I had talked with Sugawara many times, including one formal interview, and yet our rapport in the bar that night was decisively different from the past. Now we shared the perspective and spirit of robot builders after performing together on the same stage, entertaining the crowd with our robots. Directing a warm look toward me as always, Sugawara eventually posed a question to me with a conspiratorial smile: "So, has your DNA finally been activated?" I smiled back and said, "Maybe it's getting activated, but, at least, I felt today

*that I was connected to the audience through my robot. It became part
of myself." Sugawara responded, "Now you see the dream in the robot."*

The field journal allowed me to conduct a preliminary analysis during my
fieldwork. It fostered self-reflection that allowed me to maintain a critical
distance from the community I was working with. However, it also expec-
tedly revealed an emergent question about my positionality as both a participant and observer. Concerned about "how I influence" the formation
of the community as I became increasingly involved, I uncritically presumed
the community to be a fixed entity. Thus, I initially attempted to approach the
community in a unilateral manner as an outside researcher. And yet, in
keeping a weekly journal of my fieldwork experiences in a first-person narrative, I came to realize that I should be conscious of my own changes as a
participant vis-à-vis the dynamic formation of this community and Japanese
robot culture at large. This emerging technoculture did not exclusively develop within a physically bounded environment, but within broader sociocultural spheres that actively integrated social actors drawn to humanoid
robots. In the case of the Robo-One community, which I consider to be
representative of Japanese robot culture, these include not only the amateur robot builders who actively take part in the competitions, but a host of
peripheral actors as well: robotics scientists and engineers in university and
corporate settings, administrators, political and economic resources, various arms of the mass media network, freelance writers, event coordinators,
anime/manga creators, teachers in science education, robot fanatics referred
to as "robot-watchers," the general audiences of the competition, and popular
culture markets. How could an anthropologist not become part of it?

Whenever I showed my face as an anthropologist to the members of
the community, they often reacted as if they had forgotten this fact and teased
me with this quote: "go for wool and come home shorn." This perfectly cap-
tures our relationship in the field. Even if I strategically tried to have a sense
of distance from the community to retain my identity as an outside researcher, it perceived me as an insider. Once aware of this inclusive power
of Japanese robot culture, I stopped forcing myself to make my dual identities distinct. I rather let myself go with the flow of the community and kept
describing the changing process within myself and identities in the field.
This became the foundation of my reflexive ethnography.

My fieldwork ended on the day of my wedding: June 2, 2007. I invited
five of the robot builders from the Fukuoka group to the wedding party,
where we entertained nearly one hundred guests with a demonstration of
our personal humanoids. I met these informants just a few months into

my field research and subsequently developed closer relationships with them than with anyone else I met in the field. They were there with me from my first robot competition at Robosquare to my last robot demonstration at my wedding reception. The year and a half we had spent together learning to build robots transformed us and our identities as we became participants in the formation of Japan's humanoid robot culture. Several weeks after the wedding, I went back to Hawai'i, where my graduate school was located, with painful reluctance. But this pain seemed to work as a rite of passage through which I regained my identity as an anthropologist. In fact it was only in Hawai'i, nearly the opposite of Japan's hypertechnological atmosphere, that I was finally ready to write an ethnography based upon my fieldwork.

Notes

1. Kondo Kagaku's KHR series robot kit has sold more than ten thousand units to electronic hobbyists and university and corporate laboratory researchers. The kit won the Japanese Ministry of Economy, Trade and Industry (METI) 2007 robot award.
2. Robo-One regularly draws several hundred contestants who design, build, and program their own humanoid robots for competition in events such as hand-to-hand combat, sprints, dance, and soccer competitions.

Encountering Maoist Propaganda in Pastoral Inner Mongolia

HONG JIANG

IN 2001, ten years into my study of grassland changes in the Mongolian community Uxin Ju in northern China, I gained access to a set of documents I had been looking for: documents recording events and activities of Uxin Ju as a national model in China's grassland and societal transformation that occurred from 1958 through the 1970s. After studying the documents, however, the challenges I faced made me wish that I had never gained access to them in the first place.

Uxin Ju is a Mongol-dominated community in the Ordos area of the Inner Mongolia region. Situated on the Mu Us sandy land just north of the Great Wall, Uxin Ju's natural environment is dry, and its grass and shrub vegetation has long been used in animal husbandry. At the time of my last visit in 2001, the community had over five thousand people, and sheep had taken over goats as the main livestock on the increasingly managed grassland. Mongols had mostly settled down, and their grassland had been fenced up following the Chinese state's policy of land privatization. Traditional nomadic lifestyles of high mobility had largely disappeared.

I first visited Uxin Ju in the spring of 1991 to study land use changes. Pushed progressively by the Chinese who have moved into Inner Mongolia, the Mongols moved farther into the heart of the Mu Us sandy land where rainfed farming is impossible. With the policies of the Chinese Communist government promoting intensive land use, however, Uxin Ju had witnessed drastic increases in planted trees, irrigation, and cropland expansion. In tracing the origin of these intensive land use practices, I learned about a period when Uxin Ju was positioned famously in the Chinese national scene, promoted as a national model in grassland development.

In 1958, under the heavy pressure of the Great Leap Forward launched by Mao,[1] the Mongols in Uxin Ju launched a communist-style campaign to reform the grassland. That year, Uxin Ju experienced a drought, under which horse-poisoning grass (*Oxytropis glabra* in the legume family) flourished on the dry sandy grassland. The plant is the last to be grazed by sheep and goats; after a period of grazing, animals' nervous systems are damaged. From an ecological perspective, this grass acts as a regulator of the grassland ecosystem. Signs of livestock damage signify overburden on the grassland and a need to cull the livestock. But since the Great Leap Forward was so much about the numbers, a reduced number of livestock became a sign of backwardness. Uxin Ju's party branch devised a revolutionary approach to reform the grassland: they mobilized all able bodies in the area to physically remove the horse-poisoning grass from the grassland.

This was a marked change in Uxin Ju, as the local elders and Buddhist monks considered the horse-poisoning grass sacred, and its removal blasphemy. This veneration of natural elements comes from two cultural traditions. The Mongolian culture emphasizes the unity of culture and nature, and their nomadic lifestyle favors a nonaggressive adaptation to nature. Buddhism, an important belief held by the Mongols, encourages the recognition of divine source of all lives. To remove the horse-poisoning grass, the government first needed to change people's ideas about it. Mao's call to transform the landscape was first and foremost a political project of transforming people's minds. In addition, nonparticipation bore the significant risk of one's being politically criticized or even persecuted. From the start, Uxin Ju's campaign to reform the grassland was a political act. Subsequent actions included planting the moving sand with *Artemisia Ordosica* shrub and willow trees, enclosing the grassland, opening the grassland for cropping, and developing irrigation.[2] These intensified land use practices deviated sharply from the Mongols' age-old nomadic tradition, whereby people adapted to the grassland by raising livestock and shifting grazing locations to allow the grassland to regenerate naturally.

In 1964, after the disastrous Great Leap Forward culminated in the subsequent Great Famine that claimed thirty-five to forty-five million lives, China went through a short period of pulling back. Mao needed something to rouse the country. He selected Dazhai, a farming village in North China's Shanxi Province, as a national model for its self-reliance in agricultural rebuilding after a flooding disaster. Mao's exhortation, "In Agriculture, Learn from Dazhai," quickly spread all over China. In the dogmatic and "one knife cuts all" political environment of China, this meant even pastoral regions were expected to emulate Dazhai and build up agricultural fields (Shapiro 2001).

This was when the Inner Mongolia leader Ulanhu creatively followed Mao's politics while trying to save Mongol animal husbandry: he erected Uxin Ju as the "Pastoral Dazhai" model to be emulated by pastoral regions. Uxin Ju, now known as the "Pastoral Dazhai," became a national model, receiving delegations from China's pastoral areas, and even guests from Africa, to learn from its examples. Numerous sites were established for these visits, showcasing intensive land use such as grassland enclosure, tree planting, and cropland cultivation.

In researching Uxin Ju's grassland campaign, I learned that the local government had produced a set of propaganda documents to record the campaign. In the early 1970s, after the Mongolian leader Ulanhu was persecuted and many ordinary Mongols suffered with him, Uxin Ju tried to resurrect the "Pastoral Dazhai" name in order to gain political clout. The local government hired a writer to produce a series of documents about Uxin Ju's grassland campaign—this was the document that I referred to at the beginning of this essay.

I collected all materials that I could get my hands on regarding Uxin Ju's grassland campaign: photos, newspaper articles, government documents, even a film on the campaign. I conducted many interviews with campaign participants on their experiences, and visited the various sites where the grassland campaign took place. Many times, I asked the local government leaders about the set of documents that I had heard about, and each time I was told they did not know about the documents or could not find them anymore.

Then, one day in 2001, when I was visiting Uxin Ju, a former local official named Galutu who assisted my work came knocking at my door. He said he wanted to show me something. He took me to the abandoned office building of the local government. At the end of the hallway was a locked room. He stuck his hand through the broken window and opened the door from inside. I was led into the room. Spread before me were piles of scattered government documents—he pointed at the piles and said, "Here are the Pastoral Dazhai documents you've been looking for." I was shocked!

He left me alone there, with the "treasure" I had been hunting for over the years. I searched through the piles, found more than two dozen handwritten volumes of documents for "Pastoral Dazhai," mostly from the 1970s. I took the documents, reasoning that they would otherwise simply be destroyed. I never mentioned this to anyone in the local government, nor did

I tell Galutu how much I took. As far as I know, I have the only remaining propaganda material for "Pastoral Dazhai Uxin Ju."

I brought the documents to Beijing and then to the United States without difficulties—they now sit in my office at University of Hawai'i. However, it was difficult to analyze them: they were pure propaganda! After spending months reading, classifying, and translating these documents, I became so dejected that I wanted nothing to do with them. Later, I only consulted with these documents lightly, never really using them in academic writings. I understand now why they were abandoned in the first place.

When the editors of this book contacted me about fieldwork stories, I immediately thought of these documents. I felt I owed them something, some kind of closure. Having distanced myself from them for ten years now, I gained some perspective. Let me summarize the content of the documents in three areas, and then discuss the related issue of authenticity in fieldwork collections.

First, Mao's idea of humans dominating nature showed vividly through the pages. Mao perceived opposite forces in the landscape and in the cosmos (Samuels 1978). Contradictions are universal; only through constant struggle could unity be achieved. Following Marx, Mao believed that proletarians possessed all the power needed to transform the natural world. The act to reform the objective world or landscape was also a way to reform man himself. The slogans popular in China at that time announced a "battle with nature (*xiang zi ran jin jun*)" in order to "alter the heaven and change the earth (*gai tian huan di*)." The following passage from the Uxin Ju documents speaks directly about this ideology:

> [If we] use Mao's thought to equip our mind, fully mobilize positive elements in the people, dare to initiate battle with nature, then any miracles in the world can be created. This is the dialectic relationship between humans and the outside world; this is dialectics, this is philosophy. . . . How can we make the desert serve human beings? The key is the humans. In the relationship between humans and nature, humans are the primary; to change the world, we have to change people first; to change people, we have to change their minds first. Using Mao's thought to equip our mind, we can reform heaven and earth and create miracles. (Uxin Ju documents 1959–1972)

Second, direct connections between politics and nature were frequently made. I read page after page of how politics guide relationships with nature and lead to success. Who are the enemies? The rich landlords and Buddhist lamas who held "backward" views, and the sand that encroached on people's lives. In 1959, the Mongols spent the fall season planting *Artemisia* shrubs on the sandy land, but most of the shrubs died. Class enemies were quoted as saying it was wrong to plant the shrubs on the sandy land. What to do? Mao said: "All those that the enemies oppose, we are for; all those the enemies are for, we oppose." The Mongols studied Mao's work and were determined to transform the sandy land. What would happen when the battle with nature is won? Here is a description of what that might look like: "The sky has never been so blue and the grassland has never been so beautiful. People of Uxin Ju have never been so uplifted and full of spirit—they use the utmost revolutionary enthusiasm to welcome the revolutionary spring of the great Cultural Revolution" (Uxin Ju documents 1959–1972).

Third, the human body was treated as a liability, an obstacle to socialist consciousness. The body had to be soiled to be revolutionary, and the individual had to abandon personal feelings to be pure. The documents contained a description of a meeting that took place in 1963 following Mao's call to "Learn from the example of Lei Feng," a selfless soldier who prized himself as a "nail in the socialist machine." To remove bourgeois aesthetic ideals in the young people, Uxin Ju's campaign leader Baoriledai organized a discussion on "what is beauty?" Some said "Good horses are beautiful, pretty clothes are beautiful." Baoriledai renounced these understandings and explained the five beauties in Lei Feng's diary: down-to-earth working people are beautiful; workers with oil-soiled clothes are beautiful; soldiers in patched uniforms are beautiful; working people with callused hands are beautiful; faces darkened by the sun are beautiful. These are examples of beauty for proletarian laborers.

Even more extreme was a radical sentiment that sacrificing one's mortal body could help one to gain eternal life in the religion of communism. Take for example the heroic death of Sirensu, age forty-six, who suffered from a severe stomach illness:

> In order to fulfill the grass-cutting task, she carried her child and herded the sheep for over 10 km. While taking care of the herd, she cut grass. One day, her illness worsened. The production team leader asked her to return home and nurse her illness; she said, "my illness is nothing serious; revolutionaries are not even afraid of death." When cutting grass, she fainted. When she came to, her child was crying at her side. She put her baby on the donkey and

went to a nearby family. She rested a little and then wanted to get up to continue working. But she was too weak to stand up. At this moment, she thought of Chairman Mao's great image, and immediately inexhaustible strength came to her body. She recited Mao's words "resolute and unafraid of sacrifice, surmount every difficulty to win victory." She was determined to leave, but fainted again. This heroic woman sacrificed gloriously for the revolutionary course.
(Uxin Ju documents 1959–1972)

There are many similar sacrifices described in the documents: Liu Weichun, a sent-down youth from Naijing, now a veterinarian, checked on livestock during a raging unfamiliar snowstorm and was encouraged by Mao's words "first do not be afraid of hardship and second do not be afraid of death." Geligema was in her sixties and had high blood pressure, but she participated in well digging day and night, even as she fainted several times but pushed on. The stories go on.

If I treat the Uxin Ju documents as mere political discourse, I could gain insights on the grassland campaign as I described above. The issue of truthfulness does, however, plague my mind: Was what the documents described true? Did people really believe that Mao's words could bring a new heaven and earth? Did Baoriledai really say those things about beauty? Did Sirensu die with Mao's words on her lips? I chased after these documents for years, excited when I gained access to them. In the back of my mind, I thought of these documents as genuine historical archives—not fake ones. But having grown up in Mao's China, why did I expect these documents to be anything but political propaganda? Had I forgotten that writing the truth was a risky business? Going to school in the 1970s myself, I remember having to write essays criticizing Confucius, someone my father spoke of with respect privately. However, I copied all the right words from the newspapers and earned good scores.

Fictitiousness was a national "disease," and many nationally known stories during Mao's time turned out to be fictions. The "White-Haired Girl," a famed modern opera persona of a poor girl forced into the mountains by a vicious landlord, in reality was based on a white-haired deity that people worshipped at night in northern China. The Mongolian sisters Longmei and Yurong lost in the freezing snowstorm were saved by Hasichaolu, a Mongol intellectual labeled as a "rightist," and not by the hero railway worker, communist party member, Wang Fuchen, as the reports and movies said. Story writers grabbed a figment of the truth, and reworked crucial details to fit with the grand rhetoric of socialist politics and communist ideology.

These Uxin Ju documents speak to a larger question of archival collection in studying modern China. There is propaganda in all of the documents I have collected—especially those collected from the early 1970s. And earlier, in the 1960s, newspaper articles about Uxin Ju's grassland campaign were also political, full of Mao quotations and revolutionary zeal. After the 1980s, even though politics have changed, official documents are still controlled by the communist party. It is often difficult to decipher reality—real motives, intentions, and results—during field research. I could only use documents as references, and rely on interviews and recalled stories. But problems remain. I suspect the interviews were also tainted by politics and brainwashing, and hence my research results are generally complicated by "partial truths," a problem that James Clifford (1986) sees as characteristic of contemporary ethnography as a whole.

The Uxin Ju documents remain my "precious" possession, reminding me what communist politics are about, illustrating the propaganda underlying the Uxin Ju national model for grassland development. They speak silently about the daunting challenge regarding the truth claims of fieldwork material. If I have enough courage to face the documents, perhaps I could delve into them to gain more insights into the inhumanity of the communist campaign. The price of such an undertaking? Frustration and dejection—something I am unwilling to pay.

Notes

1. The Great Leap Forward was a political movement in China in 1958–1961, during which Mao ordered people in China to engage in drastic measures to build a socialist utopia. Mongols were pressured to raise more livestock and transform the sandy land.
2. Readers interested in learning about the mixed effects of these grassland changes can consult my earlier writings (Jiang 2004, 2006).

When the Field Is Your Home

Doing Advocacy Work and Academic Work in Hawai'i

Jonathan Y. Okamura

Thirty years ago in the early 1980s, I began my fieldwork with Filipino immigrants in an inner-city area of Honolulu called Kalihi for my doctoral dissertation in anthropology. I chose Kalihi as my field site because it had the largest urban community of Filipino immigrants in Hawai'i, and my research was concerned with the expression of immigrant Filipino identity and culture. I discuss below some of the advocacy efforts I have made in support of the Filipino American community, given their persisting subordinate economic and political status in Hawai'i. Insofar as I call for anthropologists to be willing to serve as advocates of the people with whom they conducted their research, my recommendation can be considered an example of "engaged anthropology." According to two of its proponents, Setha M. Low and Sally Engle Merry (2010), anthropological engagement includes: (1) sharing and support, (2) teaching and public education, (3) social critique, (4) collaboration, (5) advocacy, and (6) activism, all of which I have done at different times as I discuss below. Hardly radical, engaged anthropology pales in comparison to the direct action of proceeding as if there is no state advocated by anarchist anthropologist David Graeber, one of the major intellectual resources of the "occupy" movements that emerged in 2011.

As a result of ongoing emigration from the Philippines, Filipino Americans have become a substantial majority of the population of Kalihi, and they have transformed it into even more of a Filipino community than it was three decades ago. Over the years, I have continued my research in Kalihi and have written about Filipino Americans there as a diasporic community that maintains transnational connections with the Philippines, as in my book *Imagining the Filipino American Diaspora* (1998). Most recently, in 2013 I gave a guided tour of the Filipino American community in Kalihi for a television crew from Montreal, Canada, that was filming a documentary on Honolulu for a series on global port cities. As we walked the streets of Kalihi, I noted the many distinctly Filipino two-story houses with Spanish-style embellishments, such as tile roofs and wrought-iron railings and fences, and Filipino small businesses, including remittance shops for sending cash to the Philippines.

For my initial fieldwork, I rented a room in a house owned by a Filipino immigrant family on Gulick Avenue, one of the main streets in Kalihi well known at that time for the "purple house" occupied by the "purple man," an elderly gentleman who liked to wear purple clothes. Using their home as my base, I was the fortunate beneficiary of much assistance from the many Filipino immigrants I met and interacted with in Kalihi. These acts of generosity and kindness began with the family I lived with for more than two years who made me feel a part of their family.[1] Without them, I would not have been able to obtain my PhD degree and eventually my tenured full professorship at the University of Hawai'i at Mānoa.

I write as a non-Filipino—a local Japanese American from Hawai'i—with a much more privileged status than I had as a graduate student. As for my fieldwork, the greatest assistance I received came from my "key informants." These are community members who have specialized knowledge about their culture, and an anthropologist depends upon them for considerable guidance and help with their research. I became very good friends with one of my key informants whom I saw on almost a daily basis, and through him I was able to meet many other Filipino immigrants, which greatly expanded my network of contacts and thus my data. Besides being a well-known community leader, my friend was a travel agent and provided me with a substantially discounted ticket and invited me to travel with him and other *balikbayans* (immigrant returnees) to their hometown in Ilokos Norte province in the Philippines for the annual town fiesta. During the nearly two weeks we were there, I stayed with my friend at his home, ate with him at his relatives' and friends' homes, including numerous *bienvenida* (welcoming) parties, and was introduced by him to many of his relatives and friends as he had done in Honolulu. Perhaps thinking that he would be bestowing a great honor upon me, my friend suggested that I be the *consorte* or escort of their hometown association queen in the parade that opened the town fiesta. So, feeling somewhat embarrassed, I donned a *barong tagalog* Philippine dress shirt and rode atop a float through the town standing next to the queen who was a junior at Farrington High School in Kalihi and about half my age. I consoled myself with the thought that, by definition, participant observation can require anthropologists to do things they usually would not. But my visit to the Philippines really opened doors for me in Kalihi, because once people knew that I had been there, they seemed more willing to cooperate with my research. Visiting the Philippines with *balikbayans* also contributed to my understanding of the diasporic ties that Filipino emigrants maintained with their relatives in their hometowns, evident in the distribution of U.S. dollars and consumer goods ranging from cans of Spam to designer clothing.

My sense of obligation and responsibility to the Filipino American community led me in 1998 to take a very active role in a highly notable protest against anti-Filipino racism. This controversy has been described, admittedly in exaggeration, as the "most significant political struggle over Asian American culture in the past several decades." In 1998 the Association for Asian American Studies (AAAS), the foremost national organization in the latter field, convened its annual conference in Honolulu during which an award for fiction was to be presented to Lois-Ann Yamanaka for her novel *Blu's Hanging*. Despite being a nationally acclaimed novelist, Yamanaka had written about Filipinos in Hawai'i in some of her best-selling books in ways that I and many others considered to reinforce racist stereotypes of Filipinos. *Blu's Hanging* is ostensibly about a local Japanese family, including the young son Blu, set on Moloka'i, but it also includes portrayals of a Filipino American family consisting of the adolescent Reyes sisters and their uncle Paulo who is depicted as a sexual predator of his very young nieces and of Blu whom he also rapes.

Those familiar with the history of Filipino Americans in Hawai'i, which is certainly not limited to academics, can easily recognize that Uncle Paulo is a stereotyped representation of young Filipino men and the supposed sexual threat they posed, which had originated during the pre–World War II period on the plantations. What was especially disturbing was that in a previous book, *Saturday Night at the Pahala Theatre*, Yamanaka had already depicted Filipino men as sexually violent in her references to the character Felix, who had raped two young women, and to the "old Filipino man" who is said to cut off the sexual organs of young girls with a cane knife. Despite public protests by the Filipino American community against such racist stereotyping of them, Yamanaka chose to ignore their objections and continued with her demonic representations, which she claimed somehow challenged stereotypes about Filipino Americans instead of resurrecting them.

Prior to the AAAS conference, I wrote an essay against giving the fiction award to *Blu's Hanging* that appeared in the AAAS newsletter and was titled "When Will It End?" by which I referred to the continual denigrating stereotyping of Filipinos in Hawai'i. I stated, "I am deeply offended and outraged by the portrayal of Filipino Americans in *Blu's Hanging*, primarily the young Reyes sisters and their Uncle Paulo, who are described engaging in various sexual activities with each other or with other adolescents. . . . Bestowing an award to *Blu's Hanging* reinforces the notion already prevalent in Hawai'i that racist stereotyping of Filipino Americans is socially permissible and therefore they can continue to be maligned without fear of sanction or reprisal." I later requested Filipino American organizations in Hawai'i and the continental United States to send letters protesting the award to the AAAS board of which I was an elected member. When the board would not rescind the award to *Blu's Hanging*, despite strong opposition from Filipino Americans across the country, I resigned my position as a board member because I did not want to be a party to racism against Filipinos.

At the AAAS conference, I worked with Filipino American and other Asian American faculty and graduate students to have the fiction award to Yamanaka revoked through a resolution to be voted upon by the conference participants. Calling ourselves the Anti-Racism Coalition, we held meetings and discussions in our hotel rooms to develop a strategy to have our resolution pass. During the conference plenary session when the award was given to *Blu's Hanging*, those of us opposed to it wore black armbands and stood and turned our backs to the stage when the award plaque was accepted not by Yamanaka but by three Filipino American high school students she sent in her place. When I stood and saw that there were far more people in the audience who were sitting than standing, I doubted that our resolution would pass, but I thought it was important that we had expressed our collective opposition to the award. Thus, I was extremely surprised when it was announced later to raucous cheering that the resolution to revoke the award was approved by an overwhelming vote of ninety-one to fifty-five, although five hundred people were registered for the conference. I still consider this rescinding of the award to *Blu's Hanging* an empowering moment for Filipino Americans and other Asian Americans opposed to the racism directed against the former.

As for other ways I do community advocacy, I have been a faculty member at the University of Hawai'i (UH) at Mānoa since 1989, and this has provided me an academic position from which to serve as an advocate for Filipino Americans. Rather than anthropology, I work in the Department of Ethnic Studies, and I believe this position reflects my political orientation and values as an academic, because ethnic studies, since its inception in the late 1960s, has always emphasized political activism, community advocacy, social justice, and antiracism. The ethnic studies courses I teach on race and ethnicity enable me to discuss ongoing issues and events in my classes and to demonstrate the relevance of theories and concepts we study to understand them.

Working at the university, I have been especially concerned with the continuing underrepresentation of Filipino Americans as students and faculty at UH Mānoa and throughout the ten campuses of the UH system. The lower educational status of Filipino Americans is a significant contributing factor in their overall subordinate socioeconomic status, which they have held since Filipinos were first recruited as plantation laborers in 1906. My advocacy activities have included testifying at the state legislature in support of offering courses on Filipino Americans at the UH community colleges, giving testimony at Board of Regents meetings against substantial tuition hikes in the UH system that would result in the further underenrollment of Filipino Americans, speaking at community forums and writing in the Honolulu newspapers against the racist stereotyping of Filipino Americans by local comedians through telling jokes about them, and walking picket lines with striking Filipino American hotel workers in Waikiki. Working with others, I served on the planning committee for a national conference held in Honolulu that commemorated the one-hundredth anniversary of Filipino immigration to the United States in 2006. Over the years, I also have taught and mentored many Filipino American students, including the children of Filipino immigrants who assisted me with my fieldwork. My advocacy efforts indicate the many proactive ways that anthropologists can do engaged anthropology, including sending information from the field to disseminate news about recent problems or issues confronting the people in their fieldwork communities.

The question might arise why anthropologists should feel obligated to the people they researched, as I contend, since this issue does not seem to be as much of a concern for other social scientists such as psychologists, sociologists, and political scientists. I would argue that the reason anthropologists should have this sense of obligation results from the differences in research methods employed by anthropologists compared to other social scientists. As the basic research methodology of anthropology, participant observation involves daily contact with the people one is researching over an extended period of time, which may be as long as a year, in order to obtain the qualitative data necessary for one's study. Only through such a lengthy and intensive period of interaction with a community is an anthropologist able to acquire the ethnographic data for her study from the information, resources, and time that people share with her. Anthropologists thus should feel greatly indebted to them for making their fieldwork possible and, on many occasions, highly enjoyable. While conducting my research with Filipino immigrants, they patiently answered my many personal questions about their lives in Kalihi, invited me to family and other social functions they hosted, shared their meals with me at their homes, and generally let me hang around with them as an inquisitive observer.

It might be argued that it is much easier for me to speak or write on behalf of the people I researched because of the very large Filipino American community in Hawai'i, which is the second largest ethnic group in the islands. But precisely because of its size and many spokespersons, including academics, politicians, and community leaders, I also need to be concerned about what I say or write about Filipino Americans, because I can easily be questioned or challenged by the aforementioned people, especially since I am not Filipino. This is certainly a significant ethical issue that can arise for anthropologists who, in assuming an advocacy or supportive role for a people, can find themselves being criticized by both members and nonmembers for seeking to represent a group to which they do not belong. However, if I should be confronted about assuming an advocacy position for the Filipino American community, my response would be that I have the right to speak or write against racism and discrimination, which I believe Filipino Americans are very much subject to, no matter what group is the target. As an ethnic studies scholar, one of my primary concerns is to eliminate the institutional sources of racist ideologies and discriminatory practices in society. As such, I maintain that being opposed to racial inequality, injustice, and intolerance does not necessarily mean that one has inappropriately assumed a leadership or representative position for a community.

I fully realize that some anthropologists very likely disagree with my position that they should act, when appropriate, as advocates of the people with whom they conducted their fieldwork, because they consider academics as of far greater importance than advocacy. As an academic, I certainly take seriously the teaching of my ethnic studies courses and the research I conduct and the subsequent publication of my books and articles based on that research. However, I do not consider teaching and research as secondary to advocacy but as complementary. I like to think that I have found ways to do advocacy work through my teaching in the topics I choose to discuss in my classes and through my research in the subjects I decide to interpret and write about in my publications.

Note

1. I felt very honored when the *nana* (mother) in my "fieldwork family" asked me to give remarks at the funeral of her husband in 1983, and when their children requested I do the same for her when she died in 2009.

PART 3

Language Encounters

Voices, Discourse, Digital Practice

(*overleaf photo*) Piru Hucke Atan teaching Ira Hucke, a *hina* (granddaughter) of her *hua'ai* (extended family), Rapa Nui stories and medicinal plants at Ahu Tongariki—the largest *moai* complex on Easter Island. Such stories of place are fundamental to the meaning of the indigenous language and Rapa Nui cultural identity. Photo by Forrest Wade Young.

Introduction

FORREST WADE YOUNG

ANALYSIS OF LANGUAGE USAGE IS seen as fundamental to contemporary ethnography because cultural worlds, social conditions, and global processes are encountered through language-based communication and categories. Broadly conceived, the ethnography of language, and a sense of its importance to social and cultural inquiry, can be traced to the founding fathers of ethnography: Franz Boas and Bronislaw Malinowski. Boas encouraged fieldwork-based study of indigenous languages of the world to challenge the universality of Western-language categories and grammatical structures, and because he thought indigenous languages were "important to understand in their own right like in other great civilizations" (Stocking 1992, 91). His interest in the way language in general might limit and stabilize thought in particular ways (Boas 1911, 22) grounded the development of the famous Sapir–Whorf hypothesis, which suggests that the cultural content of one's language can influence one's habitual thought and practice. Malinowski (1965, 52) refined ethnographic understanding of the cultural constructedness of social reality by demonstrating how the meaning of everyday language use depends not upon its actual reference to things in the physical world, but its practical value in perfoming social actions in *general* and *situational* cultural contexts. Boas' insight into the cultural content of language, and Malinowski's disclosure of language usage as a cultural activity and social practice, continue to anchor contemporary paradigms of ethnographic research that analyze "language as culture" (Duranti 2003).

The ethnography of language has been updated by the incorporation of French philosopher Michel Foucault's notion of discourse. To analyze language use in the context of discourse is to understand everyday concepts and statements as articulating historically contingent "codes of normalization" (Foucault 2003, 38–39) at war with alternative discourses for authority and power. Discourses normalize "versions" of reality in social institutions (courtrooms, governments, hospitals, prisons, schools, etc.) that empower some social groups and disqualify or marginalize others. Following Foucault, ethnographers are interested in the way discourses "discipline" people to see and speak from a limited number of subject positions in social spaces—for example, as racialized inferiors, instead of as fellow human beings. Ethnographers also study how discourses can empower alternative voices and promote important global change—for example, how feminist discourses are enabling women in societies throughout the world to see and position themselves as equal to men, and how environmentalist discourse legitimates the value of conservation projects worldwide.

This section features stories that illustrate classic issues in the ethnography of language and new developments associated with digital media and discourse analysis. Naomi C. F. Yamada's "Systemic Culture Shock: Meeting Fu Lai Ming on the Tibetan Plateau" is a story about cultural categories of birds and science in China that addresses issues of the Sapir–Whorf hypothesis. She emphasizes that to learn Chinese categories she had to "unlearn" similar, yet different, concepts of Western culture. In the Boasian spirit of recording, studying, and appreciating the languages of indigenous peoples of the world, Emerson Lopez Odango's *"Shóón Pakin, sóóu tittilap:* Researching Narrative Discourse in Micronesia" documents and reflects on some of the cultural signficance of discourse markers in Mortlockese storytelling (*tittilap*) at Pakin Atoll of the Federated States of Micronesia. Forrest Wade Young illustrates in "Talking with the *Moai* on Easter Island: Placing Rapa Nui Language" how the meaning of the indigenous Rapa Nui language on Easter Island is established in ritual practices that living Rapa Nui people conduct to communicate with the ancestral spirit world. He argues that Rapa Nui language speakers, ultimately, are entangled in a political struggle for indigenous place against settler colonial discourse normalizing Easter Island as a Chilean space. Steven Edmund Winduo, in reflecting on his own experiences in "Blogging in Papua New Guinea," introduces the role of new digital media in the globalization of cultural worlds of Papua New Guinea. He argues that access to digital media is empowering Papua New Guinean communities by giving them "free, useful, and vital information" fundamental to social development.

Systemic Culture Shock

Meeting Fu Lai Ming on the Tibetan Plateau

Naomi C. F. Yamada

Before I had ever been to China, I thought that pigeons and doves were different birds entirely. In Chinese, however, one word is used to refer to both: *gezi*. Had I simply been led to believe that the symbol of peace was different because it was white and I had known it as a dove? Was it the same kind of bird as the gray beach scavenger?

The anthropologist Edward Sapir and his student Benjamin Whorf forwarded the idea that language shapes our perception of reality—that the words we learn influence our categories of thought (Whorf 2000). Learning a language is not just about learning a new set of words for the same old concepts. In some cases, it is *unlearning* the concepts that have constructed our familiar worlds.

This brings me to the scene of my story: a high school classroom in Northwest China, not far from the source of the Yellow River, on the Qinghai-Tibetan plateau.[1] It was December 2009 at twelve thousand feet. I was shivering and trying to catch my breath at altitude while the Tibetan students in the class were exuding an easy *cool*, as if to say, we've got thousands of years of red blood cell adaptation to this environment on you. A third of them were wearing baseball caps, some had bandannas on, and a particularly stylish student, with a spike through his ear, was wearing one black fingerless leather glove, and a coat lined with an unruly profusion of Tibetan wool on the inside and Chinese silk on the outside.

In front of the room were two slogans, separated by a paperboard replica of a Chinese flag: *study diligently and thoughtfully, with determination aspire to a higher level.* This particular day, the topic for the class session bore the following provocative and baffling title: *To accurately recognize the reasons, modes, and tendencies for the development of things.* A teacher was speaking excitedly about an Englishman named Fu Lai Ming.

Fu Lai Ming had made a great discovery, a discovery of *qingmeisu,* she said. I fidgeted in the seat, not sure of who Fu Lai Ming was, or what *qingmeisu* was. I wrote a transliteration of the words down in my notebook with question marks next to them. The teacher continued on, talking about how Fu Lai Ming never would have been able to grasp the opportunity when it came by—he never would have been able to discover *qingmeisu*—if there had not first been enough "quantitative change" and "accumulated knowledge." She then began to talk about internal and external factors. At the end of class, I left the room confused, hoping that over time, with a dictionary, a friend, and the Internet, I would be able to unpeel the meaning of this lesson.

I had gone to northwest China to research a national college preparatory program that was available to ethnic minority students as a "preferential policy" measure. Some people called it "affirmative action," but I found that the system operated very differently from affirmative action in the United States. To get a sense of the students' backgrounds and what they learned in school before starting the college preparatory program, I attended some classes in Tibetan autonomous prefectures of Qinghai (a province in China). I interviewed students, teachers, and administrators. Initial interviews were challenging, not only because of language difficulties, but because some of the answers I got did not initially make sense to me until I learned more about the larger systems and compelling ideas of the cultural framework that were being referenced. I used a tape recorder when permitted. The interviews got a bit easier as I expanded the base of vocabulary related to my specific interest and learned more about how the education system worked. The times that I was permitted to observe classes, however, were always difficult, and my notebooks were filled with transliterated words, question marks, half-completed sentences, and threads of ideas.

The day when the high school politics teacher spoke about Fu Lai Ming, she also talked about Chinese kings, history, and philosophers. One story was about the defeated king of Yue, who was trying to prepare himself so that he would have the strength and ability to carry through with future battles in order to achieve success. To "eat bitter" and remind himself of the humiliation of his defeat, he denied himself any luxuries, and forced himself to daily sleep in discomfort and to eat innards and bile. The proverb that comes from this story, "lying on straw and eating gall" (*wo xin chang dan*), indicates the preparation for hardship that must be endured in order to achieve success. The teacher asked the students if this preparation was related to internal factors or to external factors.

The students called out "*Neiyin* (internal factors)!" and a voice or two called out dissenting answers: "*Waiyin* (external factors)!"

She confirmed with the class: "Things develop and change on the basis of internal factors." She explained that transformation is not complete, however, without external factors. To explain the difference between the *basis* of change and the *condition* of change, she provided an example by referring to the Chinese philosopher Mencius. Mencius advocated that, in order to become a person of integrity, or a "real man," as he put it, one must not be tempted by wealth or position. Ambition was important, but one should not change oneself just to avoid unpleasant circumstances. What happens on the inside strengthens individuals so that they are not swayed by favorable or unfavorable circumstances. In other words, the basis of change happens internally, but becomes visible to others through external events and circumstances.

The teacher spoke rapidly and almost shouted out her points, and the students actively responded, repeating with her, reading phrases aloud from the book, and calling back. The teacher acknowledged the answers with a friendly "hey," and repeated the correct answers. It all seemed very unlike classes in China I had previously observed, which were quieter and less interactive. I had not been prepared for the amount of chaos and noise, the many answers being voiced at once, or the pace of the lesson in the classroom. I needed to ask the teacher a number of follow-up questions, and she apologized, explaining that it was a review day, so the pace was faster than usual. Later, I went over my notes with friends to understand the context. Even when I had gotten through some of the unfamiliar vocabulary, and had looked up some of the references on Mencius and the battles between the Wu and Yue kingdoms, I found it difficult to make sense of the notes I had taken from the lecture and copied from the board, even after translating them. This was because I had never studied this subject—dialectical materialism—before. As an adult in a high school class with teenagers, it was my first lesson.

The teacher pointed to a page in the textbook and instructed the students to take a look at a cartoon of a person lying on the ground. The teacher explained the picture: "He is saying, 'Opportunity, why do you always brush past me?' Why?" The students responded that the man did not grasp the opportunity. The teacher said that opportunity is readily available, but that certain conditions must be met in order to grasp it. The class discussed what some of those conditions might be: one needs to have a spirit of perseverance, for example, as well as to accumulate knowledge. The teacher asked the students what they were doing, and if they were accumulating knowledge.

She continued, explaining that an "accumulated amount" is the only way that *quantitative change* can result in *qualitative change*. The meaning of this is that change by degree ultimately accomplishes change of state, the classic example being the transformation of water to steam or to ice following gradual but successive temperature changes.

The teacher provided yet another example to put everything together, and this example concerned Fu Lai Ming of England, who had made the great discovery of *qingmeisu* through much trial and error. The teacher explained that for many years, he had been a lecturer who had achieved little with his research, but that internal and external factors were ultimately related to his great discovery. Without the inner discipline that fueled his prior research (the internal factor), he never would have been able to grasp or recognize the opportunity (the external factor) when it came along.

Fu Lai Ming, I found out later, is known in English as (Alexander) Fleming. For him, opportunity came in the great discovery of penicillin, called *qingmeisu* in Chinese, which was an important health breakthrough. Initially it would have appeared to the observer that his repeated experiments had accomplished nothing, but his extensive research and knowledge accumulated. This gradual accumulation represented, by degree, quantitative change. Without this background, the recognition of the opportunity, which would result in qualitative change (the discovery of penicillin), would not have been possible.

This reencounter with a famous Westerner in an unfamiliar context reminded me that fieldwork is a time when we stop not only to look but also to learn *how* to look. Not knowing the words was one problem for me, but not knowing the conceptual categories that the words described was another problem. Discovering that Fu Lai Ming was Fleming was simple enough, but understanding how his discovery of penicillin was related to a method of preparation and change—or to a defeated king's humiliation and strategy for future battle—required a little more work. For me, this "work" meant asking questions of the people around me, and relying on them to be my teachers more than my "informants." They helped me to translate not only words but also cultural categories. While the Tibetan students in the Chinese school had been doing this for years, many of them also had to learn new words in Chinese—along with different conceptual categories that suited such words.

I had learned about Fu Lai Ming and *qingmeisu* before, but I had to talk to friends in China about Marxist theory, words in Mandarin, and high school politics lessons in order to recognize Fleming and penicillin. What I had thought was foreign was actually familiar. The new context, however, made me realize that familiar categories—of birds and famous people—required rethinking. The "shock" of culture shock here is less an encounter with difference, and more a forced reevaluation of familiar categories.

Fieldwork is not just about finding the answer to a question. It is also about learning the categories in use, rephrasing the question, and culturally translating it. *How is a pigeon different from a dove?* is a nonsense question if the same word is used for "pigeon" and "dove": *How is a gezi different from a gezi?* Likewise, *how is the discovery of penicillin related to the changing fortunes of an ancient Chinese king?* would not be a question addressed in an American high school politics class.

The idea that language influences the way people see the world and even think is called *linguistic relativity.* To what degree language determines thought has been a subject of spirited debate, exacerbated by the fact that arguments in the debate must be expressed *in* and limited *by* language.[2] The issues surrounding linguistic relativity continue to be important to linguistic anthropologists.

For my own fieldwork, early interviews were hard and seemed to accomplish very little. I asked the wrong questions, and could not understand the answers I was given. Over time, I learned the vocabulary for my subject, and the categories in play. Later I was able not only to understand the comments of individuals but also to make some larger observations about the trends of the program that I was studying. Learning by degree—bit by bit—had accomplished a change in my understanding.[3] Quantitative change had brought about qualitative change.

Notes

1. The northeast portion of the Tibetan plateau, on which Qinghai province is situated, is "a historical and cultural borderland between China and Tibet" (Rohlf 2003, 455). Though not included in the political designation of the Tibetan Autonomous Region, Tibetan autonomous prefectures spatially make up much of Qinghai, and the highlands are largely populated by Tibetans. Qinghai province, encompassing 721,000 square kilometers (Stuart 1999, 1) had a population of only 5.23 million in 2001 (Goodman 2004, 379). The ethnic landscape includes Han Chinese, Tibetans, Hui, Mongolians, and Sala peoples, and places of worship include mosques as well as Buddhist temples.

2. Psychologist and linguist John Lucy has tried to study the question in a more empirical way, considering cognitive and psychological studies, and

furthermore has provided a literature review of the debated issues, with particular attention to other empirical attempts to study the question (Lucy 1996).

3. Change by degree effecting a change of state is not always positive. Tragically, a few months after my observation, there was a terrible earthquake in the area. The high school where I had my first lesson in dialectical materialism was near the epicenter. The buildings were constructed with materials too weak to withstand the accumulated pressure, and underwent a different sort of qualitative change. The high school and a girls' dormitory collapsed, and a number of students lost their lives.

Shóón Pakin, sóóu tittilap

Researching Narrative Discourse in Micronesia

EMERSON LOPEZ ODANGO

THE WAVES LAP in a rhythmic pattern along the sand. I can clearly hear the soft splashes, a result of the wind slowly shifting again. People are saying *sé ppés* (it does not stay still) about the wind, which is characteristic of the early summer months in this part of Micronesia; instead of the usual steady southeast wind, the direction changes almost hourly, moving to the west and then north, then back to the south and east. The distant chirping of honeycreepers and the shrieks of children playing in the field nearby occasionally punctuate the oscillations of the waves and the rustling of coconut leaves. The main instrument though, in this muted cacophony of sounds, is the deep baritone voice of Nicklaus Marco who begins his *tittilap* (story):

> *Pasela paseto. Raa nonno eeu pwúpwpwúlú. Pwúpwpwúlú kewe re kan nonno óón Lukunosh, ree Oou. Iit we ree Oou, sóópw ree Oou, re kan nonno iilik. Leeni we itan Leelel. Leelel, leeni we. Iwá, eman kkaláu shak naúr, raa túttúmwúnútá naúr we . . . Shóópwut we eman éésh. Seman we, eman malek.*

Drift away, drift toward. There once lived a married couple. This couple lived on Lukunosh, part of the Oou inhabitants. People of Oou was the name, the community of Oou inhabitants, they lived on the ocean side of the island. That place was called Leelel. Leelel, that place. And so, they only had one child, they cared for and raised their child (a daughter). . . . The woman was a mouse. As for the father, he was a chicken.

Nick and I are sitting on an upturned fiberglass boat, two more on either side; they are a permanent fixture here on the lagoon-side beach of Nikahlap, the largest islet of Pakin Atoll, one of hundreds of atolls within the Federated States of Micronesia (FSM). The boats have long since retired from their transportation duties, now serving as lookouts for the residents to sit and wait, eyeing the reef pass as they listen carefully for the scheduled return of boats that make the regular trip—a two-hour ride across twenty miles of open Pacific Ocean—to Pohnpei, home to Palikir, which is the capital of the FSM. Nick and I are commandeering the middle boat for an impromptu recording session. A digital recorder sits between us, the microphone trained on Nick, recording his voice and the sounds of Pakin.

The *tittilap* I recorded in that moment—a folktale about a beautiful girl whose mother is a mouse and father a chicken—is one of several dozen that Nick has shared with me over the years since I first started recording narratives as part of my fieldwork on their native language of *kapsen Mwoshulók* (Mortlockese). In a span of twenty-five minutes, Nick brought me to his home island of Lukunosh(Lekinioch), almost three hundred miles away in the Mortlock chain of islands and atolls to the southeast of Chuuk Lagoon. I have yet to visit Lukunosh, but I feel as if I have been there briefly, that I have met some of these legendary residents through Nick's masterful storytelling. People on Pakin call him one of the best *sóóu tittilap* (storytellers) for good reason: he deftly shifts into falsetto to voice different characters, he balances foreground action with background setting, and he intertwines several plot threads together for satisfying conclusions. Not everyone is a *sóóu tittilap;* it is a reputation that must be earned. Perhaps in Nick's mind, he is just sharing with me something that he loves to do, and there is nothing particularly special about the content of the story or the way he tells it. In my mind, though—the mind of a documentary linguist, a discourse analyst, an ethnographer—Nick is engaging in the performance of a discourse genre that is rich in contextualization cues (Gumperz 1982, 131), full of interesting morphosyntactic patterns, all framed in a culturally specific manner. This is partly why I find fieldwork on narrative discourse so fascinating: the stories I record provide the data for the grammatical and ethnographic description of this minority language of the FSM.

Learning how to be an attentive listener to *tittilap* was one of the main ways I gained fluency in Mortlockese as a Peace Corps volunteer on Pakin Atoll. That was also the spark of my interest in discourse narratives in the language. Over the years, as I collect more and more *tittilap* from different residents of Pakin, I have come to understand how powerful an elicitation tool it is to ask someone to share a story. Regardless of the population of an atoll community, there will always be a new story to experience. Nick is one of approximately one hundred people who call Pakin home. The *shóón Pakin* (residents of Pakin) are descendants of Mortlockese people who were relocated from their home islands after a devastating typhoon in the early twentieth century. The diaspora put down deep roots in places such as the Sokehs municipality of Pohnpei; about five generations ago, some moved from Sokehs to Pakin. Like most other minority diasporic communities, the Mortlockese who live in Pohnpei State must learn how to speak the official Pohnpeian language. Remarkably though, the Mortlockese have maintained additive bilingualism over the generations, such that to this very day, children still learn Mortlockese first as their mother tongue, and then learn Pohnpeian as their second language. Pakin is no exception. It is heartening to see and listen to five-year-olds retell and create stories in Mortlockese; I think that they are future Nicks in the making.

In doing this kind of fieldwork, it is not enough to simply hit "record" on a voice recorder and sit back. Discourse analysis provides the tools for understanding how speakers of a language both access bodies of knowledge (such as abstract grammatical patterns and generalizations based on previous conversations) and create and interpret new instances of that knowledge (Johnstone 2008, 3). "Discourse" covers a wide range of language use, but the particular type of discourse that interests me with regard to *tittilap* is the narrative, which is the means for "recapitulating past experience by matching a verbal sequence of [sentences] to the sequence of events" (Labov 1972, 359–360). The story can come from real-life personal experience or the plot of a folktale. Researchers analyze narratives for structure (for example, the beginning, middle, and end of the story) and for the grammatical techniques used by the storyteller. This includes "discourse markers," which are the words we use to move talk along, whose meaning heavily depends on the context around them. Examples of English discourse markers include *well, y'know,* and *oh* (Schiffrin 1986). Those moments of listening to *tittilap,* then, are opportunities for discourse analysis in real time.

Almost all *tittilap* in Mortlockese start with a phrase similar to *pasela paseto.* The literal translation would be "drift away, drift toward," as if that particular story were floating on the waves of a vast sea of stories, something to be caught for a moment to be shared, and then to be released again. The closest equivalent to *pasela paseto* in English would be "once upon a time." Furthermore, when the storyteller says "there lived a king" or "there was a little girl," he/she is using a tool, the phrase "there was/lived" to introduce the existence of something for the first time. In the previous extract, Nick takes an interesting approach by saying *raa nonno eeu pwúpwpwúlú,* which literally translates as "they are staying one married couple." We know that there once lived a couple, but the actual words that Nick uses (specifically, his choice of verb conjugations) to introduce this couple makes it seem as if the listener already knows about the couple, as if we were jumping right into the story. Nick prefers this technique, as many of his *tittilap* start with this *raa nonno* pattern. However, other people's *tittilap* use the Mortlockese equivalent of the phrase "there was/lived." The very first audio recording I ever made of a *tittilap* was by my host mother, Anastasia Maipi, who shared with me a folktale about two sisters. I clearly remember that night in 2007, sitting in the cookhouse, glowing embers from the dinnertime fire slowly fading away. Anastasia held her youngest child in her arms and began her *tittilap:*

> *Pasala paseto. Mi ioor eman mwáán e kai nonno óón eeu faneú. Mwáán we, naún rúaman faapwúl. Eman itan Chékchék, eman itan Sinter. Ngé itan semeer we, Rinte.*

> Drift away, drift toward. There once was a man who used to live on an island. As for that man, he has two young daughters. One is named Chékchék, the other is named Sinter. And as for the name of their father, it is Rinte.

Apart from the difference between Nick's use of *raa nonno* (they are staying) and Anastasia's use of *mi ioor* (there once was), we can already see some similarities: (1) using the *pasala paseto* phrase; (2) introducing the parents of the main characters by situating them on their land; and then (3) identifying the main characters as the children. Like other *tittilap,* Anastasia's is full of sequential action: the sisters open the door of their house to see an old man who promises to restore Rinte's sight if they vow to help him, Sinter is then married off to the old man, who later reveals his true self as a young man named Antio (whose name must be kept secret), and so on. These actions lead to plot twists, which are then resolved at the end. It really is easy to follow along with a *tittilap* once you know how to look for recurrent structural features.

Discourse markers can be difficult to define on their own, but after hearing them used in narratives over and over again, they become much easier to comprehend. Tersy Maipi—my host grandmother on Pakin whom I address as *Nohno* (mother)—told me about her experiences as a little girl living in Pohnpei during the Japanese period in Micronesia (1914–1945). Sitting along the sill of a wide window just a few inches from the ground, Nohno would share her *tittilap* with me. Some of the very first recordings I ever made with Nohno in 2007 were of her accounts of aerial dogfights between Japan and the United States; even though she was only six years old at the time, she remembers details as vivid as these:

> *Iwe, iwe. Aia wérei pwiin skooki kuftiin kewe raa kai tikeltá ngé—iei má i kai wérei llan kasto iaa úró "krrrrrrrrrrrrrr"! Eman fatal, ostán . . . ina shak má sokkon!*

> Well, okay. We saw that whole group of small planes, they were flying upwards indeed—you know like what I see now in the movies, I would say that it was like "krrrrrrrrrrrrrr"! One would walk and, I mean . . . that's exactly what it was like!

The closest translations for the discourse marker *iwe* would be "well" or "okay," with very much the same functions as in English: once you say one sentence and you want to move to the next logical sentence, you say *iwe* to keep things moving along. In the previous sentence, Nohno talks about how they would see airplanes in the main town region of Pohnpei, not far from where she lived. The next piece of information is a logical follow-up, and in order to clarify this, she employs *iwe* twice for emphasis: the first *iwe* brackets off the previous sentence, and the second *iwe* signifies that Nohno is ready to deliver something significant . . . and does she deliver! It is not every day that you hear someone tell you about World War II aerial dogfights and bombing raids. To add to this emphasis, Nohno uses two other discourse markers: *ngé* and *má,* which both mean "indeed!" in this context. In sharing her World War II experiences with me through *tittilap,* Nohno evokes emotions and experiences by using onomatopoeia, discourse markers, and other devices; her words take me on a journey.

It never ceases to amaze me how many new things I pick up on every time I hear a new story or replay previously recorded ones. During a fieldtrip to Pakin in the summer of 2012, I had the opportunity to work with a new storyteller for the first time. Forchek Nennis is about two years younger than me, but he has the storytelling repertoire and abilities of people twice his age. One narrative device that I noticed in his *tittilap* is a type of emphatic repetition. At one point in his narration of a love story, the *átemwáán* (young man) sees the *liárá* (young woman) for the first time through a window. Forcheck then says two phrases in a sequence: *liárá we aa liwinlong* (the young woman returned inside), followed by *liárá we aa liwinlong llan liimwan we* (the young woman returned inside her house). Perhaps it was because it was late at night, or perhaps it was the subject matter, but I remember at this moment, Forchek was speaking in a very quiet voice, sometimes in a whisper. There is a clear pause between the two sentences, but he did not falter in narrating this sequence. Rather than directly talking about the next logical sequence of events when the man and woman turn away from each other, he paused the narration for a moment and repeated the action of the woman going back inside, but adding a little bit more clarifying information. This small example shows me that a competent storyteller must know when to pause the action in order to add the right amount of background information at the right time. We may easily recognize this in written literature when we analyze an author's style. I am learning how to recognize this, too, in the oral literature of *shóón Pakin* as skilled as Forchek. He uses this narrative device throughout all of the *tittilap* he shared with me; only now am I realizing that Nick also does the same in some of his *tittilap*, and I will likely find variations of this in other people's *tittilap*.

I say that part of the reason why I enjoy doing fieldwork on narrative discourse on Pakin is that it is a means for collecting rich data from which we can learn more about Mortlockese grammar, narrative strategies, and culture—to learn more about the discursive practices of this speech community. It is, though, only a small part. The main draw for me goes beyond academic pursuits. There is nothing quite like the experience of forging lasting friendships and relationships with people through a shared interest in stories. It is my responsibility to learn how to become a good listener: responding verbally and nonverbally (such as raising your eyebrows to agree), or knowing when to laugh, when to stay silent, and when to ask the right questions. I also have a responsibility to discuss with any people who permit me to audio-record their stories about how they would like me to return the stories (on paper, on a burned CD, as MP3 files, etc.). Truly, it is an honor each time I am invited to be an audience to *tittilap* to realize that the *sóóu tittilap* choose to share with me something they have caught on those waves, *pasela paseto*.

Talking with the *Moai* on Easter Island

Placing Rapa Nui Language

FORREST WADE YOUNG

"EASTER ISLAND" (RAPA NUI), located in the southeastern corner of the Polynesian triangle, is renowned for the enormous monumental sculptures known as *moai* and is an important site of global ecological and archaeological imagination (see Hunt and Lipo 2012). While the archaeological and ecological significance of "Easter Island" remains of critical interest to me (Young 2012a), since my first month of fieldwork on the island in 2004 and research thereafter,[1] I have found the world of the 2,500 living indigenous Rapa Nui people much more interesting. Their interpretations of the Chilean political and legal system operating in Rapa Nui—a system that the Chilean government recently defended by state violence against Rapa Nui people in December 2010 (Young 2012b)—has been the subject that has most preoccupied my studies in Rapa Nui.

Like many anthropologists, my research has involved linguistic barriers and decisions. To access indigenous meanings of the Chilean system, I needed either to hire translators or learn the language myself. While I do consult with translators occasionally, generally I have embraced the classic stance of anthropology established by founding fathers like Malinowski and Boas, and have begun to learn the native language—an Eastern Polynesian language known as Rapa Nui, like the people and the island. While many formal features of the language were familiar given prior education in the sister languages of Tahitian and Hawaiian, some of the grammar and phonology seemed different. Upon arrival on the island, I hired a Rapa Nui woman, Evelyn Hucke, to help me learn the basic grammatical rules and vocabulary. After approximately three months of studying the language formally, it was suggested that I continue to develop my language study by hiring her elder aunt, Piru Hucke Atan, as my lead teacher. Piru's teachings radically recontextualized my interpretation of Rapa Nui culture, language, and politics. She entangled them in a complex "spiritual ecology" (Sponsel 2012).

I was both excited and scared to study with Piru. Her home is in an area named Vai Tō Iri that is next to one of the most sacred places of the island: Rano Raraku. Her backyard is the place where the world-famous *moai* statues were carved from a mountain and then transported across the island, as well as the place where hundreds of *moai* remain. Indeed, a few steps from her home one could walk to a *moai* that rests on the ancient transport roads transecting her backyard. While all Rapa Nui I knew seemed to enjoy visiting places like Rano Raraku during the day, a few noted they did not particularly like to be near there at night. As the center of the ancestral Rapa Nui world, it was recognized as a place of intense *mana* (spiritual power), and a place where ancestral spirits are thought to persist and reside.

Yet it was not only sleeping in an area permeated by spiritual phenomena that worried me. The first time I met Piru in Vai Tō Iri, an event prior to our language studies, I learned something alarming about the place. Upon arrival, I noticed that there was neither electricity nor running water. I asked her family member who was intending to stay with me there where I could get some water, and the answer was nowhere. I was told, however, not to worry, because we had a "couple of days." I asked, "A couple of days until what?" He replied, "Until we die." He elaborated that I should not worry, as we had some fruit and could stave off dehydration from juices for at least a couple of days. While everyone else was comfortable with the circumstances, I was terrified. As a man raised in suburban Los Angeles and used to having all of my food and water needs met daily, this was too challenging a condition to accept. My first visit to Vai Tō Iri ended quickly. I braved one night, and returned as fast as I could to town in the morning to get water.

In light of these concerns, it took me a few weeks to commit to studying with Piru in Vai Tō Iri. After many elders and youth alike emphasized it as an ideal context for learning, and Piru assured me that there would be water, I returned to Vai Tō Iri a month later still a little scared, but primarily with great excitement. Like a school boy, I arrived at Piru's home prepared for serious study. I brought dictionaries, flash cards I had prepared with defined words, and notebooks filled with potential grammatical rules of Rapa Nui language. Assuming that I would, in some sense, continue my study with Piru by extending the foundation I had built with her niece, I proceeded to show Piru sentences I had studied previously. Like a linguist, I asked her their meaning and the extent to which they were grammatical. Piru tolerated that for almost a day. At the end of the day she told me to leave and to return tomorrow with a number of things—for example, walking shoes and a backpack—and emphasized that I was not to bring my dictionaries, flash cards, and notebooks. In conclusion she stated, "'Apō i te po'a a Forrest he oho mai ki kampō mo oho mo hāpī 'i ruŋa i te henua ara-rua ko tō'ona taote o te roŋoroŋo!" Broadly, it can be translated thus: "Tomorrow morning Forrest will come here to the country to go study upon the land of Rapa Nui together with his professor of Rapa Nui." This statement—a kind of command—is symbolic of some of the ways in which my studies of Rapa Nui changed under Piru's leadership.

With this quick statement, Piru began to recontextualize how I was to understand Rapa Nui language, and the social conditions in which I was to learn it. The particular terms of the phrase ko tō'ona taote o te roŋoroŋo are significant. The phrase, which I have simplified in the above translation as meaning "his professor of Rapa Nui" assigns me a different social position than the one I had assumed when I arrived at her home. I arrived at Piru's home, in her eyes, as the teacher. I quizzed her about sentences and examined her answers in reference to a set of books. With her use of the third-person possessive pronoun tō'ona and the title taote, Piru establishes a different social hierarchy. This form of pronoun implies that she is potentially my superior.[2] Ambiguity is resolved by its combination with the word taote; a term generally translated as "doctor." Her command constructs a new social structure at the foundation of my education in Rapa Nui language. She demands that I return to study in the morning in a context in which she will be the doctor, and I will be the student (or perhaps patient). Piru maintained these new roles between us for the rest of my stay in Rapa Nui, and she is emphatic that they are not ever to change. Upon my return to Rapa Nui recently, she laughed that although I am now a taote of anthropology in the United States, I am not to forget that she is the taote in Rapa Nui—not me.

The command was used not only to establish Piru's pedagogical authority but also to change the method and subject matter of study. Piru's use of the word roŋoroŋo in the above phrase is also significant. The reduplicated word roŋo is generally translated as "symbol" or "message." Yet, the word roŋoroŋo is slightly different. It is most often used to mention the wooden tablets with Rapa Nui symbols called roŋoroŋo boards that Rapa Nui people often claim to be part of ancient traditions. In this context,

Piru's use of the word as a formulation for Rapa Nui language, in part, symbolizes a new subject matter of our studies. In teaching me Rapa Nui language, Piru did not conceive of herself primarily teaching me an abstract, secular, grammatical system. She saw herself teaching me a discursive practice connected to the symbolic ways of life of her *tupuna* (ancestors). Her representation of the contemporary language as *roŋoroŋo* "dialogically" (Bakhtin 2002) embedded our studies within Rapa Nui discourse of the ancestral world.

The *roŋo* (messages) of the ancestors, as her command suggests, were to be learned by *hāpī 'i ruŋa i te henua* (study upon the island). For Piru, this involved walking *te henua* (the island) with elders and youth to learn the *roŋo* of particular places similar to Hawaiian kua'āina and their teachings of wahi pana (McGregor 2007, 4–5). Sometimes the *roŋo* were literally marked upon the landscape in the form of petroglyphs. Other times *roŋo* were in place names, stories, and songs recalled about particular places and the cultural heritage and natural resources found within and around them. The important *roŋo* were not always of the ancient ancestors and places though; often *roŋo* were found in places of recent history or contexts of current affairs. *Roŋo* were also culled from engaging in ancestral Rapa Nui practices like fishing, gathering medicinal plants and shellfish, and planting traditional crops.

Piru shifted the subject matter of my studies as we studied upon the island. She also changed the subject matter by demanding, as the studies evolved, that I prepare an *umu tahu* before I could continue further work. After about a month of walking the island to learn its *roŋo*, Piru suddenly refused to teach me any additional *roŋo* until I completed an *umu tahu* ceremony. This was very frustrating to me, because from my perspective I had finally begun to acquire a deep understanding of the contextual meaning of Rapa Nui language. I did not want to delay study even one day, much less for a week or so, depending on how long it would take to complete such a ceremony. Having no idea what the ceremony was, nor how long it would take to complete, I asked Piru, "What is an *umu tahu*?" She bluntly replied, "You are the anthropologist, you figure it out."

After a few days of visiting different knowledgeable Rapa Nui people, I was able to learn the basic features of the task at hand. Broadly, an *umu tahu* is a cultural practice Rapa Nui conduct to ask the spiritual world of the *tupuna* (ancestors) to bless some activity, place, process, or thing. A living Rapa Nui is asked to receive the blessing on behalf of the *tupuna*. While living in Rapa Nui, I have seen *umu tahu* completed on a number of occasions— for example, at the inauguration of the new mayor, and at the beginning of cultural festivals. The custom involves preparing a small meal in an *umu* (underground oven) that consists minimally of a cooked white rooster and a few sweet potatoes. To make an *umu tahu*, one digs a shallow hole approximately three feet in diameter and about a foot deep. The hole is then filled with stones and firewood and the wood is burned to heat the stones. Once the stones are aglow, the remaining wood is removed quickly and the meal, wrapped in banana leaves, is placed atop the stones. Today, layers of canvas and sometimes thick plastic wraps are also often placed on top of the bundled food to improve the cooking. Ultimately, all is covered with soil and left to cook underground for a few hours. When the food is cooked, the preparer or preparers of the *umu tahu* give the meal to someone or some group on behalf of the ancestors. Those who prepare the *umu tahu* are not allowed to eat any of the food. Those who made the *umu tahu* are enjoined to give a speech to the individual or group the *umu tahu* honors and to the *tupuna* who are requested to bless the proceedings. After the *umu tahu* is completed, the hole must be refilled and restored to its original condition as well as possible.

I prepared the *umu tahu* for Piru at Vai Tō Iri. A nephew of Piru, Ioni Tuki Hucke, and his daughter, agreed to help me organize and prepare the ceremonial meal. After wringing the rooster's neck and cleaning it for cooking, I was instructed to retrieve a bundle of banana leaves from a nearby *manavai* (a planter of ancestral times composed of stone walls) in order to wrap the food to cook, and to contemplate the content of what I was to say as I offered the *umu tahu* to Piru and the *tupuna*. As I climbed over the five-foot walls of the *manavai* to reach the leaves inside, I looked at the hundreds of *moai* staring at me from nearby Ranu Raraku in Piru's backyard. The mysterious *moai* upon Rano Raraku, whom I was introduced to in 2004 in an archaeological field school to assess possible transport routes, no longer appeared as parts of an ancient engineering puzzle. Nor were they simply enchanting monumental Polynesian sculptures. The *moai* had become *te ariŋa ora o te tupuna* (the living faces of the ancestors)—as Piru liked to call them—and my conversational addressees. My later *pule* (prayer) to request permission to continue study of Rapa Nui language and culture consequently became directed to *moai* not as archaeological curiosities, but as persisting Rapa Nui *tupuna*. What I had understood as an ancient artifact since first measuring *manavai* in 2004 as an archaeology student was now clearly different; the *manavai* was now Rapa Nui culture engaged in the present. When I offered the *umu tahu* to Piru and the *tupuna*, I thanked Piru and the *tupuna* embodied in the *moai* for the knowledge they had bestowed thus far and requested they further support my studies in Rapa Nui. Neither Piru nor the *tupuna* responded in words. Piru stood like a *moai* and said nothing. However, she and the other Rapa Nui who had gathered that day did ultimately accept and eat from the *umu tahu* offered; some remaining food though was placed in the fire pit. As was customary at many Rapa Nui meals I participated in, this was food left specifically as an offering to the *tupuna*.

One of the major contemporary analytical issues in the ethnography of language has been the study of the contextual significance of language usage (Duranti and Goodwin 1992; Hanks 2000), as opposed to the formal significance of language as a grammatical system. By examining the situational as well as the general sociocultural context (Malinowski 1965, 52) of some of Piru's teachings, I hope to have shown how Piru transformed my studies from a linguistic examination of an abstract code of meaning into a linguistic anthropological investigation of Rapa Nui language as a cultural activity and discursive practice. For Piru, and other elder speakers, the meaning of Rapa Nui language is rooted in conversations with elders about the many storied places of the island such as Rano Raraku. Its meaning is connected to ceremonies such as *umu tahu*. Like those of the West (Foucault 1972, 225), the discursive practice of Rapa Nui language is thus controlled by ritual qualification and fellowship. Access depends upon "learning how to ask" (Briggs 1986) appropriate *taote* for apprenticeship, as well as the ancestral *tupuna* that persist as the faces of the *moai*.

Amid Chilean state violence and violations of their human rights to self-determination (IWGIA 2012), Rapa Nui people continue to struggle against ongoing Chilean settler colonialism (Young 2013). The discursive practice of Rapa Nui language, as opposed to Chilean Spanish, will likely continue to be an important cultural resource for the Rapa Nui people to maintain an identity and "sense of place" (Feld and Basso 1996, 11) distinguished from Chile.

Notes

1. After my initial month of research in 2004, I completed approximately a year and a half of fieldwork in Rapa Nui during my dissertation research from 2007 to 2008; subsequently, I returned in the summers of 2011 and 2012.
2. Rapa Nui possessive pronouns are different from English possessives. They involve a distinction that articulates what Whorf (2000, 147) would call a "habitual thought world" important to understanding issues of linguistic relativity. To narrate some event with a Rapa Nui possessive pronoun, one must distinguish whether the thing to be possessed is "a" class or "o" class

(and sometimes "u" class). For example, in the case of kinship one uses "o" class for parents, as in *tō'ona* (his/her) *matu'a tane* (father), but "a" class for children, as in *tā'ana* (his/her) *poki* (child). One also uses "o" class for people equal in social hierarchy, as in *tō'ona* (his/her) *taina* (sibling). Piru's use of the "o" class positions her either as equal or above me in hierarchy.

Blogging in Papua New Guinea

STEVEN EDMUND WINDUO

> "Taken together they offer the possibility of new kinds of active social and cultural relations in what is going to be in any case an exceptionally complex technological world."
>
> *(Williams 1989, 139)*

THE MOST EXCITING EXPERIENCE of blogging for me is the educational value of the content of the blog. I walked into my class on literature and politics at the University of Papua New Guinea (UPNG) one day. I asked the students to take out their cell phones. I instructed them to Google my name. The effort brought them into the entries with my name, especially the entry with the blog name. They entered the blog with no effort. I told them that for their intellectual enrichment they could now access additional materials relating to the course just through their cell phones. If they were absent from class, they only had to use their cell phones to access related materials captured in the blog: www.stevenswindow.blogspot.com. Knowing that a good number of my students are on Facebook, I also post updates in the blog to Facebook for them to access information relevant to their intellectual development. The statistics on my blog posts for the month of July 2013 reveal that the post titled "Publications Culture at UPNG Alive" recorded 958 views, the highest recorded since 2010. The simple reason is that this is a news item posted in the EMTV (a Papua New Guinea–based commercial television station owned by Fiji TV) site linked to my blog.[1] In Papua New Guinea (PNG), new communication technology is transforming the way of life and manner in which locals participate in the global world, and one can easily join without direct access to computers.

Blogging is a new experience to many Papua New Guineans. Located in the southwestern Pacific, with a population of approximately eight million people, Papua New Guinea is a country with a diversity of cultures and more than 854 different languages (Scott 2005, 24). Approximately

80 percent of the people live in isolated rural communities without the electricity, modern technologies, and accessibility to modern amenities that the rest of the world takes for granted. Though the country has only 45–50 percent literacy, its citizens have a basic knowledge of the world around it and are eager for change, like those of many other island communities in Oceania.

The advent of new communication technology has made its presence felt most in Papua New Guinea via mobile telecommunication. With the development of mobile telecommunications, interest in Internet access and Facebook rapidly increased in the past few years. Access became easier. Internet makes the local become global and the global become local. The production of space, especially the way "we conceive social processes, social flows, and the constitution of areas . . . as simultaneously an outcome and condition of social process" (Smith 2010, 29), has become self-evident to us. For Papua New Guineans, "Local transformation is therefore integral to global transformation in quite specific ways," and "arguments about global change need to be offset by an understanding of the local changes that both follow from the global and are constitutive of them" (Smith 2010, 34). The technology has influenced the way Papua New Guineans do things, send and receive information, and has helped to create new relationships with people and cultures inside and outside of Papua New Guinea.

The initial blogging experience began for me in 2006 in New Zealand. At that time I was serving as the Macmillan Brown Research Fellow at the Macmillan Brown Research Centre for Pacific Studies at the University of Canterbury, Christchurch. It was not so much the need for an Internet presence, but the experience of riding on the wave of technological innovation in this century that hooked me. I wanted to find a way to have my research and thoughts published in a digital form. I began experimenting with blogging using Google Blogger. I immediately liked working with Google Blogger, even though I tried Wordpress and Netlog.com. Developing the personal blog was slow, but as I gained the courage to master the knowledge of blogging, I sought the advice of respected journalist Malum Nalu. Nalu was running his own blog, which would later become the winner of a UNESCO Blog of the Year Award. He gave me some hints and directions on how to develop some of the tools readers see now on the homepage of my blog. The first blog I developed in 2007 was named "Manui Publishers." After a while this blog became obsolete as a result of someone hacking into my Gmail account. I was denied access to that blog. Not willing to compromise, I challenged myself to develop a new blog. The blog www.stevenswindow.blogspot.com was gestated to serve the purpose of publishing articles published in the column "Steven's Window" in the *National* newspaper of Papua New Guinea. The column appears in the "Weekender" section of the newspaper every Friday.

Digital communication was a new experience for me at that time, but one that finds currency in Howard Rheingold's discussion of the Pacific-based virtual communities: "Virtual communities might be real communities, they might be pseudocommunities, or they might be something entirely new in the realm of social contracts, but I believe they are in part a response to the hunger for community that has followed the disintegration of traditional communities around the world" (Rheingold 1996, 418). Alan Howard has further argued, "Maintaining such a community in any meaningful sense requires a core group of participants who engage in a frequent exchange of news and information . . . and a sense of collective history built from continual exposure to common lore and shared interests" (Howard 2000, 404).

As a blogger for some years now, I have gained experience making my presence known in the world through posting new entries on my blog. It is valuable to share and learn from others, as blogging and information technology become tools of survival at this moment in human history. Until recent times, I had changed little of the original outlook and design of the blog www.stevenswindow.blogspot.com.[2] The simple reason is that I had paid little attention to my responsibility as a blogger. In early January 2013, I redesigned and refashioned the blog to make it more user friendly and appealing to visitors and friends of the blog. The significant changes to the format also made it possible to view the blog using a cell phone.

There are three types of blogs in Papua New Guinea. The first type of blog is set up and managed by Papua New Guineans. This type comprises blogs carrying personal perspectives of life in PNG. A second type of blog is set up outside of the country. Individuals with long-term interests in Papua New Guinea are usually those who administrate this type of blog. This group is interested in promoting a perspective from outside of Papua New Guinea. The third type of blog is set up as a corporate marketing tool to promote products and Papua New Guinea as a commercial place for trade and the indulgence of pleasure.

All bloggers have different reasons for setting up their blogs. A few reasons motivated me to set up my blog. I wanted (1) to share what I write as a newspaper columnist with the *National* newspaper; (2) to use an electronic medium to promote the work I do; (3) to advertise the books that I write, edit, and publish; (4) to promote an intellectual body of knowledge about Papua New Guinea, arts, culture, education, books, literature, and social cultural research through the electronic medium; and (5) to network with other bloggers from Papua New Guinea. I can follow other blogs without adding new ones to my blog.[3]

Blogging provides an opportunity to explore and try out new ideas, and experience personal development in a world where digital technology has become a powerful tool of personal, social, political, economic, national, and global empowerment. The power of social networking, and the advancement of ideologies and knowledge through the effective use of this new medium, has perforated isolated communities and enabled them to adapt more immediately to the changing face of global communities.

In the nexus of the local and the global, a blogger enters into a timeless memory, created within minutes to last forever; the experience has an immediate effect. Often there is a real-time response as a new entry is made on the blog and it reaches someone at the end of the world also entering the same space in real time. There is magic in this nexus as a blogger realizes the power of words as they immediately reach someone invisible, but postgeographically present in cyberspace, reading every word a blogger writes and publishes.

Small island communities of Oceania have begun to embrace the changes brought about as a result of the advancement of new communication technology. A small island community in the Milne Bay Province of Papua New Guinea wasted no time in taking advantage of available information technology. The Catholic mission, with the help of the governor of the province, set up a broadband network around Nimowa Island—one of the remote islands of Papua New Guinea strung along the Great Barrier Reef shared between Australia and Papua New Guinea. Using this technology, the priest, Father Anthony Young, has begun to provide online education to the young people of the neighboring islands. Instead of thinking of itself as an isolated island community that the government had ignored, Nimowa has been placed by this exemplary work in a class of its own that other Papua New Guinean communities will emulate in years ahead. In my effort to network with the Hope Academy on Nimowa Island, I posted information about it on my Steven's Window blog.

Father Young arrived in Nimowa in 1964 and remained there for most of his life. I met Father Anthony Young, an Australian priest, on Nimowa Catholic Mission Station in the Milne Bay Province in late December 2012. I quickly began to admire him for his dedication and unselfish life, serving as the head priest to the people of Nimowa, Sudest Island, Yeina Island, Panatinance Island, Panawina Island, and other neighboring islands. Father Young started Hope Academy to help the large number of students unable to continue their education after eighth grade. The project depends upon a wireless broadband network covering a wide area of islands from which students can learn using modern information technologies. He was kind enough to e-mail me two documents detailing this pioneer project. Imagine e-mailing from an island cut off from the rest of PNG?

Father Young's e-mail reports, "A grant from the PNG Sustainable Development Fund five years ago financed the equipment for the backbone of our wireless network, some equipment for village classrooms, and the training of six technicians in the maintenance and handling of the network." Challenges are acknowledged as the Hope Academy gathers popularity among students in this remote part of Papua New Guinea. He emphasizes, "When we began the project, we were already tutoring twenty to thirty students to gain their Matriculation (Grade 12). Word spread, and we had more and more students knocking on the door, wanting to enroll. We couldn't turn them away, but finally we reached a stage where we couldn't squeeze any more into the dormitories or the old classrooms we were using." In 2011 and 2012 the school began the year with about one hundred students. Private donations helped pay for food to feed the students on Nimowa. With a shoestring budget, the school is struggling to meet the increasing demands for such an education. Father Young comments, "The result was that we continued work on our online Academy project on a shoestring, compared to what would normally be budgeted for the kind of work we were doing." Chatting with Father Young has helped me to see that many people in Papua New Guinea have no idea how difficult it is to provide education to those children living in isolated communities in the remotest parts of Papua New Guinea.

Use of information technology is increasing. Individuals, organizations, and institutions have benefited immensely from usage in ways that are transforming the means of production and socially productive relations. The results for communication are expected to be staggering: "Its flexible forms, in further applications of the technologies, would be fully congruous with new working relationships in self-managing agencies" (Williams 1989, 138). New communications are transforming the way we work, think, play, and interact with others in the world. In this transformation we recognize a process of "unwriting" (Winduo 2000) taking place where older discourses produced in print media are unwritten with the power of the new information technology. It is easier today to access almost anything on the Internet. It is "a significant improvement in the practicality of every kind of voluntary association: the fibres of civil society as distinct from both the market and the state" (Williams 1989, 138). Civil society has experienced a rupture of some sort, emptying its negative social cultural package out of the window to embrace the new fresh air of technological inventions; it has absorbed advantages through greater participation in the market economy and democratic processes informing and constituting the state.

The immediate recognition of this form of communication inspires me to participate in the blogging experience with awareness that I can now share information without needing permission from any organizations, institutions, or governments. I am participating in this free market economy of sharing ideas, knowledge, and cultural information about what others may not have the opportunity to know. The blog entries are based on specific social and cultural topics of value to me as a person, a writer, scholar, and someone who participates in the global education system. Rightly so, as the "use of the new technologies can add diversity and permanent availability to the most comprehensive institutions, above all in making them outward-looking, taking their own best knowledge and skills to a wider and more active society" (Williams 1989, 139).

Through blogging, a new way of participating in the centrifuging of massive amounts of information is being achieved. Consistent publishing of new information helps transform minds and perceptions of the world, improving humanity and human societies. Without updating, the world we live in becomes stagnant, unchanging, and suffocating. Papua New Guinea society has recognized immediately that empowering knowledge is now available at the touch of a cell phone or the click of a computer mouse. The digital media revolution is having an immediate positive effect on a society long denied access to free, useful, and vital information.

Notes

1. Statistics for the blog www.stevenswindow.blogspot.com reveal that since 2010 the most-viewed item, as of July 29, 2013, is the post "Publications Culture at UPNG Alive" with 958 views, followed by the post of February 19, 2011: "Lunch at the Honolulu Academy Hawaii" with 556; the post of August 28, 2010: "Book Publishing and Reprinting of Books" with 513; the post of September 14, 2010: "Reframing Indigenous Knowledge"; and the post of October 13, 2010: "Blue Eyed Angel of Kusaun" with 398 views.
2. The blog title is now changed to *The Window* on the Google search engine.
3. So far the most popular blog is Malum Nalu's blog, which had recently reached the mark of one million visitors since the blog was established. Other blogs that I follow are Emmanuel Narokobi's Masalai blog, Russell

Soaba's Soabastoryboard, Martin Namorang's TokautTokstret, and blogs by others, including Jeffrey Febi, Yana Elius, and Neles Tandamat. Some of these blogs have regular followers as well as others who accidentally arrive from other blogs. In maintaining their blogs, the bloggers have kept the interest and enthusiasm of blogging very much alive against the influence of the more popular Facebook, which is now accessible to many Papua New Guineans through their cell phones.

PART 4

Identity Encounters

Gender, Ethnicity, Nationality

(*overleaf photo*) This scene at Sinchon Station on the Seoul subway line seems to capture the desired body reflected in South Korean commercials. South Korean women have become so immersed in Western celebrity culture that plastic surgery has become as common as going to the dentist, overtaking Brazil as the plastic surgery capital of the world. In the background youngsters walk by one of the cheap eateries by the bus stations in Seoul. Photo by Hyeon Ju Lee.

Introduction

MARY MOSTAFANEZHAD

THE MYRIAD WAYS THAT GENDER, ethnic, and national identities are constructed through the complex web of culture have long been an important topic of ethnographic inquiry for social researchers. In this section, we examine these identity formations. Gender is understood as distinct from one's sex. Sex refers to biological differences between females and males. Gender is the culturally constructed associations that are ascribed to "femaleness," "maleness," and "transgendered" identity formations. Rather than being biological or genetic, gender is constructed through and varies between cultures. Ethnicity is similarly embedded in culture. It is used here to refer to culturally distinguished groups of people that share similar historical, ancestral, and cultural traditions. Nationality is distinct from ethnicity in its focus on citizenship in and/or identification with a nation-state. This means that people of different ethnicities can share the same nationality and people of the same ethnicity can be of different nationalities. Like gender and ethnicity, nationality is also socially constructed and negotiated. In this section, we consider gender, ethnicity, and nationality in several cultural contexts. Each chapter demonstrates how gender, ethnicity, and/or nationality are fluid concepts that vary in different cultural, political, and economic circumstances. By acknowledging the complex intersection of gender, ethnicity, and nationality with politics, the economy, and other cultural aspects, we can better understand the fluidity of these identity formations across cultures.

This section begins by exploring how gender identities are constructed through specific cultural practices in Thailand. LeeRay M. Costa humorously describes her fieldwork experience where traditional gender norms about men's and women's roles are made explicit when her Thai colleagues take notice of her male partner who performs "women's work" by cooking dinner as well as participating in other "feminine" activities. In an attempt to rescue her partner from being labeled feminine, several of her male Thai friends encourage him to take on a *"mia noi"* or second wife in order to demonstrate his masculinity. We then move to Guam where James Perez Viernes examines indigenous Chamorro masculinity and U.S. colonialism. Viernes begins his research believing that he will easily find willing collaborators, because he too is a Chamorro man with community ties. He is surprised when he encounters many unforeseen complications. As a result, Viernes reflects on his experience of doing research in one's home community as both an "insider" and an "outsider."

Hyeon Ju Lee examines national and ethnic identity construction among North Korean refugees in South Korea. Lee illustrates how North Korean refugee identity as *talbukja* as well as their "belonging" is constantly contested. This constructed ethnicity has many social, political, and economic implications for *talbukja* lives in South Korea. We end this section in Hawai'i, where Roderick N. Labrador illustrates the complexities of being an "insider anthropologist" as a Filipino man among Filipino communities in Hawai'i. Through his experience, he finds that the meaning of "being Filipino" is not essential or pregiven, but can shift in different geographic and cultural contexts.

Prostitutes, Menstrual Blood, Minor-wives, and Feeding the Ducks

Learning about Gender in Thailand

LeeRay M. Costa

While anthropological fieldwork, that is, the process of learning about and describing another culture through participant observation, is bounded by neither space nor time, it is undeniably shaped by embodiment. In this essay I share stories from my own fieldwork as a female-bodied woman as I sought to make sense of gender in Thailand.[1] Interestingly enough, many of these stories originate not in the formal spaces of my research on Thai women's groups and nongovernmental organizations (NGOs), but rather in my everyday experiences living as a foreign woman in Thailand, and negotiating Western assumptions about cultural "others."

Anthropologists often refer to their research site as the "field" and hold it in opposition to "home." During my graduate training, I encountered numerous stereotypes about Thailand. Whenever I mentioned that my research would focus on gender in Thailand, people automatically assumed I was studying prostitution. Thus, I resolved to avoid that topic and to focus instead on women's grassroots activism. I wanted to fight the negative stereotypes of Thai women by highlighting the many ways that Thai women were empowering themselves and creating social change.

After numerous visits to organizations and discussions with Thai friends and colleagues, I chose to study the Project for Tomorrow (PFT) because of its work with women and children in rural areas.[2] PFT had been working for over ten years on women's empowerment, rural development, economic/income projects, and children's education. They seemed to be a good fit, and, most important, Mae Somjit, PFT's president, was willing to host me and allow me to live on her property while doing fieldwork. I returned home from my exploratory visit feeling confident and excited to begin research. To my great surprise upon returning eight months later, I discovered that PFT had accepted a very large grant from the international organization Protect Our Youth (POY) to—you guessed it—fight child prostitution!

Even before beginning fieldwork, I had learned both the power of gender ideology and its global dimension. Thailand is so strongly associated with prostitution in the global imagination that the stereotype is impossible to avoid. In one notable case, an encyclopedia in the 1990s defined the capital city of Bangkok as "home to many prostitutes," provoking a firestorm among Thai leaders. And Western media regularly publish stories sensationalizing Thailand's sex trade. As I came to discover, "the prostitute" is the specter that haunts all Thai women. The prostitute is to our "whore" as the good woman is to our "madonna." For whenever Thai women are perceived to cross the line of normative sexual and gender expression, the epithet of "prostitute" (sophenee, garee) may be invoked to keep them in line. This taught me that in order to fully understand what it meant to be a woman in Thailand, I would also have to grapple with the role of the prostitute within both Thai culture and the global imaginary, whether I wanted to or not.

So what exactly does it mean to be a good and proper Thai woman? Thai womanhood is often associated with propriety, decorum, docility, and beauty. The Thai word riproi sums up the way a woman should act and dress—neatly, orderly, and quietly. Thai women should not be aggressive (except in the marketplace and in business) and are expected to abide by strict gender norms that position them in a complementary role to men that is often interpreted as inferior. Though Thai women have long worked outside the home out of necessity, more contemporary versions of middle-class womanhood construct women as avid homemakers, responsible for household and caregiving tasks.

When I moved onto the home compound of Mae and Pa (Mae's husband) in Ban Hon village, I lived on the second floor of a separate building on Mae's property. The first floor was home to the PFT organization office, and people came and went throughout the day. It was my responsibility to take care of my own cleaning, cooking, and laundry, which I did together with my partner, Andy.

One day Mae took me into the yard to show me how to correctly hang my laundered clothes. Emphasis was placed on making sure my panties were hung down low. I was told this was necessary so that Pa would never have to walk under them. As Mae explained this to me, she smiled and laughed, the irony apparent to both of us. What made this exchange so funny was that Mae, who is seen as an important rural woman leader who has repeatedly defied conventional gender norms through her activism and community organizing, was reinforcing very traditional notions about the danger of menstrual blood and by association, women's bodies. Although I already knew what she was getting at, based on my previous experience in Thailand, I listened patiently as she tried to explain that Pa's head should never have to pass under my panties, lest his power be sapped by the lingering potency of my menstrual blood.

The power of women's menstrual blood is immortalized in the story of Queen Camatewi told throughout the province where I lived. According to the tale, Queen Camatewi fashions a hat out of her undergarments and sends it to a suitor whose goal is to both marry her and assume control of her queendom. Unknowingly, the suitor places the hat on his head. This not only diminishes his strength and his ability to complete the physical challenge that will win Queen Camatewi, it eventually kills him. Today, women activists point to Queen Camatewi as an example of why women from this province are so strong.

The danger of menstrual blood also meant that, as a female-bodied anthropologist, I had to be especially careful about disposing of my used menstrual products. This is something that most cisgendered male anthropologists never have to think about.[3] The bathroom I used was an outhouse and the door was occasionally left ajar. Mae and Pa had a dog that roamed the yard as if it were his domain and his only. One day I was shocked to discover that the dog had not only ventured into the outhouse, but had rummaged through the garbage and found my used tampon. As he dashed around the yard with the tampon in his mouth, I chased him in what he obviously thought was a thrilling game. It seemed like forever until I could wrest it away from him before Pa, Mae, or anyone else could discover it. As I gasped for breath, I reconsidered my preparation for fieldwork and the implications of being a woman in the field.

Women's menstrual blood is powerful—physically and metaphorically—and by extension, so is the female body. (This is also used as an excuse to keep women out of Buddhist temples, as they are thought to defile sacred space.) Yet so much of what I had read about Thailand and gender up until that moment suggested that women were *not* powerful. This contradiction raised numerous questions for me as I sought to understand gender relations and power in Thailand. Moreover, menstruating in the field was a topic absent from the anthropological literature, no doubt a reflection of the fact that most anthropologists until the 1970s were men (Moore 1988). Yet these experiences taught me that doing fieldwork with a female body (and one that bleeds) makes a difference—both to what I experience and to the cultural knowledge I gain as a result.

While women's bodily fluids are feared and constructed as dirty in Thailand, their sexuality is also constructed in opposition to men's. This double standard around the performance of sexuality is not unlike the double standard in the United States, but it has some unique features. First, sexuality is considered appropriate for women only in sanctioned marital relationships. Any time a Thai woman exhibits her sexual being or desire, even with a romantic or sexual partner, she is threatened with the labels "prostitute" or "whore" as mentioned above. The same is not true for men, however. Men are believed to be more sexual than women and to need to "sample many flavors," as the Thai saying goes. There is a historical practice in Thailand of having multiple wives or mistresses (*mia noi*), and men accrue status based upon the number of *mia noi* they have, as it indicates both financial success and virility. Married women are normally expected to endure their husbands' infidelities while at the same time being monogamous themselves. This gender ideology means that historically men have had more freedom in terms of their activities and use of time, while women have been tied to the home or community in order to fulfill critical social roles as nurturers and caretakers. These social norms curtailing women's travel outside their home villages (without husbands as escorts) still operate in some rural areas today, limiting the work of grassroots women activists and putting them at risk for accusations of promiscuity.

That these oppositional gender roles are still the norm was reinforced both by members of my Thai household and the grassroots activists I was studying. Doing fieldwork on women's organizations meant that I was often out until late into the evening. My partner regularly had dinner waiting for me after these meetings. On more than one occasion I arrived home very late, dinner long since cold, Andy sitting on the step looking up at the starry sky. This resulted in joyful teasing by Mae, members of her household, and other NGO members. I had, it seemed, unwittingly reversed the conventional gendered relationship that made me more like Mae and the other NGO activists, and hence susceptible to some of the same criticisms. In fact, I learned that this gender role reversal could result in the hazing of women activists by members of their communities, and accusations of infidelity and even prostitution. That is, if women are out late at night at women's meetings, or working to create a better future for their children and communities, the assumption is that they are really out having sex! And that means they have cuckolded their husbands, reversing conventional gender roles and challenging men's patriarchal authority and privilege.

These ideas crystallized for me later when I learned that our *songtaeow* driver,[4] Joom, had been on a mission to find Andy a minor wife. Andy traveled with Joom back and forth to Chiang Mai to teach English while I was busy doing fieldwork. Periodically Joom would tell Andy that he needed to find himself a girlfriend. Andy tried to laugh it off, explaining that his wife was "fierce" (*thu*) and that he did not dare take the risk. One day, rather than bring Andy home, and without warning, Joom took Andy to a party at his friend's house. There Joom introduced Andy to several young Thai women and, while plying Andy with alcohol, encouraged him to take one as his new *mia noi*. Embarrassed and exasperated, Andy eventually persuaded Joom to take him home. Joom was disappointed that Andy had refused his efforts at making him into a "real Thai man."

While men taking minor wives has long been practiced in Thai society, and is indicative of the unequal power relations and double sexual standard in Thailand, there is evidence that the practice is not readily accepted by all women. Some of you may be familiar with the story of Lorena Bobbitt, the American woman who cut off her abusive husband's penis. Well, let's just say that Thailand has a slew of Lorena Bobbitts. In fact, I once gave a presentation to Chiang Mai University students about penis cutting—or what is affectionately known in Thailand as "feeding the ducks." It turns out that a number of Thai women, fed up with their husbands' philandering, have shown their outrage by simply severing their husbands' penises from their bodies. In one infamous story, the wife fled the house on her scooter, penis in hand, and flung it into the canal where it was promptly devoured by a flock of ducks. While in most cases these men have been able to have their members reattached, this poor guy was out of luck. So when Andy told Joom his wife was "fierce," and did not dare risk a minor wife, "feeding the ducks" may have been on his mind.

While humorous, these experiences revealed that gender inequality is further reinforced by sexual inequality in Thai society. Thai women are often denied full expression of their sexuality while men are encouraged to cheat on their wives as evidence of both their masculinity and social power. Yet, as philosopher and historian of sex Michel Foucault (1990) has written, wherever there is power, there is also resistance. Thai women have not accepted this sexual inequality without a fight, and as I learned with more time spent in the field, young Thai women in particular seemed to be stretching the boundaries of what it means to be a woman and a sexual being, asserting their agency in the process. Furthermore, doing fieldwork with a partner of the opposite sex and gender meant that I had access to experiences outside of my own social location as a woman. Lucky for me, having a feminist partner meant that I often had dinner waiting for me after a long, hard day of grueling fieldwork. What more could a feminist anthropologist ask for?

Fieldwork is an adventure. Neither straightforward nor sensible, it is a messy, complicated experience that, with attention and a little luck, can lead to profound discoveries. My fieldwork in Thailand often left me surprised and confused. I spent a lot of time struggling to make sense of cultural anxieties over gender, and what seemed incongruous or ironic behavior among the Thai women I met. I also became aware of my female body in a way that was not familiar, but that helped me to better understand what it means to be a woman in Thai culture, and a woman scholar in the discipline of anthropology. In that sense, doing ethnographic research is a highly visceral experience that must take into account not just the mind, but also the body.[5] The experiences, contradictions, and humorous events described above, and many more, compelled me to think through the social anxiety that exists about women's power, the ways that women negotiated social norms in relation to gender, and the vast complexity of gender as both a concept and a practice. Anthropological fieldwork can at times be embarrassing, unnerving, and infuriating, but it is always educational and transformative. And the best lessons often come when you least expect them.

Notes

1. Stories detailed here are drawn from fieldwork in Thailand during the period 1996–2000.
2. Following anthropological convention, names used in this essay are pseudonyms in order to protect the privacy of participants.
3. Cisgender/ed is a term used to describe individuals whose gender identity corresponds to the gender they were assigned at birth based upon an assumed match to their physical body/sex (for example, a child identified as "a girl" at birth comfortably identifies as female or woman). It is used in contrast to the term transgender that describes individuals who do not identify with the gender they were assigned at birth. These terms were developed by gender activists and scholars in order to acknowledge that neither gender identification is "abnormal," but evidence of regularly occuring gender variation among human beings. In Thailand, there are additional gender categories beyond man and woman. These include *sao braphet song, kathoey,* and *tom. Sao braphet song* are individuals assigned male at birth who identify as women and choose to live as such. Some scholars have glossed *sao braphet song* with the English term "transgender." *Kathoey* is another term used to describe male-bodied individuals who display

characteristics associated with nonnormative *sexual* behavior and/or who claim a female *gender* identity. *Kathoey* has been glossed with the English terms "gay," "transsexual," "transgender," "drag queen," "lady boy," and "third gender." *Tom* refers to female-bodied individuals who identify as masculine and are sexually attracted to female-identified people (itself evidence of masculinity). For more on these topics, see Costa and Matzner (2007), Jackson (1995), and Sinnott (2004).

4. A *songtaeow* is a pickup truck that functions as a taxi service in northern Thailand.

5. Attention to embodiment in social science research and theory is rooted in a critique of mind/body dualisms and an emphasis on the corporeal nature of subjectivity and identity (see Grosz, 1994). Bodies are understood as neither bounded nor autonomous. Rather they are seen as produced through their relationship to and interaction with other bodies. Such an approach has profound implications for ethnographic researchers who have no choice but to take their bodies with them into the field, and to access cultural knowledge and practice through those bodies, and their senses and emotions. Applying theories of embodiment to the practice of anthropological research raises critical questions about epistemology, social difference, and the materiality of identity, including gender and sexuality. See Mascia-Lees (2011); Kulick and Wilson (1995); and Longhurst, Ho, and Johnston (2008).

Manning Up

On Being a Chamorro Researcher with a Home Court
(Dis)Advantage on Guam

James Perez Viernes

It had been eighteen months since I moved back to Guam after having spent five years in graduate school at the University of Hawai'i. From the intellectually stimulating environment of the Mānoa campus to the good times shared with fellow graduate students, my years in Hawai'i stand out as some of the best in my life so far. But my fourteen- by seven-foot room at the Hāle Mānoa dormitory and living as a "starving student" (I use that term very loosely) had begun to wear on me. I longed for the day that I would be cut loose to begin my dissertation research back home.

I could barely contain myself on that Continental Micronesia flight in the seven hours it took to get to Guam. I filled those hours basking in nostalgia for the village life that I left behind so many years before, with the boys always ready to barbecue and drink at a moment's notice, the entire extended family within a one-mile radius, and the general comforts and security of "home." My research obligations that awaited me at home remained a secondary concern at this point.

As I have read and read about Guam's past in particular, I have been bombarded with outsider histories that told stories about the "decimation" or "obliteration" of Guam's indigenous Chamorro men. The three-hundred-year Spanish conquest of Guam beginning in the seventeenth century and the subsequent and ongoing U.S. colonialism of the island left my male ancestors a silenced relic of the past, or so the prevailing written histories told me.[1] But no matter how loudly this notion has resounded in the canon of historical documentation, I cannot help but think of my father, my uncles, and indeed, myself, and wonder, "are we not all Chamorro men and all alive?"

My mission has become to prove those histories wrong by illuminating Chamorro masculinities as very much alive, and to deliberate on the relationship between gendered identities and American colonialism in the twentieth and twenty-first centuries.

From the start, I have been adamant that my work not be based on that old-school brand of research, where I would sit in that infamous "ivory tower" spewing ideas that would be supported by books on dusty library shelves written by dead men. Instead, I have sought to pursue the island-centered/islander-oriented approach to history proposed by James Davidson (1966). I have been stirred by Davidson's acknowledgment that histories of the Pacific were all too often focused on Western histories of colonialism and ignored other narratives of the past. I have embraced Davidson's push to transcend colonially produced archives, to foreground islander ways of knowing the past and their agency in its unfolding, and to transfer focus to the islands themselves rather than the centers of their colonial administrators.

Even the radical shift Davidson inspired in Pacific history had its limitations, so I further draw from the ethnographic approach to history that grew out of the discipline of anthropology. As enthusiastic as I was about these approaches that were suspicious and often hostile toward Euro-American methods, I remain intimately tied to the Western academic traditions inherent to the very degree I am seeking. Thus, I subscribe to David Hanlon's assertion that "The decentering (or is it recenterings?) of history in Oceania is in part, then, about making the writing of history . . . but one of many possible forms of historical expression in the region" (Hanlon 2003, 34). Indeed, I remain largely vigilant of the fact that contemporary scholarship is not so much about divorcing ourselves and our approaches from those of the West altogether, as about finding what David Chappell (1995, 317) has coined a multi-vocal "middle ground" on which all practitioners, islander or otherwise, might find a meaningful space from which to articulate the past.

Looking back, I guess I would have to say that my greatest challenges since beginning my research have not so much been in the approaches themselves or in the theoretical debates over the direction of the academic discipline of history. The most immediate and challenging obstacle yet has been my underestimation of the research endeavor itself and my overestimation of myself as a researcher. I embarked on my research journey assuming that as a Chamorro male conducting research about other Chamorro males on Guam I would have the insider and home-court advantages. I approached this research with this arrogant and misguided assumption despite an abundance of warnings offered by numerous scholars about the dangers of assuming the exclusive role as either an "insider" or an "outsider" in field research. I completely discounted the reality that I, although Chamorro and doing research in my "home" field, was to become both the insider and the outsider simultaneously.

To gauge attitudes about Chamorro masculinities and U.S. colonialism, part of my initial research has included an anonymous survey of Guam Army National Guard members. The survey consisted of an individual participant completing the survey, after which we would have an open discussion about his answers, the survey questions and statements themselves, and his overall experience of participation. One of the first individuals who agreed to participate was a nineteen-year-old Chamorro male whom I will call "Joe." We were casual acquaintances from the social scene on Guam, but we were also tied to each other because our families knew each other well. Joe's contributions to the pilot survey led me to the quick realization that my attempt to get Chamorro males to talk about what constituted their manhood would not be as easy as I had anticipated.

Once Joe had completed the survey, I began to ask him about his responses. I was caught off guard when I arrived at a statement on the survey to which Joe was asked to indicate on a Likert scale the extent to which he agreed or disagreed with the statement. This was the only portion of the survey that Joe left blank. That statement read: "Serving in the Guam Army National Guard makes me feel sexually attractive." When writing the survey, my intent with this statement was to try to determine, with regard to Chamorro men, the plausibility of other studies arguing that masculinities are, to a degree, linked with male sexual prowess. It was curious to me that the survey in its entirety was completed, with the exception of this one portion.

I asked Joe why he had left this part of the survey blank. He quickly replied, "*Kåksaka, bro! Why you even asking that?!*" through boisterous chuckling.[2] I found Joe's response both intriguing and unexpected. I could not immediately understand why he left it blank, why he had questioned my motives in posing the question, why it was funny, or why it made me *kåksaka* to even ask it. Through extensive discussion with Joe, he indicated that talking about how he feels sexually with someone who was older than him and not his close friend was awkward. It was especially uncomfortable because I would have access into his personal life through our social and familial ties beyond the pilot survey. Joe indicated that those social and familial ties made him uneasy with participating in the research. "I don't want to look dumb. *Laña'*, I don't have all those degrees like you. I might say something dumb and you're going to tell my family I'm stupid!" he expressed through more laughter.[3]

I thought long and hard about my experience with Joe, because it was that very statement on my pilot survey that warranted similar reactions from my Chamorro male participants time and time again. Some left it blank, as Joe did, while others were dismissive of it, awarding a rating of 3 on the scale, which translated to "No opinion/Unsure." When asked why they had no opinion or what they were unsure about, these participants were admittedly unable to explain their response. Other statements proved daunting for participants, for example, "My service in the Guam Army National Guard makes me feel like a valued man in my family and community," about which I was asked by participants, "what's that supposed to mean?" What was most daunting about this was that their question was absolutely valid, but I was largely unable to answer it. I knew what I meant by the question, but I could not explain to them in terms they could understand or find meaningful.

I thought long and hard about the obstacles and became both troubled and discouraged by them. I had to figure out what I was doing wrong and why I seemed to keep hitting dead ends in some of the most critical areas of my research. In short, four significant problems were arising. First, being a Chamorro living on Guam, or an "insider" as I had fancied myself to be, made participants uneasy with speaking candidly about sexuality, gender, and other topics. Many expressed discomfort with the fact that they would see me regularly outside of the sterile environment of my University of Guam office in which the pilot survey was conducted. Many did not want to encounter me in places like church, funerals, parties, and other settings and have to wonder what I was thinking about them, having become privy to the thoughts that they might not otherwise discuss openly.

The second challenge that arose in this research was in the area of Chamorro cultural barriers. Many younger participants felt reluctant to speak openly about their gendered identities because I am an older Chamorro male. Cultural values demand levels of respect and deference for elders, and this is often articulated through behavior that does not draw undue or negative attention from elders to younger individuals. Now I should emphatically point out that I do not qualify as an "elder" in the conventional sense of being "elderly." But what I viewed as a mere and insignificant ten to twelve years that I had over my participants certainly disqualified me as a peer, and I soon realized the bearing that age difference would have on the research.

The last two issues that had become a problem rested in the nature of my research topic and my lack of diligence toward finding ways to make it accessible to a wide range of participants. The interaction I shared with my participants confined to the context of "research" created an uncomfortable environment in which many of them feared that my advanced, formal education created a situation that put them at risk of "looking stupid." Despite the fact that I came from similar socioeconomic and cultural backgrounds as those of the participants, my credentials put them on guard to prevent the appearance of inadequacy on their part.

I was discouraged, to say the least. The only thing that has become clear beyond doubt is that being an insider with a home-court advantage was nothing more than a figment of my arrogant imagination. With the somewhat damaged ego of an academic "put in his place," I take a lesson from Tengan, who so clearly points out, "These issues [of positionality] have become increasingly important for all ethnographers to reckon with, as distinctions between insider/outsider, home/away and engaged/disengaged have become difficult to maintain, especially in the Pacific" (Tengan 2005, 247).

Thinking back to the romantic nostalgia and the highly selective memory of Guam that beckoned me back to the island, I wonder how I could have been so foolish. Yes, I did return to the swing of life on Guam, hanging with the village boys and enjoying the splendor of living within a large extended family. But along with that came immense obligation. Many have made immeasurable sacrifices and pardoned me of numerous obligations and responsibilities to allow me the time and space to succeed as an academic. But despite my allowances to shirk obligations, one is never completely released of these responsibilities.

Try as I have to remain organized and follow a rigid timeline, all sense of organization and diligent planning can be thrown out the window at a moment's notice. Births, deaths, weddings, christenings, and other life milestones seem to occur on Guam every time the wind blows. And each time this happens, the rhythm of the day-to-day workweek seems to come to a general halt so we can practice *kustumbren Chamorro,* or Chamorro custom. The practices and obligations tied to *kustumbren Chamorro* can often take several days, or even weeks, to execute. And while contemporary practice largely incorporates cash as a means of fulfilling these obligations, the Chamorro proverb *Ti salapi' ha' a'apasi* (money is not the only way to repay) still rings loudly on Guam (see Ramirez 1993). Whether it is providing cash assistance, offering services or goods, or merely providing one's presence as a gesture of support, the need to balance career, education, and life in general with the demands of *kustumbren Chamorro* is a struggle for all people on Guam, and it has certainly been a hindrance in furthering my research.

My research on Chamorro masculinities continues, and there still remains so much to do. But what I can conclude in these preliminary stages is that Chamorro men have much to say about their identities as men, if only asked in ways that are meaningful to them. I continue to try to identify these avenues that allow Chamorro men to reveal their stories. And I am beginning to learn that while the conventions of masculinities identified elsewhere (such as sexual potency, physical prowess, and economic mobility) are very much a part of understanding evolving Chamorro masculinities in the context of continued U.S. colonialism, distinct notions of family and community obligation, custom, and cultural competence have very much become themes that I must more thoroughly explore and foreground.

I have tried to tell myself that teaching two courses each semester at the University of Guam, serving on various faculty committees, taking up contract work on the side to make ends meet, and keeping up with my communal and familial responsibilities are all valid excuses for this stalled progress. But in the end, they are just that—excuses. And they are all a part of the process I have had to go through toward finding my feet as a researcher whose "field" is at home. The time for excuses has come and gone. At the risk of sounding sexist and chauvinistic, this ongoing research really has been about "manning up" to my dual responsibilities as an academic researcher and a member of a broader nonacademic community. I remain hopeful, though, in these lessons learned and lessons to come. To cite yet another Chamorro proverb, *amanu na guaha minalagu', guaha nina'sina* (when there is desire, there is a possibility) (Ramirez 1993).

Notes

1. Guam was taken as a possession of the United States in 1898 and remains a non–self-governing territory of the United States.
2. *Kåksaka:* in general, this is an expletive in the Chamorro language with multiple meanings depending on the context in which it is used. It is also used commonly, as in the case included in this essay, among friends as an expression to indicate that one is crazy, outrageous, wildly spirited, or even fearless.
3. *Laña':* expletive loosely equivalent in this instance to the English expression "shit" or "damn."

Contested Belonging of North Korean Refugees in South Korea

HYEON JU LEE

I SAT DOWN AND WATCHED JAY, a graduate student in legal studies, taking his seat on the opposite side of a low table in a small restaurant in Seoul, South Korea. We paused briefly as we settled into our seats in a restaurant and resumed our previous conversation about North Korean refugees in China.

Jay and I had attended a small conference called "Talbuk Daehaksaeng Nonmun Balpyohoi," a conference put together by a group of North Korean refugee students in higher education in Seoul. The conference was held at a Presbyterian Church in Seodaemun-gu. There was an apparent connection between the church and the organization these students belonged to— Korea Refugees Young Christian Association (KRYCA). Jay presented a paper about difficulties North Korean refugees were facing with finding employment in South Korea. He argued that young North Korean refugees lacked enough cultural capital to be competitive among South Korean college graduates. After the conference, the presenters and some of the attendees moved to a small restaurant for dinner. On the way to the restaurant, Jay and I began to talk. As we gained rapport, our conversation took a turn from general impressions at the conference to the status of North Koreans in China and South Korea.

Shortly after we sat on a *bangseok* (flat cushion on the floor), a waitress brought in two cups of water and two wet, chilled napkins to cool off our hands. The table was soon filled with a delightful array of dishes containing kimchee, marinated vegetables, roasted dry seaweed, boiling stews in small clay pots, and steaming rice in individual bowls. Jay and I were not distracted by the luring smells and enticing colors from the small plates in front of us. We were engrossed in our conversation about the status of North Koreans often called *talbukja* in South Korea.

AUTHOR: Jay, do you think *talbukja* are refugees?

JAY: Of course they are refugees. They should be recognized and given a status as internationally recognized refugees in China. Look how many people are in trouble because they don't have the refugee status. *Talbukja* should be called refugees.

AUTHOR: But how about after they come to South Korea? Do you think they are still refugees when they are in South Korea?

JAY: (Looking perplexed and after a short pause) No. Of course they are not refugees. They are South Koreans [after arriving in South Korea]. *Talbukja* are South Korean citizens with full legal rights and privileges. They are refugees only when they are in China without legal status.

Jay and I misunderstood each other. I was asking about the overall sociocultural status of *talbukja*. Jay was concerned about the legal status of North Koreans in China. For him, the word "refugees" connoted those who "flee to a foreign country or power to escape danger or persecution," a definition commonly found in dictionaries. According to this definition, once refugees obtain citizenship or permanent residency, they are no longer refugees, legally. It was natural for him to answer my question in a legal context rather than the way I intended to ask my question. Jay had been a refugee himself and had many fearful experiences.

Talbukja literally means "person(s) who is (are) displaced from North Korea." In this context, the term *talbukja* implies that he/she is a socially marginalized refugee who does not belong to a particular country. When she is called a *talbukja,* she is not *bukhan saram* (North Korean) or *hanguk saram* (South Korean) with full cultural, historical, and legal rights as a citizen of either country. *Talbukja*'s identity as a citizen of a country is constantly contested. Her belonging to a country is also questioned continuously.

Talbukja are those who were born and raised in North Korea but left it for various reasons and are not able to return for fear of persecution and other dangers to personal safety. Many of them have witnessed or experienced illegal border crossing, human trafficking, and various forms of exploitation, displacement, and separation from the family. International and domestic mass media, novels, movies, and documentaries often feature the plight of North Korean refugees: persecution in North Korea if repatriated, vulnerable status as a displaced and illegal alien, and long and arduous migration routes from North Korea through the Chinese continent down to Southeast Asia before arriving to South Korea.[1] The period of migration can take from several months to a decade. The distances some people traverse during their migration cover half of the Asian continent.[2] For this very reason, many *talbukja* who are in transit feel that they should be given an internationally recognized refugee status so that they can safely cross the borders without the fear of repatriation and persecution. At the same time, due to such experiences, many South Koreans and *talbukja* also hesitate to call people from North Korea who now live in South Korea "North Koreans." This is in part because the term "North Korean" loses the historical and global specificity of the problems around national division and the illegal border crossing that people from North Korea experienced during their escape. Thus the term *talbukja* is commonly accepted.

The reason that many North Korean refugees in China are admitted to South Korea is due to the special relationship South Korea has with North Korea. According to the South Korean constitution, South Korea's national territory is defined as the entire Korean peninsula, which includes North Korea. The reason South Korea considers North Korea as part of the country is due to the unfinished war that broke out in 1950. Essentially the Korean War (1950–1953) has not yet ended; the physical war ended only with a truce.[3] Neither North Korea nor South Korea considers each other as a legitimate nation-state even though the division has lasted nearly seventy years. For this reason, North Korean refugees are admitted to South Korea as South Korean citizens if their North Korean identity is proven at the time of entry. During the Cold War era, North Koreans "defected" to South Korea, and until the 1990s only a few hundred "defectors" were living in South Korea.

Since the late 1990s, the number of *talbukja* in South Korea has grown from a few hundred to a few thousand. By the end of 2011, the number of North Korean refugees in South Korea had reached over twenty thousand.[4] During the first few months of their arrival in South Korea, they are placed in governmental facilities to have their North Korean identity thoroughly verified and to be culturally acquainted with ways of life in South Korean society. At a training facility called Hanawon, they receive medical treatment, lectures on a capitalist market system, democracy, computer skills, and many job-related skills. For eight to ten weeks they live in Hanawon in a dormitory. They are then relocated to a new neighborhood where government-designated housing is located. By this time, all of them receive a resident registration number, or *jumindungnokchung*, which indicates that they are South Korean citizens. From this point, *talbukja* begin to look for employment, further education, a new spouse, or other ways to begin life in a new country. Despite the newly granted citizenship, North Korean refugees are distinguished from other South Korean citizens.

The name *talbukja* had puzzled me from the beginning of my research in 2005. At the same time, I had been agonizing over whether this group should be called "refugees." The term *talbukja* separated this group from other North Koreans, South Koreans, and from all other ethnic Korean groups. It became increasingly confusing to identify this group, particularly in English, due to this name *talbukja*. As a novice anthropologist conducting long-term fieldwork for the first time, I was concerned with how to appropriately refer to the very people I was studying. *Talbukja* were not *bukhan saram* (North Koreans), nor were they *namhan saram* (South Koreans). Many of my fellow fieldworkers were at a loss about how to translate references to this group into English. Some concluded that the translation of North Korean migrants was "North Korean defectors." While I decided to stick with North Korean refugees, I wondered how *talbukja* would interpret this new group name.

Many of the North Korean refugees I met during my fieldwork in 2008 and 2009 in Seoul were bright young adults struggling to survive in a new country. They aspired to fit into South Korean culture and had aspirations to be successful. I was working as a volunteer teacher at a nonprofit organization that offered educational services to North Korean refugee youths. This place was one of my main field sites during the fieldwork. Many of the students enrolled at this nongovernmental organization called the Alternative School had limited formal schooling for reasons such as absent parent(s) at home, long-term migration throughout China in search of a shelter, and in some cases dropping out of school in South Korea. Now at the Alternative School, students were studying mathematics, Korean language, English, science, and social studies, as well as performing arts. Students often told me they liked the Alternative School because they could forget that they were different from other South Korean students and they could be themselves. Yet I witnessed on numerous occasions that *talbukja* were asked to choose a single national identity. An example of this occurred when a few students visited China in 2006 to document their past experiences. During their journey to the past, the students had to answer questions about their confusing identity once again. From their visits, the students produced a documentary film series called *The Longest Journey*.

The Longest Journey 2[5] premiered at the Art Cinema in Seoul on a cold winter day in January. The old movie theater located on the top floor of Nakwon Sanga, one of the oldest markets, was known for musical instruments in Seoul as well as for hosting independent movies. Most of the audiences were the current and former students, volunteer teachers, donors, and directors of the school. However, there seemed to be more than a handful of lay folks who came to see the film out of curiosity. *The Longest Journey 2* depicted the story of Ok, Hyuk, Eunjoo, and Chul, whose childhoods were partially or extensively spent in China. In a scene toward the end of the film, they were in Tiantan Park (Temple of Heaven) in Beijing, one of the major tourist attractions. The students had come back from visiting the border areas between China and North Korea. Ok and Eunjoo, two girls, bashfully engaged in small talk with other visitors, attempting to converse in English. They laughed and giggled in part due to embarrassment about speaking English and in part because they were having fun. In some scenes, the girls chased each other and laughed with one another, while the boys filmed the girls. A few minutes later in the film, after exchanging a few questions about who was going to approach other tourists, Ok bravely started a conversation with European visitors. As Ok started to speak to a few male visitors who appear to be European Caucasians, Eunjoo, walking next to Ok, giggled in the background.

OK: Hello. Where are you from?

VISITOR: Where are you from?

OK: North Korea.

VISITORS: North Korea?

　　　　Really? North Korea?

　　　　Which city?

(Ok looks confused at the question and at the heavy accents)

OK: What?

VISITOR: North Korea? (Sounding incredulous and doubtful)

OK (Speaking toward her friends): "Hey, are we North or South?"

　　(Then speaking to the visitors): "Oh, South Korea, South Korea."

This scene portrayed Ok's inability to identify whether she was North Korean or South Korean when speaking in English. It revealed how North Korean refugee identity is an unsettled one. When placed in a situation of having to identify their national identity as North Korean or South Korean in English, the marginality of the *talbukja* category becomes more obvious. In

South Korea, *talbukja* are accustomed to being categorized as people from North Korea. Yet when they are traveling abroad with a South Korean passport, their national identity is inevitably South Korean. Their North Korean refugee identity becomes a source of confusion regarding their affiliation with South Korean or North Korean identity categories.

At the end of the film screening, the four students in the film and mentors who were involved in producing the film held a question-and-answer session. After the introduction of the filmmakers, the floor was opened to the audience for questions. One member of the audience raised her hand and posed a question to the students who participated in the making of the film. This female viewer happened to be at the film showing by accident, unlike many others who were invited guests from the school. She said she saw the sign as she was passing and was curious to find out what the film was about. This South Korean woman did not know much about the existence of North Korean refugees in South Korea before she saw the film, and she said she was deeply moved by the movie. She then proceeded to ask the following question, which I recorded along with other observations in my field note entry.

AUDIENCE MEMBER: I have a question for the cameraman. Do you view yourself as South Korean or North Korean?

STUDENT: I wish I could be labeled not as either this or that. I don't want to be called North Korean or South Korean. I wish I could just be Josŏn *saram*.[6]

At the theater, the discussion on identity continued after the film showing. Someone in the audience asked the men from North Korea how they identified themselves. Some of the children answered that they were Josŏn *saram*. Others answered that they were North Koreans who reside in South Korea. The above scenario illustrates an uncomfortable truth about the categorization of North Korean refugee identity in South Korea. North Korean refugees were asked to choose their identity as either North Korean or South Korean, yet they hesitated to do so, due to each term's association with a political affiliation they must claim. In addition, the general perception of North Korean refugees in South Korea was that *talbukja* have "escaped" North Korea by choice and "choose" to live in South Korea. This perception also has created a general misconception that all North Korean refugees must hate North Korea and strongly wish to be South Koreans. Nicole

Dejong Newendorp (2008) in her book *Uneasy Reunions* argued that different political systems result in cultural separation even among the reunited families between the People's Republic of China wives and Hong Kong husbands. In a similar way, the migration of North Koreans to South Korea illustrates the uncomfortable union of Korean peoples. The cultural differences that each political system of North Korea and South Korea generate make it hard for *talbukja* to choose a national identity in public. *Talbukja*'s contested identity is thus a product of a complex history and uneasy definition of the modern nation-state, and the notion of national belonging. Korea's problem of continuing division complicates the national belonging of North Korean refugees. In addition, the problem is further complicated when the nation-state is an "imagined community" (Anderson 1983) in which all members assume their belonging in the same nation. Perhaps my inability to translate *talbukja* in English was not due to the lack of words but because of *talbukja* reluctance to belong to one category.

Notes

1. International organizations such as Human Rights Watch, Refugees International, United Nations Human Rights Commission, and other independent associations have produced reports on situations of North Koreans in China and other countries. These reports have been based on interviews conducted in safe houses and refugee camps. Also the *New York Times,* the *Washington Post,* and other major international newspapers and magazines have featured border-crossing stories and the dire situations faced by many North Korean refugees on their route to South Korea.

2. In recent years, the routes have typically been North Korea–Northeastern China–Southernmost Chinese border–Cambodia/Laos/Vietnam–Thailand–South Korea.

3. For a more detailed history of the Korean War, see Cumings (2011).

4. The actual number of refugees in hiding is not known.

5. The Alternative School took a monthlong trip to China to retrace the four students' migration routes before coming to South Korea. The film depicts the students' reflections on their past lives in China and their attitudes toward their transformation from fleeing refugees to visiting tourists in China.

6. In North Korea, Koreans are often referred to as Josŏn *saram,* denoting the last Korean dynasty before the Japanese colonial period (Josŏn: the name of the last "Chosun" dynasty; *saram:* a word for people in Korean). The ethnic Korean-Chinese are also called Josŏn-*jok,* meaning Joson ethnic person (*jok:* ethnic marker). In Japan, Koreans used to be commonly referred

to as Josen-*jin,* meaning Joson people. In the postcolonial period, the Koreans in Japan are called "Zainichi Josenjin," meaning Koreans within Japan (Le 2000). However, this word is not used in South Korea as the country is known as Hanguk, an acronym for Taehanminguk, the Republic of Korea, which translates literally to the "Great Country of Han People."

"You Filipino, ya?"

RODERICK N. LABRADOR

I FIRST CAME TO HONOLULU as a graduate student in July 1994. Part of the reason why I chose to attend the University of Hawai'i at Mānoa was that I had heard and read that there was a large number of Filipinos in the islands and that Hawai'i had the highest concentration of Filipinos among the U.S. states (relative to the state's total population). The 2010 U.S. Census indicated that Filipinos are now the largest Asian ancestry group in Hawai'i, constituting 14.5 percent (single race) and a little over one-quarter (single and mixed race) of the total population. Prior to arriving in O'ahu, I had also heard that unlike many Filipinos in the continental United States, most Filipinos in Hawai'i were speakers of Ilokano, one of the numerous regional languages in the Philippines and the third most-commonly spoken language (behind Cebuano and Tagalog). This was of particular personal interest to me as a native speaker of Ilokano and as a 1.5-generation Filipino American. I was born in the Philippines and when I was six years old, my family immigrated to the United States where I spent my formative years. As part of my upbringing in southeast San Diego, most of the Filipinos my family interacted with spoke Tagalog, formerly the national language of the Philippines and the language often perceived to be the lingua franca of Filipinos all over the world. I thought that going to Hawai'i would be more or less a cultural and linguistic homecoming, yet on several occasions my positionality as a "Filipino" and my authenticity as an insider were called into question. I also discovered that, although intellectually I recognized the heterogeneity of Filipinos, working through the sociocultural and political diversity of the group on the ground proved to be more challenging than I expected.

Filipinos have a long history in Hawai'i, settling in the islands in significant numbers over one hundred years ago to fill the labor needs of the sugar and pineapple plantations of the islands. The first *sakadas,* or Filipino plantation workers, arrived in 1906, and since then the agricultural labor history and a working-class consciousness have served as primary anchors for defining a local Filipino identity and often dominate contemporary state-sponsored and public discourse. However, the Immigration and Natural-ization Act of 1965, which formally ended the national-origins quotas and included family reunification and occupational preference provisions, shifted the dynamic of Filipino community development in Hawai'i. The post-1965 immigration coincided with the transformation of Hawai'i from an agriculture-based economy to one (over)dependent on corporate tourism and the defense industry, securing the islands as a global tourist destination and U.S. military colony. This political economic shift coincided with the arrival of new Filipino immigrants not directly connected to the previous *sakada* generation. Steffi San Buenaventura (1995) observed that the post-1965 immigration had two primary consequences. First, the changes in im-migration law had a numerically revitalizing effect, drawing attention to the possibility of large-scale community action and empowerment.[1] Second, the constant flow of new immigrants and growing numbers highlighted community diversity and revealed "conflicting values and concerns based on the differing perspectives and interests of the American-born and the immigrant Filipinos" (San Buenaventura 1995, 452). These consequences and the ways identity, power, and representation intersected were crucial contexts in the fieldwork I conducted among Filipina/os in Honolulu over the course of ten years (1998–2008).[2]

When I arrived in Honolulu in the summer of 1994, a university-sponsored public humanities institute called "Filipino Culture: Reclaiming a Heritage" had recently concluded and underscored the interrelatedness of identity, power, and representation. The two-week summer sessions in-stitute included a cultural fair, a film series, and a program of lectures, art exhibits, and music and dance concerts. The institute brought together Phil-ippine and Filipino American scholars, artists, writers, students, and com-munity leaders to discuss issues regarding the experiences of Filipinos in the Philippines, in Hawai'i, and in the continental United States (par-ticularly those related to language, literature, education, identity, and cul-tural values and acculturation). More interestingly, the institute posed the question "What is Filipino?" There was concern that Filipino American youth, primarily those born and raised in Hawai'i, were neglecting Philippine history, culture, tradition, and language; that they were denying their heritage. The organizers felt that Hawai'i-born Filipinos did not know what "Filipino" meant and as a result, they were disregarding or denying their cultural roots and not self-identifying as Filipino. Instead, Hawai'i-born Filipinos identified themselves as "Local," a panethnic category with roots in plantation society. As I have discussed elsewhere (Labrador 2004), I understand Local[3] as a racialized identity category; a panethnic formation composed primarily of the various nonwhite groups that usually trace their settlement in the islands to the plantation era. Thus, Local is also the label for those who are usually classified as "Asian American," "Asian Pacific Islander," or "Asian Pacific American" in the continental United States. For many Hawai'i residents, particularly those of Asian and/or Pacific Islander ancestry, Local is often the most salient category for political and sociocultural identification.

Although at that time I was new to Hawai'i, I was a bit surprised to see that in a place that had such a high concentration of Filipinos and a long history in the islands, there was a compelling need to ask "What is Filipino?" Should they not already have an idea of what it means to be Filipino? Why were Filipino American youth not identifying themselves as Filipino? And why did this matter so much to the community and university leaders? From this initial encounter, it was clear that the dynamics and character of the Filipino community in Hawai'i was quite different from both the largely military and low-income community that shaped my upbringing in San Diego and the high-income Filipino American community that I came across during my college education in New York. At that time, Hawai'i was on the verge of electing the first Filipino American governor in the United States, and as a result, the Filipino community was receiving a lot of media coverage. But perhaps more relevant to the Filipino Culture institute was the continuing media attention, both in the two mainstream dailies and in the two Filipino community newspapers, on Filipino youth gangs and their involvement in crime, drugs, and violence. As Maria Torres-Kitamura suggested in a community newspaper story titled "A Generation Lost?" in addition to the anxieties and nervousness that normally accompanies the beginning of a school year, it was also "[the] season for Filipinos to cringe as their children are described by the media as typical members of youth gangs" (Torres-Kitamura 1993, 6–7). Torres-Kitamura wondered if these young Filipinos were part of a "lost" generation.

In addition to the Filipino youth gang issue, another "Filipino problem" was the persistent low performance, low achievement, and lack of success among Filipino students at Hawai'i K-12 public schools. At the University of Hawai'i, with pending budget cuts and tuition increases, there was increased interest in issues of access, equity, and diversity and the underrepresentation of Filipino students, staff, and faculty in the University of Hawai'i system. It was hoped that the Filipino Culture institute could find the "lost" generation of Filipino youth, gang member and non–gang member alike, and address the inequities in the public educational system. By doing so, the Filipino youth could be put back on paths to success and the future of the Filipino community would no longer be in jeopardy.

Ten years later, during the heart of my fieldwork, the same issues I initially encountered were still highly relevant, especially questions around identity and what it meant to be Filipino. These issues were particularly stark and insightful in my interviews and interactions with Cliff Galvante, one of my key research participants. Cliff, like many of my other research participants, identified three primary Filipino types that are constructed along a Local–immigrant–mainland spectrum. Cliff was in his mid-twenties and self-identified primarily as "Local" (he told me he was "born and raised" in Hawai'i). He is a second-generation immigrant, and both of his parents are from Ilocos Norte, an Ilokano-speaking region in the northern Philippines. I spent over nine months interviewing him and getting to know his family and friends. In one of my early interviews, I asked him about his educational experiences. In a matter-of-fact way, he told me he went to an elementary school that was, "you know, the one by the prison" and that he went to the middle school where "you know, the one by the gym where they box." Further, mainly using Hawai'i Creole English (or Pidgin), he told me he graduated from a local high school "where they get plenty Filipinos, you know, the one by KFC. The one wit' the swimming pool that no work." Initially, Cliff thought that I was an insider, assuming that I grew up in the islands and that my upbringing was similar to his. My facial expressions and body language suggested otherwise, and that I did not understand his references. I asked him to further describe the schools he attended, and then he exclaimed, "Where you wen grad? You Filipino, ya?" In asking which high school I graduated from and whether or not I was Filipino, Cliff positioned me as an outsider of the local Filipino community. In his mind, as someone who is Filipino, I *should* know the geographical markers he used and I should be familiar with the seemingly common-sense landmarks in his descriptions (that is, the elementary school near the state prison, the middle school known for its after-school boxing program, and the high school with the nonfunctioning swimming pool). Why did he need to further explain these places in the Filipino neighborhood he grew up in? In essence, he was questioning the type of Filipino I was because I was unfamiliar with these local references. We shared Filipino ethnic identity, but we were different types of Filipinos. I was an insider because I was Filipino, but I was now positioned as an outsider because I was from the continental United States, or in his terms, "the mainland." Although he accepted that I looked as if I could be Local, where I was born, where I grew up, and my language (that is, he spoke mainly in Pidgin and he classified my speech as "straight English") marked me as an outsider. These identity dynamics demonstrate the problematics of "insider" research, depicting more what I would consider inside/out ethnography[4]—who is in/out is not always clear-cut, and researchers and research participants navigate and coconstruct the fluidities of who is considered an insider and/or outsider. In other words, what makes a researcher an insider/outsider is not solely an academic exercise but is actively and continually negotiated in the field among and between the researcher and research participants.

Cel De Guzman is Cliff's cousin. Cliff had suggested that I talk to Cel, whom he described as *buk buk* (an identity category that symbolizes a non-Local, *immigrant* Filipino),[5] to get another perspective on Filipino identity. Now in his early twenties, Cel immigrated to Hawai'i when he was twelve from Ilocos Norte. Nonlocal otherness. Although Cel and Cliff attended the same middle school and high school, there were differences in their social and educational experiences that highlighted a Local/immigrant binary. During our introductory meeting (which involved the three of us), Cel told me that he was from the town of Bacarra, and in response I shared that I was born in Zambales but my grandparents were from Laoag. Cel nodded, acknowledging the geographical proximity of the two towns (Laoag is actually one town south of Bacarra) and the possibility of ethnolinguistic similarity. During this greeting where Cel and I "placed" each other, Cliff did not understand the geographical references and asked where Laoag was, since he had never been to the Philippines. Cel admonished Cliff and exclaimed, "What? You don't know where that is? You Filipino, ya?" Cel's use of "You Filipino, ya?" is both an affirmation and rejection of Cliff's Filipino-ness. Cel recognizes that Cliff is indeed Filipino, but sees him as a different type of Filipino, perhaps one too "Americanized" and with very little knowledge of and experience in the Philippines. As in the previous interaction, Filipino-ness is being negotiated, but in this scenario, it is Cliff who is positioned as an outsider, as an "inauthentic" Filipino.

Several months later, Cliff and I attended the annual Filipino Fiesta and Parade in Waikiki and Kapiʻolani Park. There we met Cedric Surio, who was in his late twenties and had just recently moved to Honolulu from northern California. Cedric represents someone who Cliff usually categorized as "mainland" Filipino. Cliff and I introduced ourselves, and Cedric told us that he had moved to the islands not more than a year ago, and then proudly told us that he was from Daly City. I nodded, knowing that Daly City is in the Bay Area and, like Honolulu, has a high concentration of Filipino residents, albeit with a different socioeconomic profile.[6] Cliff did not know the geographic reference, so he asked politely, "Where is that?" Cedric told Cliff directly and expressively, "Come on, man! Daly City is the Filipino capital! You're Filipino, right?"

The interactions above depict ways in which individuals (and communities) align themselves according to the conditions and particularities of a historical moment, suggesting that "Filipino" identity is a fundamentally contested category. They also underscore the situations, positions, and negotiations in the identity formation process, revealing not only the mobility of identities but also their motility.[7] Here, borrowing from biology, I understand motility as active and seemingly spontaneous movement. Focusing on motility highlights the actors' agency as a type of self-propulsion where actors produce and are produced by the context, which includes power dynamics. The focus on motility also directs our attention to the gradients around which identity movements pivot. Traditional examples of identity gradients include race, ethnicity, gender, class, culture, and sexuality. My fieldwork demonstrates other types of gradients including language, speech community, towns, place-based ideologies, and immigration generation. Further, movement along these identity gradients is not necessarily a conversation between two (or more) equal agents who are in opposition. Instead, it is a multivocal conversation between agents who may or may not be diametrically opposed to one another. In other words, Filipino identity is an internally and externally contested reality, in which multiple definitions coexist and often challenge one another. For each of the interactions above, there is a privileged and enforced understanding of Filipino-ness. The privileged understanding does not deny the existence of alternate interpretations of Filipino identity, but it demonstrates how an interpretation can dominate under specific conditions, in a particular time, place, and relations of power. Motility avoids predetermination or situational essentialism by suggesting that identities are negotiated along gradients of nonprescriptive oppositions. In the end, motility embodies the shifting, relational, relative, situational, and negotiated reality of identities, suggesting that "Filipino" is not unitary and monolithic but instead involves a contested terrain of coexisting and often competing definitions, interpretations, and boundaries.

Notes

1. San Buenaventura and others have noted that roughly three thousand Filipino immigrants have arrived annually in the islands since the 1970s.
2. In what follows, I have given fictitious names to the research participants to maintain confidentiality and protect their privacy.
3. Hereafter, I use "Local" to refer to the racialized panethnic identity category and "local" to characterize a particular place or spatial location.
4. I am intentionally not using the term "native anthropology," because of the problematic native/settler dynamics in Hawai'i. For a longer treatment, see Fujikane and Okamura (2008).
5. As I have described elsewhere, the term *buk buk* is often used in local ethnic humor and everyday speech to indicate "immigrant Filipinos and is the primary marker of linguistic and cultural otherness" (Labrador 2004, 301). A Filipino who is *buk buk* is often characterized as speaking in a heavily accented English, wearing bright and/or mismatched clothes, and having a fondness for "exotic" cuisine, like black dog, pig's blood, and goat.
6. According to the 2010 U.S. Census, Filipinos constitute 33.2 percent of the Daly City population, and as Benito Vergara (2008) notes, the community as a whole exhibits middle-class characteristics.
7. The focus on mobility usually recognizes that identities move and are never static. My focus on motility acknowledges that identities are neither completely free-floating self-ascriptions nor entirely context-dependent entities.

PART 5

Close Encounters

Marriage, Kinship, Social Networks

(*overleaf photo*) Naceva village *dauvila* (firewalkers) cross the fire pit during a *vilavilairevo* (firewalking cere-mony) at the Royal Davui Resort on Ugaga Island in the Beqa Lagoon, Fiji. Traditionally performed only by members of the Sawau people on the island of Beqa, *vilavilairevo* is a prime example of a propitiation ritual that has become commodified to suit the requirements of tourism, emerging as a signature brand state-ment of Fijian national culture. Photo by Guido Carlo Pigliasco.

Introduction

GUIDO CARLO PIGLIASCO

KINSHIP EMERGED AS THE DOMINANT focus of anthropology in the period of its scientific coming of age as a discipline. Declared meaningless
and ethnocentric in the 1970s, the term "kinship" resurged in the 1990s as
a site on which to reflect on everyday experiences of intersections of ethnicity, gender, class, and power. Kinship in anthropology is an idiom generally referring to a set of coherent principles regulating relationships based
on blood and marriage. While kinship served as the main organizing principle of tribal societies, these societies have been through quite radical global
transformations that may have altered kinship categories. The case studies
outlined in this section examine how kinship principles and connections
structure social groups and many areas of social life, including economic
relations, with particular attention to contemporary issues of relatedness,
inequality, difference, implicit contradictions, and ambivalences.

This section opens with Ashley Vaughan's examination of how one
global process, the expansion of mobile phone technology in Vanuatu, affects marriage and social relations in a place particularly concerned with
protecting and reviving traditional culture. Moving to the islands of Fiji,
Guido Carlo Pigliasco explores the impasses he encounters as an ethnographer collecting kinship information to map traditional knowledge in a
Fijian village when his host refuses to acknowledge a parental tie. Navigating through village gossip, cultural faux pas, unhappy hosts, and government bureaucracies, Pigliasco unveils the local political economy of sentiment, respect, and reciprocity. Next, Pamela L. Runestad describes what it
meant, in the aftermath of the 9.0 earthquake that struck off the east coast

of northern Japan on March 11, 2011, to belong to a family, a particular community, a particular region of Japan, or even Japan itself in the minds of survivors when whole families, neighborhoods, and communities were suddenly washed away. Runestad investigates the central role of social networks as channels for relief and in the forging of new global and local connections. The section concludes with Lynette Hiʻilani Cruz's illumination of how theatrical performance artists teach Hawaiian genealogy and kinship in public culture in Hawaiʻi.

Sorry, Wrong Number!

Locating Marriage Partners through Wrong Numbers
and Text Messages in Vanuatu

ASHLEY VAUGHAN

THE PROCESSES OF GLOBALIZATION and the related growth and expansion of technologies have transformed kinship and social networking practices worldwide, in particular dating and marriage practices. With the rise of Facebook and dating Web sites, such as Match.com, "social networking" and dating in many Western countries have become synonymous with technology, mainly the Internet and iPhones. But what about places where Internet access remains limited? How are other technologies transforming social networks, and what are the effects of these technologies on cultural traditions and marriage practices?

I became interested in these questions during recent fieldwork in the village of Big Tautu on the island of Malekula. Malekula is the second largest island in the independent Melanesian nation of Vanuatu, an archipelago of eighty-three islands, sixty-five inhabited, that spans about eight hundred miles (Forsyth 2004; Goodman, Williams, and Maitland 2003). When I first visited Vanuatu in 2007, I was surprised to discover that I could purchase a cell phone—called "mobiles" on the island—and that some villagers living in Big Tautu, whom I refer to as Tautuans, were using mobile phones. I was witnessing the "Digicel Revolution" firsthand. Bimbika Sijapati-Basnett (2009) coined the phrase "Digicel Revolution" to describe the growing number of mobile phones and mobile phone services in the country. In contrast to Internet service, which remains very limited, the mobile phone service is relatively affordable and reliable. Big Tautu is near a Digicel tower, so there is great reception in the village.

Digicel is one of the two main competitors in Vanuatu's telecommunications market. The other is Telecom Vanuatu Limited (TVL). TVL's signature color is orange, while Digicel's signature color is red. Digicel red and TVL orange appear all over the island. Villagers sport red and orange Digicel and TVL T-shirts, which often come with the purchase of a new mobile phone. When I returned to Tautu again in 2010 to conduct eleven months of fieldwork, nearly every single young adult (ages eighteen to twenty-five) and most older adults I encountered had at least one mobile phone of their own. In fact, most adults had two phones, one TVL phone and one Digicel phone. Many people own two phones because both companies offer special rates and monthly deals that apply only when dialing another phone of that same company. Communicating via mobile phone became an important part of my fieldwork. While living in the village, I observed and participated in local mobile phone culture, texting, making and receiving phone calls, and sharing my mobile with my informants.

Upon returning, I also learned that one of my friends had a *niufala man* (a new man, that is, a common-law husband). I was curious. He being from Ambrym (another island), she being from Malekula, how did they happen to meet? Tara and Rodney, like many new couples in Vanuatu, met and courted over the mobile phone. Tara had received a call from an unknown number and had struck up a conversation with Rodney. Months later, Rodney took a ship from his home island to Malekula to meet Tara, and he decided to stay and live with Tara in Tautu.

When I asked Tara about this arrangement, she told me that this was not the first time she had met a man over the phone. A year or so before connecting with Rodney, she had been talking with another man who was also from another island. After several months of texting and talking on the phone, they made arrangements to meet in Lakatoro, Malekula's main urban center. Because they had only communicated via the mobile phone, Tara did not know what to expect. What would her suitor be like? She wanted to get a glimpse of him before meeting him, so she devised a plan. At the location where they were supposed to meet, Tara called him from another person's phone pretending to be someone else. When he answered, she was able to identify him. Tara did not go through with the meeting, because her suitor was "too old and ugly."

Tara and Rodney's relationship illustrates not only a new form of marriage arrangement but also the multiple meanings of marriage in Tautu. Tara and Rodney are considered *mared* (married) because they live together in the same house. If they decide to be married by a pastor in a formal church service, they will become *jos mared* (church married). If Rodney pays bride price to Tara's family, they will become *kastom mared* (customarily married). Couples can be married in only one or in all three senses of the word.

Kinship in Tautu is patrilineal, and land rights and protected knowledge are inherited through patrilineages. While patrilineality is the "rule," as on the island of Ambrym, at times Tautuans follow alternate lines in order to find a marriage partner (Eriksen 2008). Because many Tautuans are related to each other through both parents, they can follow a number of different genealogical "links" or "roads" to describe their relationship with a fellow villager (Eriksen 2008, 25). Having been adopted into a Tautuan family, I gained a village full of relatives. I could thus, for instance, refer to one of my informants as my cousin (by way of our paternal connection) or my granddaughter (by way of our maternal connection). We chose to call one another *abu* (grandmother and granddaughter in the Tautu language), because the *abu* relationship is a joking relationship (Radcliffe-Brown 1940).

Tautuans practice exogamy, meaning they marry outside of their family. There are *tabus* (taboos or rules) against marrying someone of any relation. Due to the significance of *ples* (place) in identity and in social networks, it is also preferable for Tautuans to marry a person from a different village. Combined, these customary practices make finding a suitable marriage partner challenging. In this island context, where transportation is time-consuming and expensive, using the mobile phone service is an important strategy for locating potential marriage partners.

How do people find marriage partners over the mobile phone? There are several different strategies. Some Tautuans rely on chance, only taking the opportunity to inquire about a person's marital status if an opportunity arises, for instance during an accidental dialing or answering of a wrong number. Other Tautuans, I discovered, take a more aggressive approach and actively text and dial unknown numbers. I personally received many of these inquiries. Perhaps because people are always obtaining new phones and/ or acquiring new phone numbers, it is common for Tautuans to answer an unrecognizable number. I learned to answer such numbers myself. Often it was someone I knew calling from another person's phone because she had run out of "credit" (money or minutes on her phone). On many occasions, however, I did not know the person calling, and on several occasions, after I explained that it was a wrong number, the person on the other end of the line asked me if I was married or not.

Yet another strategy is for a friend or family member to play matchmaker and set up two people via mobile phone. This technique, of arranging marriages via a third party, is not new. In Tautu, as in other areas of Vanuatu, Melanesia, and around the world, this remains a common practice. In

Tautu, it also remains common for siblings of one family to marry siblings of another family. Mobile phone communications and networks facilitate this practice. Remember Tara and Rodney? Now that Rodney is married to Tara, he is trying to find his brother a wife in the same village. His brother and Kimi, one of Tara's relatives, began talking and texting via mobile phone. When I left Tautu, Rodney's brother was planning a visit to come meet her in person.

What did Tautuans do before mobile phones? According to my consultants, before people began using mobile phones to find marriage partners, they wrote letters or traveled by ship. Then and now, all kinds of information and arrangements also traveled by the "coconut wireless" or "word of mouth." Mobile phones are used much in the same way as these older forms of communication. Now, as before, these methods of finding marriage partners underline the importance of marriage and exogamy in Tautu and Vanuatu society.

Using the mobile phone to find marriage partners, then, rather than being an entirely new development, can be seen as a transformation of traditional marriage and kinship practices. As other anthropologists have pointed out, technologies, be they medical technologies or communication technologies, are adapted to meet the particular context. In Vanuatu, mobile phones have "been integrated into existing forms of information and communication flows" (Sijapati-Basnett 2009, v). Mobile phones allow people to coordinate and communicate in customary ways and to fulfill customary goals, obligations, and desires with greater ease and convenience. Tautuans use the mobile phone as a tool to establish and reinforce important connections and to rally and organize forms of social, spiritual, and political-economic support. Jamaicans similarly use mobile phones to maintain existing social networks and in particular to manage financial difficulties, such as raising enough money for a child's school fees (Horst and Miller 2006).

Because mobile phone technology facilitates traditions like marriage and reciprocal exchange relationships, mobile phone technology has become, in a sense, a part of Tautuan *kastom* (customary or traditional culture).[1] Some aspects of mobile phone use, however, go against Tautuan *kastom*, according to my consultants. Some members of older generations complain about young adults being glued to their phones and spending time on the phone rather than fulfilling traditional duties such as working in the garden, helping their family, or engaging in *storian* (informal conversation and storytelling). My adoptive father, for instance, frequently expressed dismay regarding the time his granddaughters spent texting. He could not understand what they were doing. *Why are they always texting? It is not as if they are conducting important business. They are just wasting time and money.*

The mobile phone requires money and thus requires participation in the Western economic system, a system that most Tautuans have yet to fully join, as most people still live off the land and participate in a traditional subsistence economy (Regenvanu 2007). The desire to have cash for various goods and services, including mobile phone services, however, is a motivating force encouraging young people to move into urban centers so that they can get jobs. In this way, the mobile phone represents movement away from *kastom*. Depending on one's perspective, the mobile phone subverts *kastom* in another significant way. While it maintains the importance of marriage, the mobile phone has also created situations where traditional protocols surrounding marriage are no longer observed.

One evening, a young Tautuan woman, Lulu, left her family's house and turned off her phone. No one knew where she was or how to get in touch with her. According to her family, she had "run away" with Taso, a young man from another village. Her family did not see her for almost two weeks. I learned later that Lulu had been texting and talking with Taso for some time prior to her running away and that she had moved to Taso's house without asking for her family's permission. Her family was not happy about Lulu and Taso's actions. Lulu's grandfather was especially upset. Both Lulu and Taso had ignored *kastom;* they had failed to follow traditional protocols. Traditionally, families arranged marriages, and when a man was interested in a woman, he would have to arrange a meeting with the woman's family to negotiate bride price. Taso did not meet with Lulu's family. Nor did he make arrangements to pay bride price. Mobile phone technology enables people to circumvent these traditional marriage protocols, as it allows males and females to arrange private meetings and to communicate without their families being present.

Both Tara and Rodney's story and Lulu and Taso's story demonstrate some of the effects of globalization and the expansion of mobile phone technology on marriage practices in this one area of the world. It is too soon to tell, but it is likely that mobile phones are inciting new changes in gender norms as well. There has already been significant movement away from traditional gender separation practices. In Tautu, men and women no longer live separately. As a result of the influence of missionaries, villagers now live in nuclear families, with husbands and wives living together in the same household. There remains, however, significant separation between boys and girls and men and women. Males spend most of their time with other males, engaged in activities deemed appropriate for men, and females spend most of their time with other females, engaged in activities deemed appropriate for women. As such, males and females continue to have limited interactions. Mobile phone technology, however, provides men and women with more opportunities to be in contact. It also allows them to have private conversations in which they are able to speak more freely than they are able to in normal face-to-face interactions. This technology thus allows men and women to cross gender lines more frequently and provides a communicative space in which gender norms can potentially be played with and negotiated.

Note

1. For more comprehensive discussions of *kastom,* please see Bolton 2003; Eriksen 2008; Jolly 1982; Keesing 1982, 1989; Larcom 1990; Lindstrom 2008; Lindstrom and White 1994; Taylor 2007; and Tonkinson 1982.

The Invisible Firewalker

Negotiating Sentiment and Inalienable Possessions on a Fijian Island

Guido Carlo Pigliasco

I LEFT FIJI before the coup d'état of December 5, 2006. In the months that preceded the coup, it was becoming clear that the rule of governmental law along with customary law and the centrality of chiefly authority were at stake in Fiji. A Fijian coup is not simply a single event in which different factions compete for political or economic power. Rather, it is part of an ongoing transformative process rooted in contested views of the past that are forcing local actors to compromise and renegotiate their conceptions of their tradition, identity, and cultural heritage. Barely aware of all this in November 2004, on that boat slowly heading to Beqa Island, I was assaulted by thoughts of the potential harm I might cause to the culture and domain I was about to study.

Anthropologists often profess research interests that are not priorities for the people they study. In my study, however, I was genuinely convinced that the interests of the Sawau people of Beqa and of the Fijian policymakers working to design an intellectual property–based sui generis system to ensure protection of indigenous communities' traditional knowledge and expressions of culture would be served. One of these cultural elaborations, the Fijian firewalking ceremony (*vilavilairevo*) traditionally performed only by members of the Sawau people, is a prime example of a propitiation ritual that has become commodified to suit the requirements of tourism.

Firewalking, which early eyewitnesses reported on Beqa Island and in a few other Pacific Island communities, is associated with earth ovens used to bake the starchy roots of the cordyline plant. In Beqa, the *vilavilairevo* was staged whenever they had a large quantity of *masawe* (cordyline rhizomes) to be baked (*Na Mata* 1885, 2; Thomson 1894, 194; Toganivalu 1914, 2). This dramatic ceremony, performed by the Naivilaqata *bete* (priestly) *mataqali* (clan) of the Sawau *yavusa* (tribe), over the past two centuries has been shaped not only by the requirements of tourism but also by those of colonial pomp and circumstance. Simultaneously, it has transmuted itself into a sociocultural tool that has consistently indigenized the power of the foreign, allowing its custodians to locally sustain their community and to gain a reach and respect across the nation and beyond (Pigliasco 2010).

With the assistance of the Naivilaqata priestly clan members, in December 2004 I started reconstructing the genealogical chart of the "custodians" of the *vilavilairevo* ceremony. The chart listed 275 individuals, going back eight generations. In particular, I was convinced that the chart could amend some of the bureaucratic errors present in the *Vola ni Kawa Bula* (an official register of native landowners), and also the *Tukutuku Raraba* (oral histories of Fijian groups recorded in past centuries by the Native Land Commission), reestablishing analogical relations between past and present events.

British Native Lands Commissioners held hearings across Fiji beginning in the 1880s, soliciting historical testimony that could be used to codify "traditional" Fijian social groups and land tenure practices and link specific groups to specific lands. With the help of Bulou Ro Mereani Tuimatanisiga, sister to the Tui Sawau (paramount chief), and some of her grandfather's unpublished personal notes from 1926, I believed that we could actually challenge the "official history" of her people, offering them an unprecedented view of their prehistory, as the new chart we were constructing described a sequence of eight generations starting ca. 1800, showing that genealogical and mythical narratives are interconnected and mediate the authority of the past. I also believed that the recognition of indigenous curatorial practices challenging the "official past" was about to become another step toward the decolonization and democratization of archival practices, empowering the Sawau custodians.

The genealogical chart resulted from intense collaborative work with the community. The seventeen-page printouts of the chart were left hanging up in a place accessible to everybody who wanted to review them in the chiefly village of Dakuibeqa. The chart included illegitimate children, de facto marriages and de facto divorces, and other sensitive information that was not recorded in the Vola ni Kawa Bula or the Tukutuku Raraba. This information, nevertheless, was well impressed in the memory of the *vanua*—a complex term that Tomlinson (2009, 23) observes can be interpreted as "land," "place," or "people," the commoners, the "people of the land" as opposed to the chiefs (although the chiefs represent the *vanua*), and in its adjectival and adverbial form, *vakavanua*, "customary" or simply "traditional."

The main purpose of having this chart made was to establish the rights of co-ownership and custodianship of the iconic practice of *vilavilairevo* of the Naivilaqata descendants. In Beqa and Fiji, and across Oceania, property is not a thing, but a network of social relations that governs the conduct of people with respect to the use and disposition of things. Marilyn Strathern (2005, 104) shows that the right of ownership associated with property is "a world through which people are indefinitely interconnected through the inclusions and exclusions of property relations." On the other hand, property is not merely a relationship between persons and things. Property is a social practice including rights, privileges, powers, and immunities that govern the legitimacy of socially recognized individuals to control tangible or intangible things. In particular, property becomes meaningful only when relationships, conflicts, or claims among people are at stake.

There was only one person whose right to be on the chart was questioned, and I did not hear anything about him until the chart was basically complete. It was somebody who turned out to belong in the family tree of Samu Vakuruivalu, my host in Beqa. The person was his first son and he was also listed in the Vola ni Kawa Bula as Tikiko Korocawiri Vakuruivalu, born in 1973 to Marica Seawa, who lived in the nearby Sawau village of Dakuni. And if this was not enough of a surprise for me, Tikiko turned out to be a mysterious "competitor" of the Sawau firewalkers, organizing impromptu performances around Viti Levu. I had been chasing him for six months before even knowing his real identity, never having a chance to actually see his performances beyond some questionable pictures collected from a friend working for Japan International Cooperation Agency (JICA) in Suva.

In December 2004, Samu's son Waisea, his cousin Sake, and I were traveling from Suva to Navua; the taxi driver, who had recently watched a firewalking performance, was arguing with me that he was sure that it took place on the east coast of Viti Levu just north of Suva. I was sure that it had not; in my notes, beginning in July 2002 and diligently updated, I had listed all the firewalking venues and times of the week, the groups, and the names of each Sawau performer, including the village and clan they belonged to. Finally, I asked Waisea and Sake to explain to the driver that the Sawau *dauvila* (firewalkers) do not have any regular show on that side of the island.

Waisea and Sake started exchanging strange looks; I told the driver to turn down the Fijian reggae blasting from the inadequate speakers of the cab, and I asked Waisea to tell me what was going on. Finally, Waisea told me that most likely the performance had been organized by his brother Tikiko, a son Samu had before he married Waisea's mother, Merewai. Waisea and Sake were laughing, because Samu has never told me anything about this.

I decided to talk to Samu's older brother's son, Marika Tivitivi, who carries the name of a legendary *bete levu* (high priest of firewalking), and is in charge of one of the three firewalking teams in the village. Initially, Marika suggested just leaving Tikiko off the family tree, saying, "He is just bad news. Better if he stays 'invisible.'" A month later, however, Marika reported to me that his "brother" Tikiko had called him that morning from Nadi, asking him for some help with a large performance at the First Landing Beach Resort and Villas of Vuda Point in Lautoka. Marika also told me that Tikiko admitted doing the Robinson Crusoe Island show I saw in the pictures I had collected from my Japanese friend, and that he had asked Marika to tell the elders that this was his "last" performance. Now, regardless of Tikiko's bad reputation, considering that Tikiko was "flesh of their flesh," Marika suggested including his name on the chart.

In the course of my research, I had encountered a couple of misappropriations of the firewalking ceremony. One included the "firedancers" of Robinson Crusoe Island, an offshore budget resort on Likuri Island, a small islet north of Natadola Beach. In the pictures I had of this event, Marika thought he recognized Tikiko standing on the modest earth oven and wearing a head piece that hid his face from the camera.

Employing the heated stones of an earth oven after the food that had been cooked in it had been served to the tourists is a misrepresentation of the *vilavilairevo* ceremony. The *lovo* (earth oven) used to cook food and the one used for the *vilavilairevo* are not the same. The heating stones used in the *vilavilairevo* are typically cobbles of volcanic basalt stone much bigger than those used to cook *dalo* (taro) or any other food (Pigliasco 2009). Archaeological diagnostic exams of the earth ovens employed for the cooking of cordyline in different parts of the Pacific show a distinctive set of physical traits not found in other kinds of earth ovens: large oven size, large amount of combustible fuel, tremendous cooking temperature, prolonged cooking time, intense heat alteration of surrounding sediment, and extensive heat alteration of oven stones (Carson 2002, 362–363).

In January 2005, my collaborator Mika Tubanavau, who was helping me collect oral accounts of Sawau history for *The Sawau Project* (Pigliasco and Colatanavanua 2005), told me that at a recent *grog* (kava) gathering, Waisea showed grief and disappointment toward his father in front of the whole family for not telling me about Tikiko. I decided it was time to talk to Samu. The conversation below is taken from my fieldnotes:

12 March 2005, 17:00, Dakuibeqa, Beqa Island

GUIDO: *I owe you an explanation of why I placed Tikiko in your family tree. According to your family members he is a natural son of yours. His name also appears in the Vola ni Kawa Bula. To me there is nothing wrong with this, being a natural son of yours it would explain his ability to firewalk. . . . I understand and respect your feelings, however I would like to understand why Tikiko should be removed from your family tree, while Miriama Ciribale [an extra-nuptial daughter Samu had three years later in 1976] has become part of your family, and accepted by the Sawau community.*

SAMU: *Miriama, yes . . . it was in Bua after a vila [firewalking] at valelevu [chiefly compound], plenty of dancing, music . . . But Tikiko, no, I heard the police is looking for a black man, he is not my son, I don't know who put his name in the Vola ni Kawa Bula.*

Samu's sister Salanieta told me that Samu was trying to remove a youthful sin from his memory, and while I do agree with her, the issue of fellowship with the *vilavilairevo* also must be considered. The *isolisoli* (gift) of firewalking is still seen today as a gift to the *vanua*, in full respect of the normative codes imposed by the oral tradition of the ceremony. Tikiko, instead, is seen as somebody whose behavior is not *vakavanua*, but who is using a gift of the *vanua* solely for his own personal benefit. Although British rule and Christian influence have offered an opportunity for the growth of individuality in the Fijian character, individualism is loathed, and it is discouraged for the sake of group solidarity and harmony (Ravuvu 1987).

In Marcel Mauss' (1990) original conceptualization, the practice of gift giving is a fundamental social system; the case of firewalking, a gift mythically received by the Naivilaqata's apical ancestor, introduces another dimension of the gift practice. The Naivilaqata custodians preserve their ancestral ability, a sine qua non to maintain their solidarity and ethnic identity within the matrix of identities constituting Fijian society, where different groups possess different traditional knowledge and cultural properties. The Naivilaqata clan's gift translates into affirming their ethnic identity with their *vanua* and observing mutual respect.

In Fiji, individual activity is traditionally devoted to developing and reinforcing social relationships and promoting collective interests (Becker

1995, 16). This relational interconnectedness is integral to the concept of *vanua*. Embracing gifts and legacies of past generations, sharing resources, and maintaining stewardship for future generations strengthens the bonds among people (Halapua 2003, 200). Although gifts and commodities are often treated as ideal-type opposites, and a tradition of Melanesian scholarship has focused attention on the inalienability of gifts, the case of Tikiko indexes how the self-consciously traditional firewalking practice of Beqa Island is an inalienable commodity in the sense that it is a gift to the *vanua*. Arno (2005) elegantly emphasizes how sentiment, as a cultural system, is an intellectual rather than a material property, and, like all property, it is defined by social relationships and obligations.

Barbara Kirshenblatt-Gimblett argues, after Annette Weiner (1992), that heritage tests the alienability of inalienable possessions (1998, 149). The case of Tikiko tests anthropology's, anthropologists', and lawyers' assumption of the universal primacy of bloodlines and birth in kinship systems, showing that blood and birth can be reconceptualized as metaphors of social relatedness of situational and economic importance associated with the concept of cultural property and collective custodianship of traditional cultural practices. Kinship, in Weiner's words, becomes a decisive marker and maker of value, and not just in terms of genealogical rules. While kinship and economy may generally only appear to be "the same thing" (Strathern 2005, 205), certain productive resources, like the small, income-generating firewalking shows, can be one of the ways that kinship expresses and legitimates social relations and their cosmological antecedents.

After all, both Marshall Sahlins (2011) and Eduardo Viveiros de Castro (2009) notice that kinship, gift, and magic belong to the same animistic regime. In the village of Dakuibeqa and in the other five Sawau villages on the island of Beqa, the valued immaterial possession of the *vilavilairevo* ceremony is imbued with the intrinsic and ineffable identities of the Naivilaqata custodians, which in Weiner's terms are not easy to give away; *vilavilairevo* is safeguarded in accordance with the evolution of property patterns within the closed context of family and descent group, for its loss or failure would diminish the whole community.

"You Can Do It, Japan!"

Social Networks and Natural Disasters

PAMELA L. RUNESTAD

I settled down with a book as I left Tokyo for Nagano. A few pages in, the bus suddenly turned into a traveling bounce-house. Confused and rocking wildly in my seat, I looked out the window to see the traffic signals and signs waving erratically around us. Earthquake. BIG earthquake. I'd already been in several; I knew this was The Big One. Eventually, we returned to the depot and I had no choice but to join the millions of Tokyoites who, expelled from skyscrapers and subways seemingly simultaneously, had taken to the streets in search of a place to stay.

The 9.0 earthquake that struck off the eastern coast of northern Japan on March 11, 2011, was one of the largest in recorded history. It triggered a massive tsunami, and these two disasters caused a third: the meltdown of three nuclear reactors in Fukushima Prefecture. In daily conversation, they are collectively called 3.11. These disasters caused major shifts in social networks both within and outside Japan—but they also made it possible to see exactly how everyday social networks shift and change, something that is often difficult to visualize. In this chapter, I stress that disasters allow us to see how (1) social networks are fluid and ever-changing, (2) local social networks can be global, (3) social networks are central to the success of relief efforts, and (4) anthropologists are not outside social networks in the field, so they can contribute to relief efforts through these networks, too.

Individual connections between people form social networks. People form and reaffirm who they are as family members, friends, workers, community members, and citizens through these connections, which are in constant flux. Moreover, forging, severing, or renewing specific connections can affect relationships with others. So what happens to the self when a connection is unexpectedly lost? What happens when *multiple connections are simultaneously lost?* Considering that loss of a loved one is, in a sense, a partial loss of self, loss of several loved or familiar people can cause a shift in social networks that is devastating to personal and collective identities. On March 11, 2011, whole families, neighborhoods, and communities were suddenly washed away. What it meant to belong to a family, a particular community, a particular region of Japan, or even Japan itself, shifted in the minds of survivors—both in the region and all over the country. Further, outside Japan, concepts of Japan changed as people viewed the destruction. Almost instantly, the social networks left intact were used as channels for relief. Along the same lines, new global and local connections were forged as well.

Understanding how the three events that compose the Great Eastern Japan Disaster[1] are related yet discrete events is key to understanding the trauma that survivors experienced and how they utilized relationships—new and old—to rebuild. Yet media accounts of the disasters have been convoluted; talk is often about the earthquake, images usually portray the tsunami destruction, and lingering fear is often related to radiation. Briefly, they can be described as follows:

Disaster 1: The 9.0 earthquake, 2:46 p.m., March 11, 2011

The initial quake and numerous aftershocks that occurred on or around March 11 caused intense damage to Tōhoku[2] social networks through the loss of lives and homes. Further, destruction of commercial buildings, equipment, and infrastructure simultaneously resulted in the disruption of economic and environmental networks upon which people depend. Although it's difficult to isolate the trauma and strain to personal and professional networks caused solely by the earthquakes, we do know that many people experienced acute mental and physical traumas and posttraumatic stress disorder (PTSD). Additionally "earthquake sickness,"[3] the sense of shaking or swaying as though you are experiencing an earthquake even when you are not, was widely reported.

Disaster 2: The 30+ meter tsunami, 3:55 p.m., March 11, 2011

> *Horrified, I watched footage of the tsunami roaring into Kesennuma, Ishinomaki, and Minamisanriku (all in Miyagi Prefecture), washing*

*away buildings, cars, boats . . . I got the same sense of despair I'd had
watching the live feed from the September 11 terrorist attacks ten years
before. I knew I was watching people die, and that there was nothing
I could do to stop it. The house shook around me as the aftershocks
continued.*

To say that the tsunami compounded the damage caused by the quake
is an understatement. Thousands of people from small communities were
lost—for example, roughly nine thousand people from Kesennuma alone
perished in the tsunami. Moreover, the waters carried away homes and
businesses—the physical places that had brought communities together. In
other words, social networks were drastically changed through sheer loss
of life and loss of infrastructure that promoted social bonding. Survivors,
traumatized at the sight of the waves' destruction, feel these losses again
and again as the tsunami images are replayed on television or as they walk
the streets where familiar buildings once stood. Some also feel a sense of
survivor's guilt for having survived when so many others perished.

To summarize, victims experienced acute physical injuries and illness,
shock, grief, PTSD, and survivor's guilt due to the one-two punch of the
earthquake and tsunami. As of early 2012, there were 15,703 dead, 4,647
missing, 5,314 injured, and 130,927 people displaced (USGS 2012). Over
300,000 buildings, 2,000 roads, 56 bridges, and 26 railways were destroyed
or damaged (USGS 2012). Businesses nationwide ground to a halt; fisheries
and farming in Tōhoku were heavily damaged through loss of boats and destruction of ports, not to mention environmental factors caused by the
tsunami.[4] This is all overlaid by a third trauma, the nuclear meltdowns.

Disaster 3: The nuclear meltdowns, March 11–12, 2011

*Despite power outages in Tokyo, I arrived home the next day. The
aftershocks shook Nagano, too, but I was growing accustomed to them.
It was the nuclear fallout that forced me to consider repatriation. I wept
as I told my Japanese friends I was leaving. Was I abandoning them?
I had choices they did not. My friend Arai answered, "Go home and
show your family your smiling face. Show them you're OK and don't
worry. We Japanese won't lose to something like this! See you soon!"*

The Japanese media were banned from using the word "meltdown,"
but it is clear that is what happened with three reactors in Ōkuma, Fukushima. They spewed massive amounts of radioactive iodine and cesium into

the air and ocean following the quake and tsunami. They continue to leak; new carcinogens seep into the environment and are spread by wind, water, precipitation patterns, and ocean currents. Again, social and environmental networks are damaged, but the traumas from the meltdowns are different.

Whereas many of the tsunami and earthquake aftereffects are captured in videos and photographs, radiation is invisible; it is the donning of suits and the use of Geiger counters that is seen. Moreover, the science behind it—from the way it is measured to the way it travels through the environment to the toxicity levels—is difficult to explain and understand. People within twelve miles of the plant have been forcibly evacuated, often leaving homes that look safe but are not. Food and water, although appearing clean and healthy, may be radioactive. And finally, fear of radiation in the general public has led to fear of Fukushima, its products, and its people. Living in areas with elevated radiation compromises health, and Japan may see a new generation of *hibakusha*.[5] Whereas the earthquake and tsunami severed existing connections as people died, radiation may restrict future connections if discrimination against *hibakusha* occurs, as it has in the past.

It is important to remember that even though the physical loss and damage occurred in Tōhoku, the effects radiated across Japan and beyond. In an interview I conducted several days after the disasters, a man in Osaka, over five hundred miles from the hardest-hit areas, told me, "Ms. Pamela, I really want to talk to you. But I'm not myself today. I'm from Sendai . . ."[6] I talked to Japanese friends abroad and non-Japanese friends who had previously spent time in Japan. "I feel so helpless. I wish there were something I could do," was something I heard again and again. People around the world were affected, and many wanted to do something concrete.

Talk of rebuilding Japan after the disasters began almost immediately. But what exactly, aside from infrastructure, needed rebuilding? It turns out there is Japan, which can be physically rebuilt, and there is "Japan"—the *ideas* of what Japan is that exist in Japanese and non-Japanese minds. The latter requires rebuilding concepts of family, community, and citizenship. Social networks are essential to this. People needed to make new connections, and they needed to be able to talk with those who were suffering from similar experiences. In other words, to rebuild Japan, people all over needed to make new connections and use existing connections in new ways.

In anthropological terms, various relief and reconstruction efforts focus(ed) on addressing *social suffering*, which is a shared sense of loss caused by a traumatic event (Kleinman, Das, and Lock 1997). This involves rebuilding *physical bodies* through recognition and alleviation of the injuries, illness, and trauma experienced by individuals; *social bodies* through strengthening social networks as people take on new roles or old roles in new ways; and *the body politic* through reaffirmation of local, national, and foreign identities.

Almost immediately, Japan's Self Defense Force, international response teams, and charities such as the Red Cross were mobilized as first responders to care for victims' primary, physical needs. Note that rapid domestic response to 3.11 was possible because such networks were fostered following the 1995 Hanshin earthquake; specialized, professional systems that may be unseen on a daily basis sprang into action. The lay public responded quickly as well, often using social media such as Facebook and Twitter to check on loved ones, offer prayers and positive messages, and coordinate donations; organizations such as Peace Boat began mobilizing volunteers to help with cleanup. In these ways, relationships were renewed or forged and social bodies were supported. In an effort to support the body politic, slogans such as *Gambarō Nippon!*[7] *Gambarō Tōhoku!* and *Gambarō Ishinomaki!* were adopted, encouraging people to reimagine what it meant to belong to these areas. Despite major losses to social networks, these efforts were carried out through those that remained, and in some cases new ones were forged specifically in response to the disasters.

Below, I briefly describe how a project I am personally familiar with aimed to address the social suffering caused by the disasters, and how we made use of social networks to do it.

Adding to the trauma caused by earthquakes, the tsunami, radioactive fallout, and discrimination, thousands of people left their hometowns after 3.11. Some moved due to earthquake or tsunami damage, but many moved because of dangerous radiation levels. Every prefecture in Japan has absorbed evacuees, including my home prefecture of Nagano, which houses about two thousand evacuees. Of these, about seventeen hundred are from Fukushima, and most are young mothers and children.

I am not Japanese, but Nagano is my home. I felt an intense need to do something to help evacuees, and so did a number of my friends and family members—Japanese and non-Japanese alike. I conferred with fellow classmate Nao Nomura, and we designed Project Friendship to help ease the traumas these people experienced, by coordinating the distribution of handmade mini quilts (sometimes paired with "play in English" classes for evacuee children) and creating chances for evacuees to develop their social networks though sewing workshops. In these ways, we attempted to rebuild both the physical and social bodies of evacuees.

We found that these efforts required us to use and expand our own social networks, making the project both local and global. We contacted friends in quilters' guilds in the United States and Japan. Quilts from these group members, who had wanted to help but lacked an outlet to do so, began arriving in large boxes. At the same time, my former boss at Nagano City Hall, Mitsuyoshi Nakazawa, rallied municipal workers across the prefecture to create an efficient network capable of distributing the quilts. The Japan-America Society of Hawai'i, which had sponsored part of my research, sponsored shipping; a friend's parents' company, Yoshida Co., LTD provided the materials for the quilt workshop. Before we knew it, evacuees were connecting to longtime residents of Nagano, project organizers in Japan, and people from the United States through the project.

When quilts were distributed, this sense of connection reverberated through recipients and distributors alike:

> The children were waiting for us, bright eyes and smiles. They are so vibrant and beautiful, so mischievous and warm. Laughing together, we read stories, played games, drew monsters. And when they chose their quilts, there was a flurry of little hands as the pile was utterly dismantled—sans fighting. They showed me their spoils with big smiles, and scampered off to their mothers, to whom I explained the quilts were from my mother's group. I couldn't help but worry what would happen to these children. Would they be happy and healthy? Would they be able to smile and play outside as they'd wished for? I looked up to see one of the mothers standing before me, holding her daughter's quilt. In a strong, clear voice and impeccable English she said, "Please say hello and thank you to your mother and her friends. This means a lot to us. Thank you for playing with our children."

Project Friendship has collected quilts from five groups in the United States and Japan; these have been distributed to evacuees across Nagano Prefecture. We have held three social events and work with sponsors from Honolulu, Tokyo, and Nagano. We hope our contributions comfort evacuees as they rebuild their homes, provide them with chances to make connections in their new surroundings, and allow them to positively redefine themselves vis-à-vis the local communities. We also hoped that those who donated to the project would be able to better understand the realities of the disasters through this shared engagement, and that our work could be considered an example of how academics can use their social networks to make a difference in disaster-stricken areas while doing fieldwork.

Notes

1. *Higashi Nihon Daishinsai* in Japanese.
2. Tōhoku is "northeast" and includes six prefectures on Japan's main island Honshū: Akita, Aomori, Fukushima, Iwate, Miyagi, and Yamagata.
3. *Jishin'yō* in Japanese.
4. The effects are global. For example, the International Pacific Research Center in Hawai'i estimates that the field of debris comprises about a million tons of trash and spans one to two thousand nautical miles; most of it will sink or end up in the North Pacific "garbage patch" (Amos 2012).
5. *Hibakusha* are people who have been exposed to radiation; the term often refers to people who experienced health problems including elevated incidences of cancer and infertility after the United States dropped atomic bombs on Hiroshima and Nagasaki in August 1945. Because of these health issues, *hibakusha* were avoided as marriage partners and sometimes experienced discrimination.
6. Sendai is the capital of Miyagi Prefecture and the largest city in Tōhoku.
7. *Gambarō* means "You/We can do it." *Nippon* is Japan.

Head Candy/Gut Connection

How Reenacting a Historic Event Changes the Present in Hawai'i

Lynette Hi'ilani Cruz

In November 2011, I was invited to speak at the East-West Center International Cultural Studies Program on culture and change in Hawai'i, specifically the ongoing shifts in what is popularly called the "Hawaiian sovereignty movement." As the president of a Hawaiian civic club, I thought participation in this forum was an excellent way to share the work that our club does to enhance cultural understandings of Hawaiian sovereignty, and related terms like "self-determination" and "independence." This is a story of "indigenous anthropology" (see Tengan, Ka'ili, and Fonoti 2010) on Hawaiian performance arts on O'ahu that provide cultural education through dramatic reenactments of Hawaiian history. It shows how Hawaiian genealogy and kinship are taught in public culture, and their roles in why we do what we do, and who we are as Hawaiians.

In September 2001, a reenactment titled "Ka Lei Maile Ali'i—The Queen's Women" was first performed at the Kana'ina Building on the grounds of 'Iolani Palace in downtown Honolulu. The drama was written by Didi Lee Kwai and adapted from an article, "Strangling Hands upon a Nation's Throat," that appeared in the *San Francisco Call* newspaper in 1897. The article, written by reporter Miriam Michelson, described a meeting that took place in the Salvation Army Hall in Hilo earlier that year. A reproduction of the original article was posted by an organization called the Hawaiian Patriotic League at one of their meetings in Kāne'ohe, at the Queen Lili'uokalani Children's Center (QLCC) office on Haiku Road. Some of the people who read the article understood its significance, and envisioned it as information worthy of inclusion in an educational program for the masses in dramatic form. The reenactment as a tool for teaching and learning, both simple and effective, gave impetus for the formation of a civic club around it. In March 2003, a group of us formed ourselves into a civic club and applied for membership with the Oʻahu Council of Hawaiian Civic Clubs and, later that year, with the Association of Hawaiian Civic Clubs. We called ourselves, appropriately, Ka Lei Maile Aliʻi Hawaiian Civic Club, becoming, in essence, a lei for our Queen in the present time, as were the members of the Hui Aloha ʻĀina in times past.

I believe how we come to know and think about and understand history, especially in higher education, changes us. Learning allows us to feel good about something, about understanding the world in much the same way we think others do, even if we do not like the information or we do not agree that it is useful. Having shared knowledge helps us "fit in." We identify as part of a body of educated people that make up the community with which we identify. We feel connected. We are discerning. Part of that discernment comes about because of our interactions with teachers like Dr. Haunani-Kay Trask, Dr. Noenoe Silva, Don Lewis, and Dr. Keanu Sai.

The influence of these key figures in Hawaiian history on students, as well as the general public, has changed the way we understand the world. Dr. Trask insisted that students question texts written by both Hawaiian and non-Hawaiian writers of Hawaiian history and culture. She demanded that students research primary sources—where did these authors get their ideas? Were their interpretations correct? Were they citing each other so as to create a comprehensive body of materials that built on unproven sources, in essence giving credibility to lies? Was there particular intent in the kinds of articles or books that they published? Dr. Silva's research into the resistance of Kānaka Maoli during the time of the overthrow came about, essentially, as a rejection of the idea, promoted by supposedly knowledgeable people of Hawaiian ancestry as well as notable non-Hawaiian historians, that there was no discord and no resistance among the people back then. Her zeal to uncover the truth of history opened doors for those of us longing for a different way to understand what happened before we became the fiftieth state. From her research, Hawaiians, today, have come to view themselves as descended from historically important actors striving to hold back the transition from Hawaiian Kingdom to U.S. territory at the turn of the twentieth century. Her investigations revealed that, while change was inevitable, it was by no means desired. Hawaiians began to see that they are as important today as they were a century ago. Don Lewis, former realtor and co-owner of Locations, Inc., and later founder of Perfect Title Co., laid the groundwork for the major challenges that came about during the mid-1990s. He changed how we understood history by challenging how we understood land ownership. Prior to Perfect Title Co., no one questioned the genealogy of land titles in Hawai'i. No one really understood enough legal history to question title transfers. But as soon as researchers began to rethink history as more than the history of the victimized, a different story emerged. Spearheaded by David Keanu Sai, the research in this area challenged the very foundation of the view of Hawaiians as oppressed, and offered instead the view of Hawaiians as in control of much of their destiny. Dr. Sai's research into the legal and political history of Hawai'i within the context of international relations shifted for so many people the idea of indigeneity as part of their identity, moving many of us away from a view of ourselves as "natives" indigenous to the nation of the United States toward recognition of ourselves as nationals, citizens of a country somehow lost. Knowing ourselves in a historic context lets us know that our claim of nationalism today is well founded. In their capacity as teachers, each of these individuals helped Hawaiians know, today, who we are and who we are not. From Trask to Sai, a continuity was established for historians of contemporary history that pointed in a particular direction.

Sometimes there is a hunger to know the truth when what has been presented as truth in historic texts is proven to be incorrect. Lies about history, especially when those lies build on each other, imply intent—there is a safety for the dishonest author/academic who condones lies that have provided benefit to those in power. Their position among their peers is affirmed. But there is no stopping those who are hungry for truth. This is what surfaced for the general population of activist Hawaiians when Dr. Silva brought home to Hawai'i the truth of resistance at the time of the overthrow and so-called annexation of Hawai'i to the United States. A hunger for knowledge about those who signed the petitions protesting annexation of Hawai'i to the United States thrust upon many of us an awakening of those who did not necessarily claim genealogical ties to the ali'i (chiefs). Suddenly, genealogical connection to ordinary maka'āinana (common people) became as important as connection to the chiefs, perhaps even more important. The petitions were signed by nearly everyone, including those descended from chiefly lines. Every person who signed was as important as every other person, and together they made a difference. The petition became the great leveler, an example of participatory democracy in action. As the people rallied around Queen Lili'uokalani in 1893–1897, they provided us with a model for behavior and resistance action that makes sense for us today. And herein is expressed the story of the Ka Lei Maile Ali'i Hawaiian Civic Club.

Hunger for knowledge is not necessarily abated by feeding the intellect. Perhaps the real hunger is for intimate connection to the past so as to understand how we are connected in the present—a desire for both head and gut connections. Our civic club has two major activities that provide opportunities for connecting at both levels: a dramatic reenactment titled "Ka Lei Maile Aliʻi—The Queen's Women" and an art display, which might be described as a monumental art project we call the "Kuʻe Name Signs Project." The first is a drama depicting a meeting held in 1897 at the Salvation Army Hall in Hilo, Hawaiʻi, hosted by the Hui Aloha ʻĀina o Nā Wāhine, the Women's Branch of the Hawaiian Patriotic League. The meeting featured guest speakers Mrs. Emma Nawahi and Mrs. Kuaihelani Campbell, who attended on behalf of the Queen specifically to ask that the people present sign the petition protesting annexation of Hawaiʻi to the United States. Such meetings were being held on almost all the islands, spearheaded by the women and men who were members of the League. Present at that meeting was Ms. Miriam Michelson, a reporter for the *San Francisco Call* newspaper. Ms. Michelson took notes and, on her way home to San Francisco on the steamship *Australia*, she wrote an article that was subsequently published on the front page of the *Call*, titled "Strangling Hands upon a Nation's Throat." In 2000, just over a hundred years later, that news article surfaced at a meeting of the organization calling itself the Hawaiian Patriotic League in Kāneʻohe. Some of the women obtained copies and considered adapting the article as a short drama.

In 2001, Didi Lee Kwai, artist and musician, crafted the first draft of "Ka Lei Maile Aliʻi—The Queen's Women," which recounted the story of the meeting and allowed history to come to life by allowing the voices of the people to be heard through members of the audience. The script was written as a re-creation of the meeting. People from the audience, armed with scripts, stood up and voiced their concerns, as they did at the original meeting, using the same words. During the role-play, participants, very often, became the people they depicted in the process of reenacting the scene. Anecdotal stories confirmed that "acting the part" and being the part amounted to the same thing. Real people being real people, the great-grandchildren of Hawaiian patriots told the stories of their ancestors as if they were their ancestors, and in the process of participation, collapsed time and became their ancestors. Hawaiian historic narrative, shared through the process of dramatic reenactment, and in particular this point in time and place, allowed participants to focus on ancestral experiences and become them.

The reenactment is part of a process of education that targets a broad audience, providing information about the often incorrectly described history of Hawai'i. In the process of delivering information, people learn about how and why the Hui Aloha 'Āina, members of whom are integral to the drama, was formed. But they also discover that what they had been taught in grade school, and even in college, is incorrect. Sometimes audience members are insulted by what they hear and witness, as if the information were meant to cause injury. Before the reenactment begins, a history is provided as context, generally conveyed by Dr. Keanu Sai, but in the past also shared by Dr. Kūhiō Vogeler and Leon Siu. All of them are members of Ka Lei Maile Ali'i Hawaiian Civic Club. The reenactment is cued by words provided by the director: "She wrote the article on September 22, 1897, on the deck of the passenger ship *Australia,* on her way home to San Francisco." Thereafter, the story unfolds toward a climax of testimonials delivered by audience members. Selecting participants for this part of the drama is generally an uncertain process, depending on who is willing, who can relate best to Hawaiian experience, or who has genealogical ties to Hawai'i. Preferred are those who are Hawaiian by ethnicity, who thus can connect genealogically to that period in time. The director walks through the audience and hands out scripts to those who appear interested, requesting that each person share his or her short one- or two-sentence part with feeling. Regardless of who accepts the speaking parts, once they stand up and enact history, they are affected. Everyone in the audience, including those who may be passive in the drama, feels as if they are in an earlier time. They feel the urgency of the situation back in 1897 and respond as if they are there, even as they realize that the scene playing out before them is a role-play. For Hawaiians, anger surfaces. For non-Hawaiians, often there is shame. The story loses its historic flavor and manifests in the present the indignities and hurt felt by Hawaiians a hundred years ago. More than just history, the reenactment illustrates a real and present injury situated in the present time. The only thing different is that the players have changed. The sentiments expressed are the same today: "I am telling you the truth, the great majority of the people on Molokai completely oppose annexation. They are fearful that if annexed to America their lands will be lost. The foreigners will gather the benefits, and Hawaiians will be put in a worse position than they are today."

Not much has changed, except for the players. In essence, this is why the reenactment, and drama in general, works so well in providing people with more than information. Drama makes space for emotion, for the Hawaiian sense of na'au (feeling settled in the gut, akin to emotional intelligence that allows us to feel calm and satisfied) to surface in acceptable ways. As one audience participant once commented, "When I play this part I feel like I am my ancestor and I can say, with feeling and out loud, that 'I am very strongly opposed to annexation. How dare the Americans rob a people's independence? I want the American government to do the correct thing. America helped to overthrow Liliʻuokalani. She must be restored. We will never consent to annexation.'" By the end of the drama, during the question/comment period, inevitably four or five people, often more, will comment that they felt as if they were really at the meeting and that their ancestors were with them in the room. The emotional response is generally overwhelming, and their tears flow as they reconnect with ancestors two or three generations removed whom none of them have ever met.

Ka Lei Maile Aliʻi Hawaiian Civic Club's second major activity, and one we have continued to actively practice and prepare for since 2009, is an activity called the "Kuʻe Name Signs Project." We decided to honor individually the signatories of the Kuʻe Petition of 1897, which is highlighted in the reenactment, by creating signs with their names on white placards, 6" × 24" with black lettering and feet made of metal wire, to be placed in the ground, somewhat resembling headstones in a cemetery. One side of each placard has the person's name, age, island, and district where they signed on, as well as the page number in the Kuʻe petition book where their names can be found. The other side carries the words "No Treaty of Annexation." On February 16, 2009, on American Presidents' Day, the signs were laid out for the first time and arranged around the statue of William McKinley on a school grounds in downtown Honolulu. Six hundred signs were prepared for this first showing. A design was created for the layout, and thirty volunteers helped place them in the ground. Since 2009, the display has traveled to the grounds of ʻIolani Palace and Thomas Square, and the number of signs has increased to nearly twenty-two hundred. This year, in 2012, they will be making the journey to Washington, DC, to be displayed on the National Mall in conjunction with the Association of Hawaiian Civic Clubs Convention in mid-October. From our point of view, our kūpuna will be making their second appearance after a century, but the message they will be delivering by their presence is the same: no treaty of annexation, which translates at this time to no federal recognition.

Since 2009, the Kuʻe signs have been displayed eight times and documented via photos and videotaping. Those familiar with cemeteries and the fascination many people have for looking at names on headstones can relate to what they see at the sign displays. Local visitors seem to be reading every name, possibly looking for familiar ones. Those of Hawaiian ancestry seem to recognize almost every name. There are typical scenes: Grandmother says to grandchild: "This is your tūtū [grandparent]. You were named after her." Then the family gathers around the sign, takes photos, sits down, and "visits" with their kupuna (elder, ancestor). One young man said, "I just found my tūtū and took a picture with my cell phone and sent it to my mother on Big Island. She called me back and she was crying." Another young man from Maui found his tūtū's name and asked if he might oli (chant, asking permission of the ancestors to acknowledge ancestral connection in a public way) to her. Then he chanted a welcome to his tūtū while the rest of us watched in awe. Another woman, currently running for election as a congressional delegate, brought a lei to drape on her great-grandfather's name sign. She introduced her brother and pointed out her mother, who waited underneath a shady tree. Then she presented the lei to her kupuna. Photos document these instances of people finding connection to ancestors whom they have never met and who are only now being seen as significant players in the political history of Hawai'i. If these kūpuna had not signed the petition protesting annexation of Hawai'i to the United States, there would have been a treaty annexing Hawai'i to the United States. But because they *did* sign, no treaty exists today. This is the message that is embedded in every sign. It is the same message in every signature on the petition, and in the words spoken by every person who attended any of a multitude of meetings where they were asked to defend their country and their queen.

There are certain markers that tell us when change occurs in our lives. Both activities described above are reenactments. The first change occurs when the drama becomes the real thing, when the words spoken by actors become the words of our ancestors, and the evidence or marker of this change is that people cry and they feel the anguish felt by their ancestors. In a sense, time stands still and, for a short time, collapses. We are them and they are us. And in our utterances of the words shared, our ancient and present selves merge. Because we now know our history and what our ancestors experienced a century ago, whenever we hear these voices and see these names laid out in this particular way, we are reminded that we are in the presence of our ancestors. As one present-day kupuna noted, "There is sweetness in being in their presence. But that means we have a kuleana (responsibility) to honor and protect them and make sure their voices are heard." In this present time, we take that to mean that where once there was passive acknowledgment of our history, there is now active desire to mālama (to care for as a family member) those who bravely stood up and spoke up in the face of threats and fear for their own future by actively participating in giving new life to our ancestors, those whose one shot at saving the future was to invest in a document that would carry their message to us today. It is our inheritance and their legacy. Owning it is what has changed and is changing us.

PART 6

Economic Encounters

Class, Development, Inequality

(*overleaf photo*) A bowl of *tsukemen* at rāmen shop Benkei in Asakusa, a famous tourist destination in Tokyo. *Tsukemen* literally means "dipping noodles" and is enjoyed by serving cold noodles that are dipped in a tasty broth before being eaten. The popularity of *tsukemen* has grown since the beginning of the century and they now have their own dedicated food festivals across Japan. Photo by Cyril Calugay.

Introduction

MARY MOSTAFANEZHAD

ON SEPTEMBER 17, 2011, thousands of protesters gathered at Zuccoti Park in New York City's Financial District to demonstrate their frustration around the continued growth of economic inequality at the national and global levels. This demonstration came to be known as the "Occupy Wall Street Movement." Millions of people around the world protested in city halls, parks, university campuses, and other public spaces. The slogan that unified this truly transnational movement was "We are the 99%." This slogan points to the growing disparity between the rich and the poor. Today, more than 50 percent of the world's population lives on less than US$2.50 per day, 22,000 children die every day because of poverty, nearly one billion people cannot read or sign their names, and 25 percent of the world's population lives without electricity (Shah 2010). At the same time, the wealthiest 10 percent consumes 60 percent of the world's material goods, the gross domestic product of the forty-one most indebted poor countries is less than the combined wealth of the seven richest individuals, 25 percent of the world's finances are controlled by just 0.13 percent of the world's population, and if corporations were countries, they would represent more than half of the richest countries in the world (Shah 2010). How this massive economic and social inequality is maintained through complex webs of power is the subject of the chapters in this section. While the communities described in the chapters that follow confront different threats, they share a mutual desire to defend their economic and political futures in the face of corporations, organizations, and development agendas.

The chapters in this section illustrate some of the complex ways economic structures and processes articulate in the lives of Samoans, Japanese, and Hawaiians. Fa'anofo Lisaclaire Uperesa conducts "homework" in American Sāmoa that illustrates how the intensification of transnational flows of goods, people, and ideas in the late twentieth and early twenty-first centuries have transformed local values about cars, mobility, and social status. Satomi Fukutomi studies the meanings of rāmen consumption in Japan. Through an examination of its popular consumption, Fukutomi illustrates how identities based on class are created, maintained, and challenged in rāmen noodle shops throughout the city.

Mary Tuti Baker, a Kānaka 'Ōiwi (Indigenous Hawaiian) woman raised on O'ahu, introduces us to struggles between subsistence and cash economies on Moloka'i, Hawai'i. Her ethnography highlights Kānaka 'Ōiwi spiritual values of aloha (love as reciprocity), kuleana (responsibility to community), and mālama 'āina (stewardship of the land) threatened by the globalization of Moloka'i by corporate development projects.

Tales of the Talā (Dollar)

Notes on Cars, Consumption, and Class in American Sāmoa[1]

FA'ANOFO LISACLAIRE UPERESA

"HOW'S YOUR DAD DOING? . . . I saw him the other day waiting for the bus and I felt so bad for him!" It was dropped in the middle of a conversation with one of my high school friends in Sāmoa.[2] I had been home a couple of weeks on a research trip and was catching up, one by one, with old friends. Her voice was full of concern as I reassured her he was doing fine, and liked getting his exercise out walking. We breezed on to other topics, and set up a lunch date for later in the week, but the small comment stuck. It came back to me a few days later as I was writing my notes at night:

> Yesterday I was thinking about a few things, one of them being the car issue. So I was talking to Malia [a pseudonym] on the phone the other day and she was saying how she saw Dad catching the bus recently and she felt so bad for him . . . I guess part of it is his age and the condition of his knee, so for him having to get around with difficulty. But it got me thinking—the mobility that the car has introduced makes a big difference between having one and not having one.

My father is in his sixties. As a former athlete and health educator he tries to stay active; he also has a higher threshold for the pain that his old knee injuries and recent arthritis inflict with regularity. This was before his knee replacement, and getting around took a bit of effort and probably a bit of pain as well. We live mountainside in a village in the town area, where houses are built largely on communal land.[3] Moving down from the mountain toward the malae (village green) and the area of flat land that borders the main road and the ocean, you enter one of the main government and business hubs. The village lies adjacent to one of the largest deepwater harbors in the area, known locally as Pago Bay. The area was the site of the early twentieth century U.S. Naval government. When the territorial administration was transferred to a civilian government under the Department of the Interior, it remained the seat of government (although today the main official government building stands in nearby Utulei and new developments in the Tafuna plain have created a rival hub). On the ocean side of the main road are small shops, McDonald's, the renovated marketplace, and a multilevel waterfront plaza. Centrally located stand the Fono (legislative assembly buildings) and several other government offices. Buses are plentiful, but you have to walk down and up the road that bends at a steep incline to our house. Across the road from the market is a taxi stand; the drivers knew our house well.

The comment was one of concern that someone at his age, with his ailments, would have to regularly make the hike up and down the mountain road just to get around. But there was more to it—it stayed in the back of my mind until I was able to put it into context with other recent observations about cars, mobility, and status.

Looking Back: Car Culture Emerging

I remember the first car our immediate family had when we lived in Sāmoa. It was not anything fancy—a small used sedan (a Toyota, my mother says). What I remember about having a car was it meant that we could visit my grandparents in town for to'ona'i (Sunday family meal, usually following church service), go to Burns Philp for groceries, or the weekend rugby matches in Pago. Later when we moved closer to town, we still had the car and still used it a lot, but it did not give the same kind of freedom as when we lived farther out from the town center, down the long offshoot from the main road that passed through the village of Tafuna. That was back before the current movie theaters in Nu'u'uli (Haleck's Theaters were farther out), or the new McDonald's, Pizza Hut/KFC, and Cost-U-Less near the development known as "Ottoville," before there was a Bank of Hawai'i branch or the new Bowling Alley; before all the retail development that has grown up in the Tafuna plain.

By the time we moved into town the car was sold (or given away, I am not sure which). These are the stronger memories of transportation and movement: catching the āiga bus everywhere,[4] listening to Samoan songs or the ubiquitous UB40 or Bob Marley tunes. In those days cars were still something of a rarity, more often accessible as government vehicles, and a new car for a household caused lots of excitement. By high school we saw them more and more often; they became something of a staple for many extended households all sharing the same car. If someone had access to a car, and preferably a truck, we would pile into the truck bed and go for a long ride out to one side of the island or the other. On flight night the excitement was to go and see who was at the airport hanging out or waiting for friends and family to leave or arrive. Still, for us and for many of my classmates and their families, the trip to school was on foot or by bus; so were grocery shopping and trips to the hospital.

I returned for a summer while I was in college, and one of my cousins had made a down payment on a Toyota 4Runner, so that my grandmother—who was aging and ailing—could access hospital services more easily. When I came back some years later for my brother's high school graduation in the early 2000s, we still had the car but it was getting old and rusty. I remember seeing lots more new cars on the road, and it was the first time I remembered being in bad traffic—the kind that slowed to a crawl along the two-lane road, where the people walking on the sidewalk moved faster than you did. I overheard people talking about who just got a new car, how much their car payments were, and wondering how they could possibly afford it. This form of evaluation, or gossip, likely betrayed a bit of envy but illustrates the kinds of changes in consumption practices that were taking place. Cars were becoming not just the occasional luxury, but a perceived necessity—one that conferred status on the owners and their household. I think that was the first time I saw the flashy yellow Hummer moving along the road. There were also 4Runners, Escalades, and Explorers. Some government workers requested that new vehicles be SUVs, ostensibly so that they could visit their clients on the steep mountain roads. Was this a new thing? Not necessarily—there is a long history of foreign goods being incorporated into Samoan ideas of value and status (Linnekin 1991). Cars are not exactly new to the islands. However, a change was occurring that was not clear to me until I returned home for fieldwork, or in my case, "homework" (Teaiwa 2004; Uperesa 2010).

Transforming Everyday Life in Sāmoa

As I thought about my friend's remark over the next couple of weeks, I could see that there were important shifts during the snapshots in time, which came into bold relief because they were punctuated by periods of absence, or being "off-island" as people say. Many things had changed in Tutuila between my childhood years in the 1980s, high school and college days in the 1990s, and graduate school in the mid-2000s. While there is a longer history of transnational flows of goods, people, and ideas throughout Sāmoa, the particular movements associated with globalization of the late twentieth century mark an important shift in the frequency and volume of these flows, as they do for other places and peoples across the globe. With the 1950s and 1960s military and church-related migration that established Samoan communities in the United States, trips off-island for work, family visits, fa'alavelave or kinship exchanges,[5] and college attendance were highly valued. In ensuing decades they became more common, fueled also by expanded scholarship opportunities through the local government, schooling opportunities at the local community college that better positioned students to continue their pursuit of bachelor's or master's degrees, government-funded professional development trips, football and other sport-related scholarships, continued military enlistments, and expanded family networks.

Rather than subsistence agricultural production (centuries old) or even small-scale production for export (such as the copra exports of the late 1800s and early 1900s), the mid-twentieth century was a period of targeted infrastructure, bureaucratic, and private enterprise development aimed at building a capitalist economy in Tutuila. Imports and consumption, as well as remittances from abroad, became much more widespread in the latter part of the century, and now inform the more contemporary local ideas around consumption, status, dignity, and shame. Increased consumption, dependency on the U.S. funding streams, and the shift in people's thinking about money and proper social behavior was a widespread topic of conversation when I was doing my research. It came up during interviews and casual conversations in places like the new cafés, which are themselves a testament to the rise in either disposable income or spending choices, or both.

As I wrote in my field note, the mobility that the car has introduced makes a big difference between having one and not having one, enabling access to different consumer items for wider swaths of local people. Without a car you walk to the bus and shorter distances; you often have to rely on stores closer to home and do smaller batches of shopping, since taking your purchases on the bus is less than convenient, or you rely on relatives and friends for rides. After the first couple of weeks of our basic diet, I took a friend up on her offer to take me out to the other side of the island to do some shopping. Since I had my toddler in tow on the trip and she had some food allergy issues, I wanted to keep more or less to her regular diet, and add to it rather than disrupt it completely if I could help it (turns out she loved faʻi, or boiled green bananas!). Since the local market was temporarily moved to the next village while they renovated, fresh produce was not as readily available, and, with the exception of the weekend meals, we ended up eating a lot of canned or prepared food during the week (there is a reason American Sāmoa is overrepresented in rates of diabetes, gout, and other "lifestyle" diseases, and it is not merely an issue of food choice). After one of our afternoon walks, my friend took me out to Cost-U-Less (a warehouse store, like Costco or Sam's Club) and Aveina Bros. to do my shopping. On the way back, I paid for dinner at the new Carl's Jr. in the Laufou Shopping Center as a small thanks for taking me shopping. We would repeat this trip several times over the course of the summer, and thereby be able to access foods and consumer items that would have been inaccessible without my friend's generosity.

In addition to accessing consumer goods more easily, car culture has enabled the transformation of everyday patterns of movement for many on the island. Over the course of the trip, I noticed that things like business and organizational dinners, special events, and evening shopping all required access to a car, since the āiga buses stopped running at dusk. Being able to wear an appropriately fancy puletasi (local dress for women) to an awards banquet, for example, required traveling by car rather than by bus. It was a tremendous option for personal mobility that I had not recognized before: older parents could meet friends to socialize at McDonald's instead of being confined at home; young adults went out to the bars or clubs instead of staying at home on a Friday or Saturday night; people had the option of shopping for better/pricey/imported foods instead of basic canned items; one could be "seen" out on the road rather than remain at home or in the village. The cost of owning and operating the cars (and more often trucks or SUVs) would seem to prohibit widespread ownership, but this was not the case.

Class, Status, Wealth

While the islands have long been part of globalizing processes, these shifts in daily patterns of movement and consumption, and associated ideas of properly dignified modes of travel, appear to be relatively recent.[6] Because of their link to the cash economy, they also suggest changes in local social organization, where one's social status is not always primarily determined by one's relation to ranking titles (although clearly this is still very important). While theories of class and consumption have traditionally centered on industrialized or postindustrial societies (Marx and Engels 1978; Weber

1946; Bourdieu 1984), the existence or emergence of classes in societies traditionally organized by rank and status has been less clear. Still, the rise of postcolonial elites and their rearticulations of cultural meanings and practices have been well documented (see Lawson 1997). One day in passing as I remarked on seeing particular people featured in the paper, or out for dinner, a relative noted that there was indeed a "high society." As we talked and identified those who seemed to belong, it was clear that many of those circles overlapped: local business leaders, well-placed government employees, and certain military families (with access to VA housing loans, the Army Exchange or PX, or pensions). This loose grouping was not limited to high-ranking chiefs as may have been the case in decades past, but included the high ranking *and* "well-to-do."

Even with the changes inspired by intensified global movements—especially the spread of capitalism and the cash economy—Samoan cultural traditions that redistribute wealth through exchange and gifting have long been seen to prevent widespread inequality and the emergence of classes of "haves" and "have-nots." Those who were able to become wealthy would eventually bow to cultural obligations of gifting and reciprocity and gift away some of that wealth. This is why colonial administrators and development and modernization proponents of the early 1900s saw traditional Samoan cultural practices (like fa'alavelave) as a barrier to "progress," because with all of one's obligations it was impossible to save enough money to invest in long-term, profitable capitalist enterprise.

In the relentless development and modernization discourses of the twentieth century, modernity became associated with wealth and consumption, while tradition contained undertones of poverty. It is within this context that American Sāmoa's territorial relationship with the United States is seen by some as a Faustian bargain: attaining wealth and a measure of modernity by sacrificing aspects of Samoan culture. On the other hand, independent Sāmoa is often understood to be maintaining traditional culture at the price of material success. This is a viewpoint shared by many in the islands and the global diaspora (as any sampling of conversations, blog posts, letters to the editor, and so on, would attest). This deceptively simple view ignores the long histories of social transformation in independent Sāmoa, which are themselves intimately bound to globalization and movement abroad. It also relies upon problematic assumptions about authenticity, and a narrow and somewhat static view of culture. Drawing on respected Samoan historian Malama Meleisea's (1987) contention that the fa'asāmoa, or Samoan cultural practice, is strong in its tenets but flexible in details, and esteemed anthropologist Marshall Sahlins' (1988, 1992) work on cosmologies of capitalism, what we see across the Samoan islands is a complicated story of selectively interweaving indigenous Samoan institutions and practices with those from outside the islands, with a variety of consequences entailed. Far from a simple story of "McDonaldization," this incorporation is producing new sociocultural formations, where these practices and commodities are resignified in the local context. In some cases this can be read as "homogenization," but it is perhaps more accurately described as both a process of transformation and a push for cultural differentiation. While Sāmoa is distinct, it is also part of a global economy, society, polity, and so on.

Changes linked to what is often described as globalization mean that things like remittances, veteran loans, military enlistment, and formal education or employment abroad are not supplementary cash or in-kind contributions to subsistence family or village-based agricultural production, but have become for many families the basis of subsistence and are therefore seen as necessary in Sāmoa. In the effort to support one's family and to meet familial obligations, many move off-island and back (or circulate between) as the circumstances demand. When I thought of many families in our village, I saw that most of the young adults were in the military, away at college, playing sports abroad, or were otherwise employed in the continental United States or Hawai'i. The one or two siblings in a family who were at home were working and helping parents who themselves worked.

These material shifts are enmeshed with symbolic ones, where measures of status and assessments of appropriate action (particularly for those seen as part of "high society" or who are otherwise accomplished) have also shifted. Having to resort to the bus to go to work or school, or transporting packages, is not just inconvenient, it has become less dignified. For some, taking something unpleasantly fragrant—fish, for example—on the bus for a long ride home may now be a source of intense embarrassment (māsiasi) in a way that was not part of everyday life in the recent past, because luxuries like a private car were still beyond the reach of most. Since today many if not most households own or have access to a car, to be without one is to show one's lack of wealth, resources, and/or dignity, and therefore to expose oneself or one's family to gossip (particularly if household members have jobs that one associates with higher status). This is the wider cultural context within which I came to understand my friend's comment, and although I would not attribute this meaning to her, it is how I eventually came to understand it.

As I write this story I am back on-island for another family visit and research trip. In our discussion about this essay my father reiterated the conscious decision to keep our family physically active as long as possible by walking as much as possible (especially in light of poor family health history). Still, in advancing age, he bought a car recently, and as one would expect, it has made everyday life activities that much easier. He is also able to travel in a way that many see as appropriately dignified for a college graduate and retired professional.

Notes

Fa'afetai tele lava to my father, Tu'ufuli K. Uperesa for his thoughtful comments on an earlier draft, and for giving me permission to include him in it. Thanks also to the other friends and relatives who generously shared their time, cars, and hospitality with us.

1. A note on diacritics: There is an ongoing debate about the use of diacritics in written Samoan, but I have chosen to use them here to promote best language use among this collection's early undergraduate audience.

2. For ethnographic specificity, this chapter is focused on the island of Tutuila. For the larger American Sāmoa island group, the U.S. Census 2010 enumerated 55,109 residents. In terms of "ethnic origin and race," 95.8 percent reported one race only (86.5 percent of those identified as Samoan, 9.1 percent as other Pacific Islander, 2.8 percent Asian, and 1.4 percent White), while 4.2 percent identified as mixed race (most as Samoan and another group). Over 36 percent of the island residents at the time were foreign-born (outside American Sāmoa, the United States, and its other territories), which speaks to its status as a migration node within Pacific networks. Household sizes (just over six people) are larger than in the United States overall, and the average income per household was $26,093. In terms of language use, over 90 percent reported speaking Samoan at home, and although Samoan and English are used in school and government settings, Samoan remains the language most people use in daily interaction.

3. Large tracts of land are held in common by an extended kin group; by custom, authority and administration of the land is invested in the person chosen to hold the family's chiefly title as matai. The majority of land in Tutuila and Manu'a (except that under authority of the American Sāmoa government) officially remains communally held.

4. Since there is no public transportation system on the island, family- or individually owned buses provide this service. The buses are converted from large trucks and renovated to provide larger seating capacity, and are usually styled with colorful detailing and sound systems.

5. Fa'alavelave are gifting obligations usually associated with supporting one's āiga, or immediate and extended family, in life-cycle events such as weddings, funerals, and chiefly title investitures.

6. Some of the most well-known anthropological texts on Sāmoa focus on the areas of traditional Samoan culture and society (Mead 2001; Shore 1982). However, others have addressed the importance of historical context and taken a longer view of sociocultural transformation (Salesa 2003; Tcherkézoff 2000).

Working-Class Hospitality and Etiquette in a Bowl of Rāmen Noodles in Tokyo, Japan

Satomi Fukutomi

Rāmen is a popular noodle soup in Japan. Since its introduction to the Japanese palate over a century ago, it has been associated with class-specific connotations.[1] Initially rāmen was considered a "low" class food. Originating from China, ramen had a low status partly because of the Japanese defeat of China in the Sino-Japanese War (1894–1895). Japan's military power was superior to China's, and there was a contemporary anti-Chinese movement in Japan. Outside Chinatowns, working-class Japanese people began to sell rāmen at street stalls to laborers and poor students. Around the 1990s, decades after rāmen became fast food for the masses, middle-class consumers began to treat rāmen as an object of connoisseurship, although rāmen maintained its working-class characteristics: low price and quick preparation. Former white-collar businessmen and university graduates began to open upscale *rāmen-ya* (rāmen noodle shops), while many old *rāmen-ya* (opened prior to the 1990s) continued to serve rāmen in blue-collar environments. I examine the ways in which employees and customers at the old *rāmen-ya* valorize a bowl of rāmen without losing the working-class characteristics of the food.

I conducted ethnographic fieldwork as a novice employee in one of the old *rāmen-ya* in Tokyo, Rāmen Hideyoshi. From the owner's viewpoint, the ideal employee would be someone who was willing to practice the craft of cooking rāmen. Yet, finding employees with such a motivation was a luxury for Rāmen Hideyoshi. Employees constantly complained about working conditions such as long hours, hard tasks, and low pay. One of the employees told me, "Work at *rāmen-ya* is neither easy nor popular compared to McDonald's or Starbucks Coffee [in Japan]. They are cleaner and neater and require only a few hours of work a day, and the tasks are simpler than here [Rāmen Hideyoshi]." As an employee at Rāmen Hideyoshi, my primary task was to wash dishes in the open kitchen.

During my "internship" with Rāmen Hideyoshi I examined the ways in which the owner and the employees acquire cultural competence and valorize rāmen. Pierre Bourdieu describes how a person's cultural competence reflects his or her education (Bourdieu 1984, 13). Middle-class children acquire cultural competence from their parents, and formal education paves the way to future success. For children of lower classes, it is work experience rather than higher education that enables individuals to acquire cultural capital. For the owner and employees at Hideyoshi who are high school graduates or high school dropouts, work experiences are important if they want to be successful in their careers.

The ambience of Rāmen Hideyoshi is in many ways representative of a typical blue-collar eatery. The shop is set up for efficiency and speedy service. Both the interior and exterior walls are used as temporary storage areas for boxes of vegetables and piles of wet hand towels. An exposed kitchen, rather than an open kitchen, is situated in the middle of a U-shaped counter with twenty customer stools. It is merely a pragmatic use of space. All the customers and employees, men and women alike, share a single restroom adjacent to the kitchen at the end of the customer counter. Furthermore, unlike upscale restaurants, Rāmen Hideyoshi does not have a nonsmoking section.

In the blue-collar environment, the owner of Rāmen Hideyoshi emphasizes a *kyakushōbai* business philosophy to please customers. *Kyakushōbai* means customer-oriented service; it is captured in the English adage, "The Customer Is King." The owner bluntly explained to me, "We cannot run a business without customers. We need to offer them good service." He uses *kyakushōbai* to discipline his employees and empower the customers, as well as to remind them of their roles. The integration of this philosophy distinguishes Rāmen Hideyoshi from other blue-collar and fast-food eateries.

The *kyakushōbai* philosophy emphasizes the *tatemae-honne* (public face vs. private/true feelings) dichotomy. This distinction between public and private self-presentation defines social relationships in Japan (Doi 1986; Lebra 1976; Nakane 1970).[2] However, in Rāmen Hideyoshi, the exposed kitchen and counter where customers watch the chefs and other employees work can make it difficult for the employees to maintain a distinction between public and private acts. In this environment, the employees are made to "perform" their roles. The employees nimbly switch between front and backstage roles through voice modulation and varying speech patterns. Sometimes the employees treat the exposed kitchen as a backstage where they grab a snack, but they do so while squatting down to conceal these private activities from customers. Standing up with a mouth full of food would cross the boundary between the frontstage and backstage.[3]

Using a code language is a common technique for maintaining the boundaries. An occupation-specific jargon provides shorthand for relaying work-related messages while masking backstage practices. Much like other eateries and department stores, in Rāmen Hideyoshi, certain numbers are used as a frontstage code to signify places or actions. For instance, an employee would say the number three, meaning he needed to step out of the kitchen to use the restroom, or number two to take a meal break. Using a number code was seen as a rule of etiquette. The assistant manager explained, "Customers do not want to hear the word *toire* (toilet/restroom) while they are eating." However, one wonders about the efficacy of such a code, given that the restroom is in plain view of the customers. Rather than simply disassociating excretory functions from food, such codes enable employees to separate their private actions from their public performances.[4]

The employees of Rāmen Hideyoshi must perform within the frontstage/backstage boundaries and *kyakushōbai* philosophy in every moment. If these performances step outside the boundaries, they will be noticed by others. For example, the owner mentioned an unacceptable blunder committed by one of his employees. This employee made the mistake of calling a customer *kyaku* (customer) instead of by a formal honorific such as *o-kyaku-san* or *o-kyaku-sama*. The customer was furious and yelled at the employee, "I am not *kyaku*; I am *o-kyaku-san*. What kind of shop is this?!" Although the customer's reaction might be considered just as immature and low-class as the employee's gaffe, the perceived gravity of this incident illustrates the *kyakushōbai* treatment customers expect.

This incident also illustrates the cultural competence that blue-collar workers must acquire through work experience. The owner's daughter repeatedly asked me during my job interview: "We have snobby customers, like company presidents, sometimes. Can you [a PhD student] be humble when interacting with them?" Her mention of snobby customers in a working-class eatery did not strike me as ironic. Rāmen Hideyoshi is located near a well-known historical monument in Tokyo, and rāmen has burgeoned as a popular food, so it is not unusual even for blue-collar *rāmen-ya* to have customers from different classes.[5] I simply took her question as a warning that acting humble was part of *kyakushōbai* philosophy.

Using the extended metaphor of a restaurant as dramatic theater, Karla Erickson (2007, 21) writes that "every player has their role." Within any social space, actors tailor their roles to suit the events and circumstances therein. Customers are just as important in creating an eatery's culture as restaurant owners and their employees, since word of mouth is powerful and often the only advertisement for *rāmen-ya*. Additionally, the type of customers who frequent the eatery facilitates the formation of the shop's image. Regular customers become critical judges, encouraging cooks to expand their business or decorate the shop in a certain style.

Rāmen Hideyoshi's regular customers are deliverymen, students, senior citizens, local residents, office workers, and taxi drivers. They often come at the same time and on the same days of the week. For example, one table with six stools at the end of the counter and by the large window is informally "reserved" for a group of deliverymen, because they stay longer than other customers and smoke after meals.

Longtime customers often know more about the rāmen than the newer employees. These aficionados mechanically break their wooden chopsticks apart just before their bowls are served, knowing precisely how long it takes for their food to arrive. Some customers check to see which cook is on duty before ordering, as they believe that each cook produces a slightly different taste. One regular customer whom we employees dubbed "Baseball Man" regularly eats the store manager's miso-flavored rāmen on Wednesdays. However, if the store manager happens to be out of the kitchen, he changes his order to another menu item. For the customers, too, the exposed kitchen at Rāmen Hideyoshi plays a practical role.

The relationship between regular customers and employees is unique. Employees and customers know each other's habits but rarely communicate verbally or exchange names (which is why the employees often resort to nicknaming the customers). Unlike upscale establishments, where customers and waiters socialize through short conversations and services (for example, the waiter offers water, or asks whether the dishes are satisfactory), customers and employees maintain a personal distance at Rāmen Hideyoshi, communicating only through the rāmen. Rāmen is consumed as a quick meal, and employees do not bother even regular customers with unnecessary chitchat. Employees greet customers with a hearty "Welcome," but customers rarely respond while they wait to be seated. When customers leave, they might say "Thank you," and a few comment on their meal, saying "It was good." On rare occasions one might say, "Sorry for not finishing it," as they rush off. For the most part, a simple bow suffices. The majority of

Rāmen Hideyoshi's customers do not expect the shop to have upscale service and they act accordingly.

The boundary drawn by customers between public and private is thin. Customers consider Rāmen Hideyoshi an *uchi* or "inside" space; *uchi* means family or household.[6] Dorinne Kondo (1990, 141) describes *uchi* space as "the world of informality, casual behavior, and relaxation," as opposed to the *soto* (outside) space of the formal, public world. *Uchi* is not a site for socializing, but a more private, homey space. Rāmen Hidesyohi's unpretentious interior blurs these frontstage and backstage and public and private spaces, which permits customers to engage in semi-homey behavior.

There are no dress codes or restrictive middle-class rules of decorum in Rāmen Hideyoshi. Wet hand towels are provided by the employees so customers can cleanse their faces and necks while waiting for their bowls of noodle soup to be served. It is also common for customers to keep their jackets on while they are eating, since the eatery does not have a place to hang one's jacket. I once observed a customer who left his backpack on while eating. Male office workers often drape their ties over their shoulders to avoid stains. Some male customers provide evidence of their extreme comfortableness in the shop by taking off their shoes and massaging their feet while waiting for their order to arrive. Once the soup comes, the emphasis is on the food rather than the environment in which it is served. Customers normally take no longer than twenty minutes to finish their bowl; some spend barely five minutes to finish a bowl of rāmen.

Eateries are complex entities involving communication, food, ambience, and service. Some restaurants aim to be extensions of the home, while upscale restaurants attempt to differentiate from the domestic. Restaurants also represent a kind of "third space" where the private blends into the public and vice versa (Sutton 2007, 202). Customers' acts follow the codes that are embedded in the social space of the *rāmen-ya*. Rāmen Hideyoshi provides a space with blurred frontstage/backstage boundaries for working-class consumers, creating a homey space where they can comfortably enjoy their bowls. The blue-collar working-class environment offers customers a few moments of leisure in a casual atmosphere without pressure to socialize. David Plath (1964, 9) asserts that the difficulty of separating the mindsets of work and recreation motivates people to seek out such sources of leisure to restore their well-being. Rāmen Hideyoshi's homey space allows customers to disconnect from work and relax for a moment, although they may rush back to their jobs soon after finishing their meals.

To some extent, all eateries in Japan follow the *kyakushōbai* philosophy, yet the ways in which they manifest it varies greatly. Rāmen Hideyoshi's interior and the service its employees provide are quite different from up-scale eateries aimed at white-collar customers. This blue-collar environment implicitly defines Rāmen Hideyoshi as an inexpensive fast-food eatery. However, Rāmen Hideyoshi employees are fully aware of their duty to please their customers; they do so by offering a cozy environment with a bowl of rāmen. At the same time, rāmen consumers, particularly regulars with their rich experiences in rāmen consumption, play just as critical a role in the creation and maintenance of its blue-collar environment.

When you go to *rāmen-ya* next time (or the first time), enjoy employees' and regular customers' "performances"; they add an extra flavor to your rāmen.

Notes

1. Merry White (2012) discusses changing class and gender connotations of coffee in Japan.
2. *Omote-ura* (front/public and back/private self) is another way of expressing the public-private dichotomy.
3. The idea of a frontstage/backstage dichotomy resembles Goffman's discourse analysis of face-work, yet my study details the boundaries that are strictly limited within the workplace.
4. Employees are required to take off their uniforms (white apron and bandanna/cap) when they go to the restroom. This is ostensibly for hygienic reasons, but it also signals a separation between front- and backstage activities.
5. Customers usually vary from one establishment to another, because where one dines out is associated with one's position in class hierarchy. In the case of rāmen, the association between types of customers and *rāmen-ya* is not as strict as in other eateries, but new-wave *rāmen-ya* still have more middle-class clientele than old-school *rāmen-ya*.
6. *Uchi* can be stretched to include groups with which one regularly associates, such as a corporation, school, club, or nation.

Entering Moloka'i Hawaiian Style

MARY TUTI BAKER

MOLOKA'I IS KNOWN AS "the most Hawaiian island."[1] Although a mere
twenty-five miles from O'ahu, the urban center of the state of Hawai'i,
Kanaka 'Ōiwi[2] on Moloka'i fiercely protect their rural Hawaiian way of life
in the face of globalization. The residents of Moloka'i are engaged in pro-
tracted struggles with large landowners to keep access to hunting and fishing grounds open and to stop state-sponsored and private economic development schemes that threaten the island's fragile social and ecological
systems (Yamashita 2008). I conduct "homework" (see Teaiwa 2004) as a
Kanaka 'Ōiwi scholar on cultural and economic resistance to the forces of
globalization on Moloka'i.

The fifth largest in the Hawaiian island archipelago, Moloka'i is di-
vided into three distinct regions: the mountains and valleys of East Moloka'i,
where most of the population resides, the central plain of Ho'olehua, where
much of the agricultural activity takes place, and the open terrain of West
Moloka'i, which is the center of real estate holdings of Moloka'i Ranch.[3] Native Hawaiians are the majority of the island's approximately nine thousand
residents. By state of Hawai'i standards Moloka'i is a distressed community.
Unemployment hovers around twice the state average, and many residents
live below the poverty line (Hawaii Business Research Library 2007).

In conversations with me, Walter Ritte Jr., a Kanaka 'Ōiwi from
Moloka'i, has emphasized that "Moloka'i residents live in two economies:
the subsistence economy and the cash economy." In a subsistence economy,
wild and cultivated renewable resources are used for direct personal or
family consumption as well as for barter or trade (McGregor 2007, 16).

Many on Moloka'i supplement their household income with subsistence practices like fishing, hunting, and gardening (McGregor 2007, 243–248). "In order for me to survive on this island," stresses Ritte, "I had to hunt. I never had money so I had to trade my meat. Somebody fixed my car I traded for deer meat" (*Mo'olelo Aloha 'Āina* 2010a).

Kanaka 'Ōiwi on Moloka'i stress the importance of traditional Hawaiian knowledge and practices in their social and economic life. "The first rule with regard to the land, ocean, and natural resources is to only take what is needed. Wasting resources is strongly condemned" (McGregor 2007, 16). These practices are primary principles of aloha and mālama 'āina. Moloka'i resident Joyce Kainoa explains, "Aloha 'āina is survival. It is independence. The Hawaiians of yesterday lived the same way (as we do today) except we get modern tools, modern house, but the values are the same" (*Mo'olelo Aloha 'Āina* 2011).

Participation in a cash economy includes selling products in a market or working for a wage. On Moloka'i most Saturday mornings there is an open-air market in Kaunakakai, the municipal center of the island. At this market, artisans sell goods like clothing, jewelry, and other crafts, and farmers and backyard gardeners sell surplus produce. Teachers and other public employees, retail workers, agricultural workers, hotel maids, and the like earn wages by working for someone else. The largest employers on the island are the State of Hawai'i and Monsanto, a biotechnology corporation that produces genetically modified seed corn on the island.

The cash economy is often in conflict with the subsistence economy. Transnational corporations like GuocoLeisure Limited, the corporation that owns Moloka'i Ranch, and Monsanto exist to produce profit from their landholdings. These corporations are not concerned with the subsistence requirements of island residents. This is the socioeconomic climate that I encountered when I first arrived on Moloka'i in 2009.

I have been intrigued by the "Hawaiian mystique" of Moloka'i since my childhood in a suburban Hawaiian family on O'ahu. My mother kept the house and raised the children, and my father commuted to work in Honolulu. My mother's Hawaiian parents, who lived next door to us, were the anchors to my Hawaiian roots. We ate Hawaiian food, sang Hawaiian songs, danced hula, and, curiously, we always referred to Hawaiian culture in the past tense.

Life on Moloka'i is similar to the life my grandparents knew growing up on their home islands of Kaua'i and Hawai'i Island. Like many Hawaiians of their generation they left home to pursue their fortunes in the "big city." In Honolulu they met, married, and successfully assimilated into the

American economic system. My grandparents maintained their connection to the places where they were born though, and as a family we often visited their home islands. We never traveled to other islands in the archipelago though, because, as my grandmother used to say, we do not go where we do not belong.

I went to university in the continental United States and when I returned home, Honolulu had expanded into a metropolitan city with freeways, traffic jams, and a proliferation of suburbs. Tourism had replaced sugar and pineapple production as the state's major economic engine. The population was booming, as was the economy. However, protests erupted over fears that in this post-statehood boom "old Hawai'i" would be lost. A renaissance of Native Hawaiian cultural practices grew out of these protests, and Native Hawaiian spiritual values such as aloha (love as reciprocity), kuleana (responsibility to community), laulima (many hands working together), and mālama 'āina (stewardship of the land) guided a movement for Native Hawaiian sovereignty and self-determination.[4]

During this time of Native Hawaiian activism, a small but powerful political force was growing on Moloka'i. In 1975, island residents fought Moloka'i Ranch to maintain public access to the island's hunting, fishing, and cultural sites. Their successful protests inspired movements to reclaim Native Hawaiian land rights throughout the state (McGregor 2007, 268–269). One such grassroots movement was the campaign to stop the bombing of Kaho'olawe, an island that the U.S. military had used as a training range since 1941. Moloka'i activist George Helm led this campaign (see Morales 1984). "He (Helm) came up with the term aloha 'āina to explain what we were doing and why we were doing it," recalls fellow activist Ritte, "and that was the birth of aloha 'āina again. In the old days aloha 'āina was a political party in Hawai'i" (Mo'olelo Aloha 'Āina 2010b). Aloha 'āina became an organizing principle for the movement to reclaim land for Native Hawaiians (see Silva 2004, 123–163).

Observing political activism emerging out of living on the land inspired me to study the relationship between land-based economic practice and self-government in indigenous communities. Based on what I knew about the island, Moloka'i appeared to be an ideal community in which to begin this investigation, but I remembered my grandmother's admonition that we do not go where not invited. How do I enter? What kind of invitation do I need? This childhood lesson is closely tied to research protocols that Māori scholar Linda Tuhiwai Smith writes about in Decolonizing Methodologies. Researchers working in indigenous communities, Smith writes, must respect the knowledge, the values, and the spirit of the indigenous community being researched. She presents a research protocol to follow when working within an indigenous community that includes two key elements: the community must be involved in the research process, and researchers must share their findings with the community in a meaningful and productive way (Smith 1999, 118–120).

In July 2009 an opportunity opened up for my first visit to Moloka'i. I was invited to attend a conference titled "Sustainable Moloka'i the Future of a Hawaiian Island." "Sustainable Moloka'i" is a play on "sustainable" and "'āina." As implied in the title, this conference presented models of economic development that would provide long-term good for people while protecting the land from overuse. The conference program vision statement emphasized that

> Moloka'i is the last Hawaiian island. We who live here choose not to be strangers in our own land. The values of aloha 'āina and mālama 'āina (love and care for the land) guide our stewardship of Moloka'i's natural resources, which nourish our families both physically and spiritually. . . . Our true wealth is measured by the extent of our generosity.

The organizers of the conference were primarily Kānaka 'Ōiwi, and the one hundred or so participants included longtime residents and the newly settled on Moloka'i. Residents were encouraged to attend for free, and registration for nonresidents was by invitation only. The organizers wanted to ensure that people attending the conference not from Moloka'i would be productive contributors to the event. In keeping with the economic development and self-sufficiency themes of the conference, a colleague and I from a Kanaka 'Ōiwi artists' cooperative were invited to provide information to Moloka'i artists about working within a cooperative business model. On this first trip to Moloka'i, I sat in on a number of talk-story sessions with Moloka'i residents.[5] The visions I heard of the economic and political future of Moloka'i involved projects based in aloha 'āina and mālama 'āina. The ideas that were generated included locally owned visitor operations and investments of outside capital that would provide benefit to the community as well as profit for investors.

In one talk-story session at the conference, residents alluded to tensions within the community about how best to preserve the balance between the subsistence and cash economies. Participants told me that the conference was an attempt to heal the rift between factions in the community over a plan to develop Lā'au Point, a pristine shoreline and productive offshore fishing ground. As part of an earlier community-based planning process, the Moloka'i Enterprise Community (a community-based organization funded by the U.S. Department of Agriculture to create economic development projects on Moloka'i) and Moloka'i Ranch developed a Community-based Master Land Use Plan for the Ranch. The plan incorporated preserving open space and providing jobs for Moloka'i residents. In exchange, Moloka'i Ranch expected community support to develop two hundred one-acre multimillion-dollar house lots at Lā'au Point.

A large segment of the Moloka'i community objected to this development. Fishermen were concerned that developing Lā'au Point would adversely affect offshore fishing. Farmers insisted that there was not enough water on the island to support the development, and many residents were concerned that the development would negatively affect the island's lifestyle. Residents challenged the corporation's private property rights. They invoked their traditional responsibility to take care of the land, and they were critical of the potential concentration of wealthy landowners at Lā'au (Yamashita 2007). The advocates of the plan argued that it provided an opportunity for the community to participate in the managed growth of their island and that reopening the corporation's resort would provide jobs for residents. These arguments did not sway the community, and because of community opposition, Moloka'i Ranch abandoned the Lā'au Point project in November 2007.

My research into economic practices on the island also took me to Halawa Valley, on the east side of the island. Halawa Valley once provided kalo (taro), a staple food in the Hawaiian diet, to communities as far away as Hana on the island of Maui. I worked with a man who is slowly returning family land to kalo production. He invites school groups and individuals like myself to come to help open up lo'i, the ponds where kalo is grown. Although he works on O'ahu, he returns to Halawa Valley regularly to grow kalo, to preserve the ancient varieties, and to share his knowledge with all who work with him in his lo'i. Kanaka 'Ōiwi on Moloka'i not only engage in resistance activities to protect their island; they also provide urban dwellers like myself the opportunity to practice aloha and mālama 'āina.

The struggles are ongoing between subsistence and cash economies. In lo'i, in community meetings, and on the protest line, Kanaka 'Ōiwi on Moloka'i continue to work to balance their subsistence and cash economies. In conversations, Ritte has emphasized to me, "Subsistence rights are continuously challenged by large landowners." Moloka'i residents say that their island is the "last Hawaiian island," and after spending time on the island talking story with and working alongside politically engaged residents, I see clearly that they are determined to hold on to Hawaiian traditions even as the island deals with social and economic globalization, the challenge of the twenty-first century. My time on the island has shown me that Kanaka ʻŌiwi on Molokaʻi are united by shared values of aloha and mālama ʻāina. Even though they may not always agree on strategies for political action, these shared values contribute to their ability to resist detrimental economic forces that threaten the balance between subsistence and cash economies on their island. Indigenous peoples throughout the world who are also dealing with powerful economic forces that exploit their homelands with little or no benefit to their community (see Hall 2009) can draw inspiration from the perseverance of the Kanaka ʻŌiwi on Molokaʻi in their dynamic and vigourous efforts to protect the ʻāina, the source of sustenance, and to live a life governed by the maxim that "generosity is the true measure of wealth."

Notes

1. See http://visitmolokai.com (accessed October 24, 2012).
2. I use the term Kanaka ʻŌiwi to refer to the Indigenous People of Hawaiʻi. It is synonymous with Native Hawaiian but, unlike Native Hawaiian, does not carry a connotation of blood quantum. In this essay, I use the terms interchangeably.
3. Molokaʻi Ranch, the largest landowner on the island, was created in 1897 and in the late twentieth century transitioned into property development. Molokaʻi Properties Limited is the legal name of the corporation that is a wholly owned subsidiary of GuocoLeisure Limited, a corporation headquartered in Singapore. See http://www.guocoleisure.com/invest.html (accessed August 16, 2012).
4. ʻĀina is a complex word that is derived from ʻai, to eat, signifying the reciprocal relationship between Kanaka ʻŌiwi and their homeland, as expressed in the Hawaiian proverb "Take care of the land and the land will take care of you."
5. Talk-story sessions are people gathered to discuss an issue in an unstructured format.

PART 7

Green Encounters

Environment, Sustainability, Restoration

(*overleaf photo*) ʻĪmaikalani Aikau, son of contributing author Hokulani Aikau, observes the loʻi kalo (taro field) being restored at Heʻeia, Oʻahu. Loʻi restoration is a fundamental component of Native Hawaiian resurgence projects to fortify traditional land- and water-based practices. The restoration of loʻi kalo reconnects Native Hawaiians to the knowledge of kūpuna (elders) and ensures the health and well-being of future generations. Photo by Hokulani K. Aikau.

Introduction

MARY MOSTAFANEZHAD

AS WE MOVE into the twenty-first century, the influence of industrialization on the environment has emerged as one of the most pressing issues of our time. To address these issues, social scientists examine how humans interact with the environment. A focus on human–environment relationships provides insights into how we are affected as well as how we affect the environment. While this topic is addressed from various disciplinary perspectives, what links these perspectives is the continued interest in the diverse ways humans engage with their environment and how this engagement contributes to cultural, economic, and political diversity. Hence, the topics in this section focus on the complex interplay of the environment, economy, culture, and politics. In each case, ecological knowledge is examined from multiple perspectives in order to highlight the diversity of "ways of knowing" about the natural world that surrounds us.

We begin with Joseph H. Genz's exploration of the revival of indigenous navigation in the Marshall Islands. Genz's primary question is, "How do Marshallese navigators orient themselves at sea?" By ethnographically exploring this question, Genz illustrates where Marshallese and American navigators' ecological knowledge converge and diverge. Mary Mostafanezhad's and Keith Bettinger's chapters examine ecological degradation as well as environmental conservation from a political-ecology perspective that highlights the historical, political, and economic context of environmental issues. Mostafanezhad examines how the conservation agendas of Thai host community members, nongovernmental organization coordinators, and volunteer tourists converge in ironic, contradictory, and complex ways. The result is that some environmental agendas are privileged while others are marginalized. Bettinger's chapter is situated in the Kerinci Seblat National Park on the island of Sumatra in Indonesia. Examining the forced relocation of thousands of local people for the implementation of a conservation area around the Sumatran Tiger habitat, Bettinger studies how saving tigers in Indonesia conflicts with local coffee farmers' livelihoods. Both Mostafanezhad and Bettinger ethnographically demonstrate the complexity of the question, "conservation for whom?"

This section concludes with Hokulani Aikau, Nahaku Kalei, and Bradley Wong's in-depth analysis of ecological restoration in Hawai'i. They explore the process of kalo (taro) restoration on O'ahu through the revitalization of indigenous ecological knowledge gained from six kūpuna (elders, grandparents). The revitalization process was carried out using ArcGIS software to digitally map the area. This chapter reflects on the intersection of this software with indigenous ways of knowing as well as outlines some of the potentials and limitations of this method for indigenous communities and ecological knowledge revitalization.

From Nuclear Exodus to Cultural Reawakening

A Navigator's Journey in the Marshall Islands

JOSEPH H. GENZ

WE HAD BEEN SAILING west against high storm-driven winds and seas for thirty-six hours without sighting a single star amid a completely overcast sky, when the navigator showed, for the first time during this voyage and since I had known him for over a year, signs of uncertainty. Based on his learning as a child and over thirty years of experience at sea as a government ship captain, Korent Joel, known locally as Captain Korent, expected already to have felt a reflected wave pattern—a navigational "sign"—that would lead us toward land.[1] He estimated that our target, a low-lying coral atoll, was about twenty miles to the northwest of our present location, but that the tops of the coconut trees would only be visible from ten miles offshore. He scanned the seas to the starboard (right) side of the vessel, hoping to sight the wave patterns that he could not feel. As time passed, it became clear to him that either the wave was not present or its characteristic signature was masked by the dominant storm swells. Unsure of our location, he was about to direct the helmsman to sail closer to the wind and head to the northwest in search of land.

We were sailing in the western chain of the Marshall Islands, a group of thirty-four low-lying coral atolls and islands spread out over aproximately 750,000 square miles of ocean in the western Pacific in an area conventionally referred to as Micronesia. Our voyage left the populous atoll of Kwajalein,[2] the site of a U.S. missile-testing range that, when combined with the capital atoll of Majuro, contributes about two-thirds of the country's fifty-five thousand residents. The other third of the population lives in villages of a few hundred people on the outer islands, such as Ujae, an atoll about 120 miles west of Kwajalein toward which we were sailing.

This voyage was the culminating event of a long-term collaborative project to document and revitalize a unique wave-based system of navigation (Genz et al. 2009; Genz 2011). Since I was documenting the track of the vessel with a handheld global positioning system unit, which I compared to the navigator's estimates of where we were, I was aware that we would soon see an intermediate small coral atoll, Lae, as well as Ujae within the next few hours if we held our course and speed. If we tacked and steered Captain Korent's proposed new course to the northwest, however, there was a remote chance that we might come upon two outlying atolls about four hundred miles distant. If we missed those sightings, we would be sailing out of Marshallese waters, and the next landfall in that direction was Japan, nearly three thousand miles away! This was by far the most intense moment of my anthropological fieldwork.

Thoroughly complicating this precise moment in my mind was the fact that the two likely consequences of Captain Korent's impending decision—finding land or becoming lost at sea—were linked with ancient cultural beliefs of tremendous importance and continuing relevance. On the one hand, this voyage served as a final navigational test that, if successful, would elevate Captain Korent to the socially recognized and chiefly sanctioned title of *ri-meto*, a "person of the ocean," or navigator, an event that had not happened in living memory. On the other hand, several consequences would likely follow from getting lost at sea. Most immediately, Captain Korent would not become a navigator since he had failed the test. The revival of voyaging would likely come to a halt, as Captain Korent was one of the last elders with navigational knowledge. Of more pressing concern, Captain Korent could enter a state of *wiwijet* (loss of direction, panic), in which, according to *bwebwenato* (oral traditions), a navigator loses his way, becomes confused, and sails toward his death.

And yet another form of death haunted Captain Korent. Between 1946 and 1958, the U.S. government detonated sixty-seven atomic and thermonuclear bombs in the Marshall Islands as part of its nuclear weapons testing program. In 1954, Korent Joel was a young boy when a thermonuclear bomb codenamed "Bravo"—a massive fifteen-megaton device equivalent to one thousand Hiroshima bombs—was detonated over Bikini. The resulting nuclear fallout on his neighboring home atolls of Rongelap, Rongerik, and Ailinginae had such massive physical and social consequences for his family and community through forced exodus and relocation, sickness and medical experiments, contamination of terrestrial and marine resources, stigmatization, and loss of traditional ways of life (Barker 2013; Johnston and Barker 2008) that it effectively terminated the transmission of navigational knowledge to the last-known group of traditional navigation students in the Marshall Islands, including the young Korent.

Up until this time, and despite a violent history of colonialism and militarization, an older generation of navigators, including Korent's grandfather, had kept the knowledge alive. Afterward, Korent became a captain of large government transport ships and continued to teach himself the various wave patterns for more than thirty years, but the strict protocols of sharing specialized knowledge were still maintained (Genz 2011). He could not be called a navigator until, with the permission of his chief, he put his knowledge to the test at sea. This involved an intellectual awakening called *ruprup jọkur,* which literally translates as "breaking open of the turtle shell," and metaphorically means that his mind would fill with new knowledge. Now, if he could successfully find land without becoming lost or misjudging landfall, the chief would bestow the title of *ri-meto.* If he failed, the pathway to becoming a navigator would be forever closed.

By the time I started my fieldwork in 2005, I had spent two summers on an outer atoll, Ailuk, with a host family, for immersion in the Marshallese culture and language. My family lived in a cement house in the center of the main village at the edge of the beach on the lagoon side of the atoll. Each morning the family members would launch their twenty-foot sailing outrigger canoe into these protected lagoon waters. With strong trade winds, the crew would deftly sail the canoe with the outrigger just skimming across the surface of the water for balance, and quickly vanish from sight in pursuit of bountiful fishing grounds. Usually, just before sunset, the canoe would arrive back with reef fish, turtles, octopus, clams, and, if the winds had been high enough for trolling in the deep ocean waters, fresh tuna that was consumed raw on the spot. On other days we ate a variety of dishes made from breadfruit, pandanus, and coconuts.

My host father, Kilon Takiah, was the eldest master canoe builder in the Marshall Islands. He took me under his wing and, with much patience, taught me about the components of the canoe, how to make coconut sennit for lashing and rigging, and much more. His son, Russel, took me sailing and fishing. His daughter, Alimi, showed me how to do many of the women's activities, such as cooking, husking coconuts, and preparing pandanus and coconut leaves for weavings. She also refined my knowledge of Marshallese customs and language. During my first summer visit in 2003, my constant companions were the family's children, since my own cultural knowledge was in its infancy. By the end of my second summer visit in 2005,

I had gained enough cultural and linguistic competence for Kilon to say with pride that I was his son, and over the course of my fieldwork I gained quick rapport with the broader community by relating my family connection to Kilon.

When I shared with Kilon my plans to eventually work with Captain Korent on navigation, Kilon's usual playful smile vanished. This was to be far different from having Kilon demonstrate, say, how to make a fishing line out of the fibers of pandanus aerial roots. It was clear from Kilon's countenance alone that I was no longer a neophyte cultural learner. For him, navigation was the most specialized, prized, and secretive type of knowledge, and Captain Korent was the most distinguished navigator. My thoughts concentrated on how I was going to humbly present myself to such an esteemed navigator, who was like a Marshallese version of the famous Satawalese navigator Mau Pialug.[3]

My first meeting with Captain Korent and Alson Kelen, my counterpart researcher, took place at a Chinese restaurant on Majuro. The most memorable aspect of this key event was the different expectations that we each held. Within the span of a few minutes, before we even got a chance to order our meal, Captain Korent shared vital information that launched a totally new trajectory for my fieldwork. Alson and Dennis Alessio, the former director of a local canoe-building organization named Waan Aelon in Majel (Canoes of the Marshall Islands), had been under the impression that Captain Korent was a titled navigator because he had approached them several years earlier expressing an interest in sharing his knowledge. At this current meeting, however, Alson and I learned that Captain Korent had just been given permission by his chief to share his knowledge for this revival project, but that he had yet to take his first traditionally navigated voyage, his *ruprup jọkur* test. Just as I had been expecting to work with a master (titled) navigator, Captain Korent had been expecting to work with an expert researcher such as Ben Finney, my academic adviser at the University of Hawai'i at Mānoa, who had extensive experience in voyaging revival projects in Hawai'i and throughout Polynesia (Finney 1979, 1994, 2003).

It became instantly clear to me that I would have to work incredibly hard to convince Captain Korent that I had the expertise and perseverance of someone like Ben Finney to not merely document Captain Korent's knowledge, but to facilitate his learning by collaborating with other elders and oceanographers who could help to explain the wave patterns, and with assistance from Alson, to enable him to take his belated *ruprup jọkur* navigation test. Since this was my first day of formal fieldwork, I had no way to know yet what exactly was at stake—namely, his pathway to becoming a navigator would close forever if he failed this test, with the likely impending cessation of the voyaging revival, and, as the antithesis of *ruprup jǫkur,* Captain Korent would enter a state of *wiwijet* and possibly sail in a crazed condition until his death.

Over the course of a year of land-based research and learning, as well as sea-based wave studies, I was able to establish a strong rapport with Captain Korent. This had as much to do with impressing him with my abilities as a researcher and facilitator as with simply talking story with him for several hours each day. Knowing what was at stake, we then planned Captain Korent's first voyage. As the voyaging canoe of Waan Aelon in Majel was undergoing repairs at the time, we enlisted the help of two yachtsmen from Kwajalein. The plan for the navigation test was to sail a yacht from Kwajalein to Ujae and back, with the condition that I would cover the compass with duct tape and stow all other navigational instruments to prevent any inadvertent use of modern technology.

Captain Korent's impending decision to tack to the northeast (and unknowingly sail past Ujae) was at hand. It is no wonder Captain Korent was starting to feel disoriented, given that the storm-driven seas had masked the subtler navigational wave patterns for the past thirty-six hours and that the crew had difficulty maintaining Captain Korent's intended course in such strong seas with no celestial guides. Captain Korent had been searching to starboard (right) looking for wave patterns that could be followed toward land. From an indigenous Marshallese worldview, distinctive waves and currents serve as navigational "signs" that indicate both the distance toward land and the direction of land. In this case, Captain Korent was searching for either the visual patterning or the sensation of motion of a wave called *jur in okme* to help him remotely sense Ujae. He envisions that a dominant trade wind-driven swell reflects seaward from land in a radiating curve. This curve is the same shape as a land-based *jur in okme,* "a pole for harvesting breadfruit." To facilitate Captain Korent's learning of this and other wave patterns in preparation for his *ruprup jǫkur* voyage, his uncle, Isao Eknilang, had woven and lashed thin sections of aerial pandanus roots into a latticework of lines and curves. Commonly referred to as a "stick chart," this indigenous wave model graphically represents the multiple kinds of ocean swells and wave-based navigation signs (Ascher 1995; Finney 1998).

Then, for just a moment, we saw a speck of land appear to port (left), and then quickly disappear as we slid into the trough of a wave. Captain Korent halted his command to tack. At first, he thought we had somehow followed a circular wind pattern during the night and that we were now sailing back toward Kwajalein, at which point he thought about turning around (which would have brought us back to Kwajalein!). As we drew closer and the configuration of land became clearer, Captain Korent identified it (correctly), based on his years of experience sailing throughout the archipelago, as the tiny atoll Lae. Then, an instant clarity of mind settled over Captain Korent, and he knew that we had been heading in the right direction.

Although the navigation was not yet complete, I believe this moment was his intellectual transformation of *ruprup jọkur*. Everything fell into place after that. With a newfound sense of confidence, we sighted land the next day. We never did feel the *jur in okme* reflected wave that would have remotely indicated the presence of Ujae. But our sighting of the tops of the coconut trees coincided with observing a school of dolphins about ten miles offshore of Ujae. In addition to wave-based phenomena, Marshallese navigators also draw upon their spiritual beliefs of the ocean to help find their way. As elaborated in chants and songs, this school of dolphins was a different kind of navigational "sign" specific to Ujae. These dolphins were associated with a spiritual being called *ekjab* (sea life) that could benevolently guide a lost navigator toward land. Marshallese oral traditions describe additional forms of *ekjab* near various atolls, taking the form of birds and other marine life. The presence of this *ekjab* school of dolphins further solidified Captain Korent's understanding and appreciation for the more ancient, esoteric aspects of navigation.

Although the storm system still presented a completely overcast sky on the return voyage to Kwajalein, the rough seas had diminished just enough that Captain Korent could detect a few navigational "signs," such as a different type of reflected wave emanating from Kwajalein called *kāmeto*, literally meaning "fly seaward." In addition, the constant westerly wind provided pleasant downwind sailing. After a direct course with only minor course adjustments, observing the street lights of Kwajalein islet gave a sense of finality to the navigation test. An air of excitement filled the crew, and although we still had several hours of sailing to do before reaching land, Captain Korent was finally able to rest and reflect on what he had just accomplished.

We sat on the deck together, gazing ahead to the increasing glow of light, thinking of so many possibilities for the future—especially plans to teach his young grandson by the traditional forms of instruction on his home atoll of Rongelap. What extreme emotions in just a matter of days—from anxiety at the thought of Captain Korent losing his way and entering a state of *wiwijet* to the most fulfilling moment of my fieldwork when I realized that I had played a part in this historical and, for Captain Korent, very personal event. My questions and copious notetaking on the deck at that moment and Captain Korent's customary terse answers could not possibly have done justice to capturing the emotions he must have been feeling. Days later, in a very quiet manner without a public ceremony, the chief sanctioned Captain Korent as a *ri-meto,* a true person of the ocean.

This story of Captain Korent's becoming a traditional navigator in the wake of extreme social and cultural changes in the Marshall Islands illuminates broad issues of indigenous ecological knowledge and political ecology. Successive waves of militarism in the past century—including the Pacific theater of World War II, the era of nuclear testing, and the (ongoing) missile range shaped by U.S. Cold War policy—has left the Marshallese, and to some extent other island communities throughout Oceania, with strong impressions of America's wealth, power, and knowledge. This has led to an implicit devaluing of traditional practices and epistemologies despite their sustainability, while valorizing development, modernity, and scientific ways of knowing (Walsh 2003). Yet recent studies of indigenous epistemologies in Oceania have emphasized a plurality of knowledges with equally valid ways of knowing (Gegeo and Watson-Gegeo 2001; Lauer and Aswani 2009; Meyer 2001; Nabobo-Baba 2006). In the Marshalls and elsewhere, perhaps those who have lost the most are the keenest to turn once again to their ancestral past to selectively and creatively forge new solutions for the uncharted future. Captain Korent, whose ancestral homeland still remains unsettled due to the forced relocations from nuclear fallout, has forged a path to recovering the specialized and esoteric knowledge of navigation. Within the complex postnuclear political ecology of the Marshall Islands and the broader region of Micronesia, I am optimistic that Captain Korent's incredible accomplishment will awaken the Marshallese and broader Pacific community to the importance of indigenous ways of knowing for their cultural survival.

Notes

1. This essay is based on fieldwork conducted between 2003 and 2009 as part of a collaborative and interdisciplinary revival project. I would like to especially acknowledge Kilon Takiah and Captain Korent Joel for sharing their canoe-building and navigational knowledge, Alson Kelen for his collaborative research, Ben Finney and Mark Merrifield for their guidance, and Iroijlaplap (Paramount Chief) Imata Kabua and Iroij (Chief) Mike Kabua for their permission to conduct the project. The views expressed herein are those of the author and do not necessarily reflect the views of NOAA or any of its subagencies.

2. The spellings of Marshallese words follow the new orthography as reflected in the Marshallese dictionary (Abo et al. 1976), but I revert to older spellings of place-names for ease of recognition.

3. Mau Pialug, now deceased, was a traditional navigator from Satawal in Micronesia who was instrumental in the Hawaiian and Polynesian rebirth of voyaging. Mau navigated the double-hulled voyaging canoe *Hōkūleʻa* 2,500 miles to Tahiti, and later instructed Nainoa Thompson (now a master navigator) in the arts of navigation (Finney 1979, 1994).

"They Came for Nature"

A Political Ecology of Volunteer Tourism Development in Northern Thailand

MARY MOSTAFANEZHAD

WON, A TWENTY-SIX-YEAR-OLD Thai woman and mother of one, works six days a week at Pu Khao Eco-Lodge in Mae Nam Village, located fifty kilometers outside of Chiang Mai, in northern Thailand. Won had barely worked at the lodge for six months, yet she had already met dozens of "Farang" or Westerners. While washing dishes one evening after dinner, Won asked me what the volunteer tourists—tourists who pay money to participate in development and environmental conservation projects—were up to. "I believe they are drinking rice whiskey and playing cards upstairs," I responded. I could tell that Won was confused about something. We began talking about the conservation project that the volunteer tourists were working on. I then asked Won why she thought the volunteer tourists were drawn to her village. Won explained to me that Farang volunteer tourists come to Mae Nam Village because they want to see nature. "But don't they have nature at home? Why would they come all the way to Thailand?" I asked. She paused for a moment and then explained to me: "The Farang volunteers come to my village because they have already destroyed their own natural environments. Thailand still has nature. The Farang come here because they are trying to escape traffic jams and big buildings and have an experience in nature." Won's response is echoed by other Thai host-community members as well as Farang volunteer tourists involved in conservation-oriented volunteer tourism. In Mae Nam Village, the explicit goal of Farang volunteers is to contribute to environmental conservation. Won and other Thai community members, however, do not necessarily view environmental conservation as a pressing need. Won, for example, explained: "We have lived in harmony with nature for over two hundred years on this land. We know how to take care of it."

In this chapter, I examine the sometimes contradictory perspectives of Thai host-community members, nongovernmental organization (NGO) practitioners, and volunteer tourists, using a political ecology framework. A political ecology framework allows me to highlight the complex historical, political and economic context of environmental conservation in Mae Nam Village. Using this perspective, I argue that the Northern environmental goals (goals that originate in the Global North or those countries identified by the World Bank as "developed") and the strategies of Farang volunteer tourists and NGO practitioners tend to overlook preexisting local environmental knowledge, values, and practices that have allowed Mae Nam Village residents to maintain their "pristine forest" over the centuries. In this way, the sometimes disparate perspectives of volunteer tourism participants converge in ironic, contradictory, and complex ways, resulting in some goals that become privileged while other goals become marginalized.

Mae Nam Village has a complex mixed economy of barter, cash crops, subsistence, and tourism. The local community is bound by strong social ties and a partial barter economy, in which people exchange money as well as goods—such as fruit, vegetables, tea, and chickens—and services. In addition, almost every household has family members working outside of the village, in Chiang Mai or Bangkok. Community members' ancestors were attracted to the area by the fertile land suitable for tea and other crops. Of the fifty-five families who currently live in Mae Nam Village, forty-eight grow tea. Their main crops are *cha-miang* (pickled tea leaf)—a traditional crop of northern Thailand—and more recently, coffee. The adults in the community harvest crops five to six days per week. They collect around 10.5 kilos of *cha-miang* per day, which they exchange for approximately 63 baht (US$2). Tourism is another growing source of income, representing 7 percent of the annual yearly income for the village. While fourteen households reported income from tourism, only three households benefit from the majority of this income.

The relationship between Mae Nam Village and Borderless Volunteers—the NGO that operates the volunteer tourism program in the community—began in 2000, five years prior to my first arrival in 2005. Tom, the founder of Borderless Volunteers, approached Mae Nam Village because he saw it as an ideal environment for ecotourism development. Tom and his partner sought to create an ecotourism lodge in Mae Nam Village. They developed an agreement with the village whereby the village would benefit from the lodge profits, and in ten years' time their NGO would become the beneficiary of the ecotourism trails to be built in the villages. At the time of my research, the only community members to be directly involved in the development of ecotourism were the headman (village leader) and his extended family. Most community members had minimal interaction with the volunteers.

Since the 1980s there has been a rise of NGOs focused on sustainable development practices in northern Thailand. Mae Nam Village, in particular, has been targeted by several NGOs in the area. The goals of these NGOs have tended to be in line with environmental concerns of the Global North. Interactions between the NGO practitioners, volunteer tourists, and host-community members in Mae Nam Village, for example, are often based on Northern environmental conservation discourses. Discourse, according to Michel Foucault, refers to how knowledge is constituted through social practices and relations of power (Foucault 1981). In other words, discourses are ways of thinking and producing meaning, and as such, they create realities. Importantly, these realities are embedded in relations of power. The concept of discourse is important here because we can consider how people talk about conservation to better understand how some practices are privileged over others.

An example of these competing conservation agendas is illustrated in Mae Nam Village where the environmental agendas of Borderless Volunteers did not always subscribe to the same environmental concerns of the local community. Even when local discourses of environmental conservation were recognized, they were often still undermined by Northern conservation discourses. Northern conservation discourses tend to privilege scientific knowledge over other ways of knowing. While Tom, the founder of Borderless Volunteers, identifies local knowledge as a key aspect of environmental conservation in the area, he and his organization also seek to "educate" the local people by encouraging them to adopt Northern discourses. He states, "We can learn as much from these people as they can learn from us. With ecotourism and environmental science, we look at the forest here and the knowledge that these people have of the biodiversity. It is quite amazing. That's not a simple thing. It's fairly complex. You can't say these people have gone on unorganized. They've done it. They've looked after that forest for two centuries." Yet, despite Tom's appreciation for Mae Nam community residents' conservation of the forest, in his brochures he explains that he seeks to enhance environmental awareness for local people.

Mandy, a twenty-seven-year-old American NGO coordinator who worked for Tom, echoed his interest in enhancing environmental awareness for the villagers. Mandy saw an advertisement for her position on Idealist.org—an online network dedicated to promoting social justice agendas. She explained to me that she was interested in sustainability issues: "I definitely want to work only in the environmental field. . . . Anything that is sustainability and that covers social, environmental, and economic responsibilities is where I want to work. I want to benefit the community here, and I think teaching sustainability is how I can do that because that is where my passion is." Many of the volunteer tourists at Borderless Volunteers also admitted that that they came to Mae Nam Village because they wanted to conserve the forest. Jan, a twenty-one-year-old sustainability studies student from England, explained that she wanted to try out sustainability modeling, a technique she learned at her university. For Mandy and Jan, their understanding of environmental conservation has developed around a specific set of conservation and sustainability strategies and discourses that they learned in their Euro-American universities, such as labeling, calculating, and categorizing plants.

When asked what she thought about environmental conservation, Ratana, a Thai host community member stated, "I think it is about living how we already live. I think we have conservation in our hearts and it is our way of life." When the question of how Mae Nam Village benefits from the volunteer tourists arose, she commented, "We benefit from the tourists paying money to come to our village." And when I inquired about benefits from environmental education, Ratana responded, "I haven't seen that. We only benefit from the money that comes in." She explained that she was not quite sure what the volunteers were doing in her village: "I don't know what they are doing. I am not sure what the volunteers do besides bring money. They are teaching something, but I am not sure anyone is listening. We already know how to take care of our forest, but they want to label everything. We are not sure what the point of all this is."

One afternoon while sitting on the veranda at the Eco-Lodge with Mandy, Tom informed us that the next project would be the development of a biodiversity modeling program. As part of this program, the volunteers would identify and monitor plants in the surrounding forest in order to better understand the quality of soil and to gain knowledge about the types of plants in the area. I immediately asked how they were going to identify the plants, because to my knowledge none of the NGO practitioners or volunteers had a background in the local ecology. Mong, a Thai man from the village, had stated that he could help identify the plants for the project. When Supat, a young Thai woman from the village, asked about the purpose of the biodiversity modeling project, it was explained to her that it was to be incorporated into the environmental education program for the local school children. As Ratana expressed above, this type of labeling is unfamiliar to local people in Mae Nam Village, and it is seen by many as a cause for discomfort and confusion.

The irony of this project is that the local community was asked to identify local plants for the environmental education program so that they could be taught about the plants and conservation, presumably, by nonlocal volunteer tourists! This experience exemplifies what West (2006) refers to as "conservation-as-development," by which she means government policies that envision conservation projects as development strategies, in and of themselves. While NGO practitioners, volunteer tourists, and local people appear to be working on the same project, ethnographic investigation reveals their very different ideas about what development is and how tourism should be used to achieve this.

Such developments can also be seen as a form of "eco-governmentality," or the "productive relations of government—with their emphasis on 'knowing' and 'clarifying' one's relationship to nature and the environment as mediated through new institutions" (Goldman 2004, 168). Environmental labeling, in other words, can be seen as a form of colonialism where environments are classified and colonized through labeling practices. This type of practice leads to what Linda Tuhiwai Smith refers to as "research through imperial eyes," by which she mean research that not only does not help local communities but also contributes to the colonization of the mind, whereby local ways of knowing are perceived as inferior to Western knowledge systems (Smith 1999).

A key feature of political ecology is the recognition of environmental knowledge and practice as a product of competing discourses. As discussed above, the production of knowledge is intimately related to power. Economically and politically marginalized groups are often excluded from "official" knowledge production. Highlighting the construction of knowledge and discourse, Paul Robbins explains how "Rather than simply pursue the goal of the 1970s bumper sticker, 'Question Authority,' Foucault pressed us to more radically 'Question Reality,' " (Robbins 2004, 109). When considering how conservation discourses are constructed, it may be important for us to question the "reality" of our understandings of environmental knowledge and practice.

This questioning is especially important in the context of volunteer tourism, where people from different historical, economic, and cultural backgrounds come together around a seemingly common conservation goal. In Mae Nam Village there are radically different perspectives, strategies, and

ideals that complicate what may at first have seemed to be a mutually ben-
eficial project. These frictions call into question what may appear to be
politically quite neutral discourses of conservation. In particular, local
environmental knowledge is a significant area of contention, as the NGO
practitioners' and volunteer tourists' Northern discourses of environmental
conservation seek to dominate Thai host-community members' perspectives
and downplay their local environmental knowledge.

Debates on political ecology have important implications for
conservation-oriented volunteer tourism, in that questions such as "What
are we conserving and whom are we conserving for?" complicate such projects. By exploring these kinds of questions through a political ecological
lens, we foreground the political and social nature of environmental knowledge. In this way, the ways in which knowledge is discursively produced
through a broad range of potentially complicated and contradictory perspectives on conservation become apparent.

Discourses of conservation are complex, fluid, and differentially entangled in local historical and political and economic contexts. Anna Tsing
uses the concept of "friction" to describe local people's experiences of globalization. The concept of "friction" suggests that global capitalism contributes to complex encounters between peoples from sometimes disparate
backgrounds, which can often lead to the creation of "zones of awkward
engagement" (Tsing 2005). By describing these interactions as "zones of
awkward engagement" Tsing calls attention to people's diverse interests and
the resulting misunderstandings and miscommunications that often take
place in these ecological spaces.

The concept of friction is a useful description for the volunteer tourism experience in Mae Nam Village. On the surface, people appear to have
the same interests in environmental conservation, yet a closer look reveals
radically different perspectives that rub up against each other. Borderless
Volunteers and its volunteer tourists seek to promote environmental conservation in the forest that surrounds Mae Nam Village, an area that is widely
recognized as "pristine forest." All participants describe the local community as exemplar stewards of their forest. It is ironic that NGO practitioners
and volunteer tourists seek to develop environmental education programs
and promote conservation in this village. While each group is mutually interested in conserving the forest surrounding Mae Nam Village, what "conservation" means and the best ways to achieve it remain unsettled.

Conservation discourses can be contested within everyday interactions between people. It is through these moments of exchange that the
power dynamics mediating conservation discourses are revealed. Volunteer

tourism raises important issues regarding how to best examine the sociopolitical aspects of environmental conservation. When policymakers and local people have radically different interpretations, is it possible to develop a coherent plan of conservation? An ethnographic perspective can shed light on some of the nuances of conflicting understandings of environmental conservation as well as the power dynamics influencing relations between local community members, national policymakers, and international conservationists.

The Forest of Contradictions

Coffee Versus Conservation at Indonesia's
Kerinci Seblat National Park

Keith Andrew Bettinger

Several contradictions always seem to crop up around protected areas in Southeast Asia: livelihoods versus global priorities, struggles over representation, conservation versus development, and the letter of the law versus the peasant moral code. This story describes some participant observations made during a year of fieldwork in Kerinci Seblat National Park (KSNP)—a large protected area on the island of Sumatra in Indonesia—where, in a valley called Lembah Masurai, thousands of farmers have been illegally moving into the park to grow coffee.

At the end of another five days of hacking through the dense forest near Lembah Masurai, I was as tired as I had ever been. On this particular outing, I was observing and participating in the activities of the Sumatran Tiger Protection and Conservation Team, an elite group of handpicked, specially trained rangers tasked with catching tiger poachers and destroying their traps. I had been on forest patrols before, but this particular patrol took place during the Muslim holy month of Ramadan, and so my colleagues were fulfilling their ritual obligation to fast from sunup to sundown. Though I cheated from time to time with a discreet pull from my canteen or a couple of sips from a package of condensed milk, nothing in my previous field experience or the training I underwent as an auxiliary forest policeman prepared me for this particular experience. I had to push myself to the limit just to keep up with the nimble rangers; they seemed to float effortlessly through the same jungle that appeared intent on entangling me at every turn.

For those who have never been there, the rainforest is not what you might expect. Although replete with flora and fauna of all sorts, there are no playful monkeys waiting to greet you, no singing birds enlivening the place with their bucolic voices. There is no transcendental communing with nature; no epiphany; no Zen. The rain forest is a rough place; it is hot and humid, and there are all manner of biting, stinging, and just generally annoying insects lying in wait. There are snakes and leeches, thorns and briars everywhere. It is an exhausting, inhospitable place.

It is also inhabited—not just by the aforementioned flora and fauna, but by people who enter the forest to take things. Those who have moved to Lembah Masurai see the forest not as a biodiversity resource or as a storehouse of genetic diversity and habitat for endangered and endemic species; rather, they see it as land to be opened up for cultivation. This is the kernel of the forest's first contradiction: the very *definition* of the resource and for what it is used. People see the forest as a place to extract the raw material needed for subsistence, or, more commonly, commodities to be used in exchange for hard cash. Though the economic system driving it has changed, the pattern of extraction has persisted for hundreds if not thousands of years, and so the people of Sumatra see the rain forest as potential: potential for feeding one's family, for making a living, for getting a leg up, and in some cases for getting rich. You can see their traces everywhere: a footpath cut across a ridge, a skeletal structure built from young trees for camping, a snare set for a tiger or deer (deer meat is sold for about US$5 per kilogram; tigers are poached for their skin, bones, and organs and fetch far higher prices). Though all of these activities are technically illegal, the forest supports this peripheral lifestyle in its vastness, and in turn its vastness leads many to the conclusion that the forest is inexhaustible. Here we can see the second irony in our "forest of contradictions": the opposition between technical illegality, or behaviors that are proscribed by national law, and what James Scott (1977) refers to as the "moral economy of the peasant": sanctions on activities seen as legitimate survival strategies. This also illustrates the messy convergence of priorities formed at different spatial scales; conservation priorities[1] originate from the global and national levels, whereas land clearance and poaching are manifestations of local-level agendas. This scalar *friction*[2] is the forest's third irony. Though the Tiger Protection Team was formed to deal with poaching, the scope of forest clearance for coffee cultivation at Lembah Masurai has become a problem for them, as forest encroachment nibbles away at the tiger's last remaining sanctuary. Complicating this is the fact that forest rangers are outnumbered about a thousand to one, so there is not any easy way for the park to solve the "problem." I was following the Tiger Team to observe their interactions with the encroaching farmers in this uneasy situation.

On the way out of the forest, my team bivouacked at the hut of a hospitable coffee farmer named Bambang. I sat on Bambang's bamboo veranda enjoying the freshly ground brew, harvested directly from his one-hectare plantation.[3] As the sun set across the Masurai Valley, we chatted about the ups and downs of coffee cultivation. Bambang told me that he had been farming coffee in the valley for five years now, and that the profit from the harvest has enabled him to put two of his four children through college. He was especially proud of this fact given that he had only finished primary school himself. Bambang is one of an estimated eighteen thousand farmers currently cultivating coffee here. Most of these farmers come from other provinces and districts, some from as far away as Lampung province, more than five hundred kilometers to the south. They come because of the unparalleled fertility of the soil on the slopes between two extinct volcanoes, Gunung Nilo and Gunung Masurai. Coffee cultivation is very profitable in this area and offers tremendous opportunities for those who otherwise have few, for those who are willing to pull up stakes and move to this out-of-the-way place. Bambang's story was consistent with those of other farmers I had met and interviewed on previous trips to the area.

But what would seem at first glance to be a shining example of smallholder farmers pulling themselves up by their bootstraps is in fact much more complex. The main problem is that most of the land cultivated by the "newcomers" is legally classified as conservation forest and national park. As more and more farmers have moved into the area, the price of titled land has skyrocketed, which pushes newcomers into frontier areas. Tree crops like cinnamon and rubber have been cut down to make room for coffee. And newcomers hoping to cash in have started to move into Kerinci Seblat National Park, the second largest terrestrial protected area in all of Indonesia. The gigantic park protects a wide variety of ecosystems ranging from lowland tropical to montane forest. It is the largest remaining habitat for the critically endangered Sumatran tiger (*Panthera tigris sumatrae*) and protects habitat for hundreds of other species of endemic plants, mammals, birds, reptiles, fungi, and insects. The park also protects the watersheds of three of the largest rivers on Sumatra, which provide water for millions of farmers and households downstream. The park's forests are said to help regulate the local and regional climate and hydrology as well, and it has been designated as a World Heritage Site[4] due to its biodiversity and contribution to carbon sequestration.

The farmers' story is simultaneously compelling and vexing. Compelling because of the outcomes—according to Bambang and the other farmers I interviewed, this was not a case of a massive transnational corporation greedily plundering the rain forest; this was a case of the little guy taking the initiative to improve his lot in life. Vexing because of its seemingly dichotomous juxtaposition of development and conservation. Are these really mutually exclusive goals as they seem to be at Lembah Masurai? When I started my research, this was the ultimate question. I had been trained as an environmental geographer with concentrations in development and conservation. My decision to go to graduate school long ago was motivated by the desire to help in efforts to promote economic improvement without sacrificing the environment or the livelihoods of the poorest, the most vulnerable, and the most marginalized. My idealism was (and still is) rooted in social justice and "green" ethics, and I was convinced that all of these goals could be achieved at the same time. When I started doing fieldwork, though, I realized that it is not always so easy to tell who is right and who is wrong; these are oftentimes subjective considerations that depend on the scale at which you look at a certain issue. Moreover, actors contesting the fundamental meaning of resources as well as issues of access to and control of those resources struggle to frame the issue;[5] different actors attempt to forward different discourses to portray their side as the most "correct."

This simmering concoction of contradictions began to boil over in 2010. The crux of the problem is that the park boundaries are absolutely not subject to negotiation; there are no provisions in the conservation law for agroforestry, cooperative management, or any other kind of compromise. Kerinci Seblat Park is a strict conservation area, and the farmers' activities were a violation of national law. Thus the district government faced increasing pressure from the national government as well as conservationists to take action. In response, on August 31, 2010, Nalim, the headman of Merangin district, where Lembah Masurai is located, issued an edict ordering more than ten thousand people to vacate land they had been cultivating, in some cases for more than a decade, within two months. The immediate trigger was a nongovernmental organization (NGO) report about the level of encroachment into the park. As the eviction date approached, various NGOs attempted to portray the situation in different ways. Each of these NGOs has attempted to portray the situation there in keeping with their agendas and priorities, and the battle over the way the story is framed has been at times quite pitched. On one side there are NGOs that are concerned with environmental issues, including Flora and Fauna International (FFI) and their local NGO clients who make up a regional network of NGOs known as the

Aliansi Konservasi Alam Raya (AKAR) network (Grand Nature Conservation Alliance). These NGOs have long been active in and around Kerinci Seblat National Park and have worked to backstop the park's conservation efforts. One of FFI's main priorities is to protect the Sumatran tiger, whereas
for the most part the members of the AKAR network run programs aimed
at improving the capabilities and livelihoods of local villagers so that they
exert less pressure on the park. FFI and the members of AKAR have been
monitoring events at Lembah Masurai for several years due to its proximity to prime tiger habitat.

On the other hand, the farmers had the advantage of sheer numbers.
There were also several Indonesian NGOs concerned with farmers' rights
advocating and agitating in favor of the farmers. These include Sarekat Pet-
ani Indonesia (SPI), a nationwide group that is active across the archipelago, and the Community Alliance for Pulp and Paper Advocacy (CAPPA).
SPI and CAPPA had also been active in the area, but their activities focused
on organizing and mobilizing the encroaching farmers and helping them
establish a legal basis that would enable them to maintain control over their
land claims. Because of this, these NGOs were at loggerheads with FFI and
AKAR, and the conflict that emerged between the two NGO camps became
quite bitter and ended up erasing the tradition of cooperation that had existed between CAPPA and AKAR. This bitterness stemmed from the nature of the conflict; it was not just between two groups with different philosophies, but rather between people and personalities. One of AKAR's
member NGOs claimed that one of the leaders of CAPPA, who had previously worked closely with AKAR, copied important documents and pictures
from AKAR's computers and then erased the hard drives. These documents
were then leaked to other sources, whereas some photographs were altered
to show AKAR members wielding firearms at Lembah Masurai, suggesting that AKAR was a participant in plans to forcefully remove the villagers.
These pictures spread rapidly and strengthened the argument that farmers'
human rights had been and were continuing to be violated. This story was
then picked up by the World Rainforest Movement and highlighted on their
Web site, which includes a letter and petition addressed to the president of
Indonesia, Susilo Bambang Yudhoyono.

Finally on November 12, a multiagency taskforce, including national
park rangers and district and provincial police, attempted to enforce the order. The task force had the support of the governor of Jambi province as well
as the district headman, but the heads of five villages in the area refused to
cooperate with the eviction. As the officers began burning farmers' pondoks,
they encountered stiff resistance and suddenly found themselves greatly

outnumbered. After several days the taskforce withdrew, the job unfinished. The farmers went on tilling the land. To this day newcomers continue to move into the area to open up more land in the park.

The Lembah Masurai "problem" is far from being solved. A number of contradictions have come together to create a more or less intractable situation at Lembah Masurai. Conflicting priorities originating at different scales (for example, the local and the global) have found their champions in the NGOs that forward contrasting portrayals. These diametrically opposed portrayals of the situation create a rigid bifurcation between development and conservation; a zero-sum game where one side decries a crime against nature while the other depicts a crime against humanity. Is there a mutually agreeable solution to this case where the needs of locals can be balanced with national and global conservation imperatives? Maybe. But the strategies employed by each side at Lembah Masurai and the increasing tension between them make this sort of solution less and less likely with each passing day.

Notes

1. At least, as they are articulated in national park-based conservation. However, many scholars have described and documented systems of *traditional ecological knowledge* (TEK) whereby indigenous groups and/or local communities conserve or carefully manage environmental resources. These conservation imperatives are rooted in local-level priorities. Fikret Berkes's *Sacred Ecology* (2008) is a good place to start for those interested in learning more about TEK.
2. Here I allude to Anna Tsing's (2005) characterization of "friction" as "zones of awkward engagement" stemming from the interaction of actors, agendas, and forces originating from different scales.
3. A hectare is about two and a half acres; a hectare is about the size of two football fields.
4. KSNP, along with Gunung Leuser National Park in northern Sumatra and Bukit Barisan Selatan National Park in southern Sumatra, has been designated the Tropical Rainforest Heritage of Sumatra World Heritage Site.
5. For more on how different actors attempt to frame discourse, see Tanya Li's (2007) outstanding account of development and conservation in Indonesia. Also see Brosius, Tsing, and Zerner (1998).

He'eia Kūpuna Mapping Workshops

Unearthing the Past, Inspiring the Future in Hawai'i

HOKULANI K. AIKAU, NAHAKU KALEI, BRADLEY WONG

As we climbed through yet another hau grove and hacked our way into more California grass, the 90-degree, humid weather was starting to get to us. Being out in He'eia wetland all morning looking for 'auwai and stream diversions was not an easy task. The goal was to find the stream diversions so that we could use the stream water for lo'i crop production. The wetland, once 300 acres of lo'i kalo, was now covered in thick grass 6 feet tall, dense hau bushes, shrubby java plum trees, and monstrous Jobe's tears. There were five of us that day, including Brad, Nahaku, and Christine, trudging through the vegetation trying to find any remnants of the old 'auwai systems that we believed once flowed through the area.

As we finished up, tired, sweaty and hungry, we talked about our struggles throughout the day looking for streams we only knew existed from old maps. As we sat and talked, we agreed that maybe, just maybe, we should ask the people that lived in the area when lo'i still existed— the kūpuna—where the 'auwai were. This was the inception of the He'eia Kūpuna Mapping project.

The Kūpuna Mapping Workshops started out as an attempt to help Kāko'o 'Ōiwi, a Native Hawaiian non-profit organization working to restore lo'i kalo (irrigated terraces for growing taro) on the windward coast of O'ahu, find the 'auwai (irrigation canals) that once connected the lo'i to the streams.[1] We saw the workshops as an important part of the Māhuahua 'Ai o Hoi project, which means to restore food production in Hoi, the ili or land parcel where the first loʻi kalo was restored. From this ʻāina (land), new loʻi are being unearthed and kalo (taro) replanted, nurtured, harvested, and eaten in Hawaiʻi.

The kūpuna (elders, ancestors) we engaged with in the workshops were some of the last living individuals with firsthand knowledge of how the wetland loʻi system in the Heʻeia ahupuaʻa functioned in the first half of the twentieth century.[2] They grew up in a time when Heʻeia still provided food, goods, and livelihoods for the local community. We looked to these kūpuna to provide a historical context that would inform Kākoʻo ʻŌiwi's restoration and development process. This was not an anthropological salvage mission (see Rosaldo 1993); our workshops were intended to reconnect our understanding of the loʻi system while also unearthing the Hawaiian frameworks of the people of old that could be adopted by contemporary Hawaiians. By conducting indigenous ethnographic "genealogical work" (Tengan, Kaʻili, and Fonoti 2010) with the kūpuna, we saw the interviews and maps as repairing the familial ties that bind us to our ancestors, the ʻāina and the kalo.[3]

The site of this restoration project is quite unexpected, because it is taking place on the edge of a suburban neighborhood on the very urbanized island of Oʻahu. Most people do not think of the windward coast of Oʻahu when they think of vast acres of land devoted to loʻi kalo. Hokulani certainly did not when she first visited Māhuahua ʻAi o Hoi in 2009, a few short months after Brad, along with a group of his friends, and under the supervision of an elder from the area who had cleared the land and planted the first kalo. She met Kanekoa Shultz, executive director of Kāhoʻo ʻŌiwi, at a Starbucks across the street from the Windward Mall in Kāneʻohe before following him down Kamehameha Highway through suburban neighborhoods and past King Intermediate School. Just before they reached the bridge that would take them over Heʻeia stream, Shultz pulled off to the side of the road and waved her over. He got out of his truck, opened a gate, returned to his truck and drove through the gate. She followed him and was blown away when she saw acres of green fields framed by the Koʻolau Mountains in the background. From her inexperienced eye, it appeared they had been transported to another time when the land was not burdened by the weight of development and urbanization. What she would learn, however, was that although the land appeared to be pristine, it was in fact inundated by nonnative species of plants and animals that take valuable nutrients and oxygen out of the soil and water, making it nearly impossible for native plants and animals to thrive. More than two hundred acres of invasive grasses would need to be removed before kalo could be replanted.

In bridging the past and the present, we were blending the traditional "talk story" technique with new forms of technologies. The idea for going high-tech came from Christine Feinholz of NOAA Pacific Services Center, who had conducted participatory mapping workshops with community members along the Kona coast on the island of Hawai'i using the mapping program ArcGIS and eBeam technology, an interactive pen that allowed facilitators to turn any wall into a drawing surface using a projector.[4] These new technologies appealed to us because it would allow kūpuna to spatially and temporally situate their stories on maps and aerial photographs of He'eia during different historical periods.[5] For all of us, the intersection of technology with the Hawaiian practice of "talk story" expanded our vision of the possibilities for retrieving important traditional knowledge that could be used to inform the restoration process.

Admittedly, we were a bit nervous about using the technology because we were not sure how the kūpuna would respond to it. Would they find it alienating and would it cause them to shut down? Or, optimistically, would they embrace it? Since the issue of technology was already a worry for us, we felt that we needed to make sure that we establish a trusting relationship with the kūpuna and create a setting that was familiar and comfortable to them. Given that Nahaku, Hokulani, and Christine were not from He'eia, we relied on Brad, with his familial connection to the ahupua'a and his role in Kāko'o 'Ōiwi, to be our lead contact person. Because of his experiences with Kāko'o 'Ōiwi, he was familiar with the needs of the organization and personally knew the kūpuna involved with the Māhuahua 'Ai o Hoi project. Conversely, the kūpuna knew about the work that he had been doing and they trusted him. Building on this relationship with kūpuna and the community was very important, because without their backing and trust, we knew it would be difficult to get sincere participation.

We also chose a venue for the workshops that was geographically close to the homes of the kūpuna. Originally, we wanted to have the workshops at the wetlands, which we hoped would organically inspire memories. However, we decided against the wetland, because we did not want the kūpuna to become distracted by the everyday bustle at the farm. Indeed, the use of "high-tech equipment" including laptop computers, a projector, the eBeam tablet, and power cords for all of the equipment required electricity, which is not available at the farm. All of these questions and concerns pointed to returning to the site where the restoration project began—the Ko'olaupoko Hawaiian Civic Club offices, a place the kūpuna knew well.

On the day of the workshops, the interview team unloaded the equipment at the Hawaiian Civic Club offices and spent the morning setting up. When the kūpuna arrived, we greeted them with aloha and encouraged everyone to make a plate of food. With everyone settled, Brad and Nahaku formally introduced the two members of the NOAA staff who were assisting with the project, Christine Feinholz and Gabrielle Fausel, and described what their roles would be during the workshop.

Once the workshop began, Nahaku assumed the role of facilitator and guided the conversation around the interview questions and topics. Brad was the driver and controlled the computer and projected and manipulated the images on the wall and on the eBeam tablet. Christine was the note taker. Even though eBeam software will record voice audio and screen images at the same time, the note taker is essential, because she would document the major themes that would later be used to contextualize each attribute. Because we were able to simultaneously project images onto a wall and on a tabletop tablet, kūpuna could either stand up and illustrate their stories on images projected on the wall or they could stay seated and work on the tablet. The flexibility of having both options was important because after a brief introduction to the technology, the kūpuna had no problem drawing features on the tablet as they told stories about growing up in a very different environment than the one we have today.[6]

Each interviewee gave us illuminating flashbacks to a time when they were keiki (kids) running around playing outside. Their stories reveal a level of familiarity with the entire ahupuaʻa that for Brad, who was born and raised in the area, was inspiring. The uncles who were well-known fishermen talked about how when they were kids they would leave the house early in the morning not to return home until nearly sundown. They did not pack a lunch because when they got hungry they would get fish and prawns from the stream, build a fire, and make themselves lunch. Because they spent their free time in the wetland, mountains, and in the ocean, they were familiar with the entire ahupuaʻa and knew where ono (delicious) food could be found. These experiences were invaluable as they grew up and used their knowledge of the resources from the land and sea to feed their families. They knew where the best limu (seaweed) could be gathered, where to get oysters, and what time of the year they could and should fish. Their knowledge of the ʻāina was a product of living with the natural world that they interacted with on a daily basis.

The kūpuna also talked about how the land and sea were momona (fertile), filled with enough resources to feed them and their community. For Nahaku, these interviews entirely changed the way that she saw Heʻeia.

Through the stories of the kūpuna she could see their young, bare feet running as fast as they could across kuāuna (the vegetated walls that separate loʻi kalo) producing a vast grid spanning the basin floor. ʻAuwai ran through the backyards of each house, and like sunlight touching one place and then the next, neighbors shared fresh water, filling one ʻauwai for a time and then closing it and filling the next. She saw ʻāina so rich with water and sun that farmers and families alike planted and grew crops in such abundance that you could not possibly eat all that was available, and therefore you shared unrestrictedly with those around you. As a part of a generation that has never eaten an entire meal grown exclusively from her town, Nahaku was really in awe at how extensively she had underestimated the ability of our ʻāina to feed us.

But the vision of the kūpuna was not narrowly focused on feeding their immediate family; they were always thinking about themselves in relationship to the community. For example, one uncle told us about fishing for honu (turtle). He knew that not only would he need enough honu to feed his family but he would also need enough to feed the families along the route to his home. He explained that this was important because it nurtured the relationships in the community; it ensured that when his neighbor went to the ocean to fish, a part of his catch would be shared with them. In a society obsessed with the individual, these stories gave us hope that we can live differently, more cooperatively, that sharing really is caring.

The kūpuna mapping project was important because it reminded us that the land was once momona and can be again if we restore our traditional land-based practices. The stories, memories, and skills the kūpuna shared with us remind Kanaka ʻŌiwi Hawaiʻi (the indigenous people of Hawaiʻi) that we have an inherent, unbreakable bond between ourselves and our ʻāina. The creation of the Hawaiian Islands is generally credited to Papahānaumoku, or Papa who gives birth to islands, and Wākea, the upper province of the sky. The significance of this genealogical account is not only that it communicates the godly forces that gave birth to the Hawaiian archipelago but also, more importantly, that it embodies the familial relationship shared between the Hawaiian people and their beloved lands. This familial relationship sets forth the stewardship responsibilities that Kanaka ʻŌiwi bear as the descendants of Papahānaumoku and Wākea, while inspiring key Hawaiian philosophies of aloha ʻāina (love of the land) and mālama ʻāina (to care for the land), which influence Kanaka ʻŌiwi behavior and attitudes when dealing with ʻāina. It is this mindset that defines the relationship of Hawaiians to ka ʻāina, our land, and ke kalo, the food staple of the Hawaiian people. When taken together, they nourish the lāhui, our nation and community of individuals. Despite the familial ties that bind us to our 'āina, many kānaka are disconnected from the knowledge of our kūpuna and the knowledge that comes directly from the 'āina. The Kūpuna Mapping Workshops help each of us to reconnect with the 'āina, and we are confident that when we listen to the stories our kūpuna have to tell we will be reminded of the power of mālama 'āina; when we care for the land, it becomes abundant again, thus nourishing our souls, our bodies, and our communities.

Notes

1. The workshops were sponsored by Kāko'o 'Ōiwi, the Ko'olaupoko Hawaiian Civic Club, The Nature Conservancy of Hawai'i, and NOAA Pacific Services Center.

2. The He'eia ahupua'a is a pie-shaped land division that extends from the uplands of the Ko'olau mountain range through alluvial and coastal plains, through a restored fishpond to the fringing reefs. In addition to its geographical dimensions, an ahupua'a also represents a historical system for administering land, resources, and responsibilities among the different 'ohana (extended families) living within the region. Although the geographic boundaries of ahupua'a are still recognized, the land management system that governed the use and distribution of resources has transformed with changes to the Indigenous land tenure system and economic realities of contemporary Hawai'i.

3. "Genealogical work" involves "the search for, production, and transformation of connections across time and space" (Tengan, Ka'ili, and Fonoti 2010, 140).

4. The Participatory Mapping project was part of the Hawai'i coastal and marine spatial planning, one of nine National Priority Objectives established by the National Ocean Policy Council. The base participatory mapping methods used in the kūpuna workshops were developed by Mimi D'iorio (as part of her dissertation) from the NOAA Marine Protected Areas Center in Monterey, California, to engage public and private stakeholders in mapping how humans use the ocean environment both for recreation and commerce. These techniques were modified by the NOAA Pacific Services Center and The Nature Conservancy in 2011 to achieve the goal of mapping traditional land management practices as told by the kūpuna of He'eia.

5. We digitized aerial images of the He'eia wetland from 1928, 1958, 1965, 1977, and 2005 and had them available at each workshop.

6. Three different GIS feature types can be created: points, lines, and polygons. Initially, we created files within the geodatabase that included all three of the features to make it easy for us in the post-processing. We quickly

found the three feature types to be cumbersome and difficult to manipulate when using the digital pen. The kūpuna were using the eBeam pen like a regular pen! In following interviews, we changed up the geodatabases to include only the line feature type to avoid any confusion. It also meant a little extra post-processing work, but this made it a lot easier for the kūpuna.

PART 8

Political Encounters

Power, Conflict, Resistance

(*overleaf photo*) Independence activist and traditional leader Benny Wenda gives an address in front of the Morning Star flag—a symbol banned in his native land of West Papua. Wenda is the head of the Free West Papua Campaign, based in England, and has traveled the world raising awareness of issues in his homeland. His organization and many others use digital technologies and social media as platforms to promote their quest for independence. Photo courtesy of the Free West Papua Campaign.

Introduction

FORREST WADE YOUNG

POLITICAL ANALYSIS in contemporary ethnography centers upon questions of power in sociocultural worlds and global conditions. As power relations are increasingly thought to saturate the conditions in which all human events, objects, and lives occur and have meaning, it is common for contemporary ethnographers to politicize all facets of human life and question aspects that are normalized. Political encounters are thus not limited to actions within official political systems of social control and conflict resolution, but occur within everyday practices of power, conflict, and resistance.

The stories of this section represent conflicts over social identities, natural resources, and political territories in Asia and the Pacific Islands. Each reflects upon contemporary acts and social practices of resistance: a topic of increasing prominence following the late twentieth-century seminal work of James C. Scott (1985, 1990). Melisa Casumbal-Salazar's "Narratives of the Vulval Curse in Bontok and Kalinga, Philippines" examines gendered indigenous resistance to the Chico IV dam and hydropower development project in the Cordillera Mountains in the northern Philippines. She argues that the disrobing tactics of women against the development project have become inspirational not only to indigenous groups, but to broader feminist struggles. James Stiefvater's "Digitalizing the *Wantok* System in West Papua" takes readers into the grounds of West Papuan refugee camps in Papua New Guinea and online into their transnational virtual communities, as he reflects on the role of digital social networks in West Papuan struggles for independence from Indonesia. Ty P. Kāwika Tengan's "Embattled

Stories of Occupied Hawai'i" introduces readers to Charles Kānehailua, a Vietnam veteran reinterpreting his life, Hawai'i, and the United States in the context of developing a Hawaiian national identity he had largely forgotten through enculturation as an American soldier. Tengan's story of friendship with Kānehailua illuminates some of the everyday social interaction involved in the deconstruction of American identity within the Hawaiian community. Finally, in "Ta'aroa Is Great, Good and Mā'ohi," Lorenz Gonschor examines the politicization of religion and spirituality in contemporary Tahiti. Proindependence political parties in Tahiti, historically, have been strongly aligned with Protestant Christianity. Gonschor illustrates that a new religious group in Tahiti, Te Hivarereata, is increasingly persuading Tahitian nationalists to reclaim ancestral religious practices and disentangle Christianity from their identity.

Narratives of the Vulval Curse in Bontok and Kalinga, Philippines

MELISA CASUMBAL-SALAZAR

THE BONTOK AND KALINGA are two state-recognized indigenous groups of wet rice subsistence farmers whose ancestral lands are located in the Cordillera Mountains of northern Luzon. In the 1970s and 1980s, they successfully resisted a four-dam hydropower project, called Chico IV. The project, if built, would have inundated dozens of Bontok and Kalinga *ili* (villages),[1] requiring the relocation of approximately fifteen thousand families, or one hundred thousand people, from their ancestral lands (Carino, Carino, and Nettleton 1979, 59).

Bontok and Kalinga villagers organized to oppose the Chico IV project in many ways. Five delegations of leaders lobbied local and national officials. An anti-dam petition campaign gathered the signatures of thousands of villagers throughout the Cordillera, as well as their supporters in Manila, for presentation to the martial law president, Ferdinand Marcos. A well-coordinated media effort targeted international journalists, whose reporting incited European and U.S.-based activists to pressure the World Bank to withdraw support for the Chico IV project (Finin 2008).

Some popular and activist discussions of the resistance, however, focus less on these forms of opposition than on the direct confrontations that occurred between Bontok and Kalinga villagers and Chico IV project engineers working for the Philippine National Power Corporation (NAPOCOR). NAPOCOR workers arrived in the villages accompanied by an armed militia composed of Philippine Army soldiers and Philippine Constabulary police officers. At various sites along the Chico River, zones of confrontation emerged. The soldiers and dam workers were confronted by various tactics.

Villagers—primarily women—tore down dam workers' and soldiers' camp-sites, threw their construction lumber into the Chico River, and created human barricades to prevent them from accessing their equipment. With tremendous support from allies throughout the Cordillera region, in Manila, and internationally, the villagers exerted so much pressure that the Chico IV project was never built.

Dumaloy ang Ilog Chico (And so the Chico River Flows), a children's book published in 1995 by the General Assembly Binding Women for Reforms, Integrity, Equality, Leadership, and Action (GABRIELA), a national coalition of Philippine women's organizations, emphasizes a unique form of resistance by women. The narrator—a Kalinga woman elder from the *ili* of Duppag—describes how a confrontation between villagers, dam workers, and soldiers escalated:

> After several months, the prisoners were released. We all went home rejoicing. But when we returned to our village, we saw that the dam builders had built a bigger and stronger camp. Again, we fought and we fought hard. We used our hands, our feet, our bodies. Some used stones and sticks. Some used arms. But the dam builders were so many, and they had more arms. We could not drive them away.
>
> "We have to stop them," we cried.
>
> Then, in a final gesture of resistance, an old woman cried out, "HWOOO-OW! HWOOOW!" and shed off her clothes. One by one, our mothers, sisters and aunts followed. We held each other by the arms as we all disrobed.
>
> "We are your mothers, sisters and aunts," we told the dam builders and soldiers. "Why are you doing this?"
>
> The dam builders and the soldiers were put to shame. They left covering their faces with their hands. (Carino and Villanueva 1995)

When I first encountered this narrative, I was intrigued. While it is well known that indigenous women all over the world are active in political struggles to protect their ancestral lands, I had not encountered accounts of this particular tactic occurring elsewhere. What was the significance of the women's exposure of sexed body parts in these confrontations? I investigated further, and found a few brief accounts of Bontok and Kalinga women's use of this tactic in the 1970s and 1980s to oppose industrial mining projects as well. In these accounts, the tactic is generally described in the discourse of "breast-baring" or "disrobing." But these brief accounts, primarily published in nongovernmental organization (NGO) newsletters, did not address my many questions. What was the genealogy of this tactic? What made it effective? What does this embodied mode of confrontation suggest about Bontok and Kalinga ethics regarding feminine bodies? How are narratives about this tactic deployed, decades later, for specific political ends?

I did one year of fieldwork in the Cordillera seeking answers to these questions. My archive included ethnographies, historiographies, oral literature, and media accounts gathered from universities, newspapers, and NGOs. Working with translators, I interviewed more than fifty people—scholars, activists, villagers, officials, NGO workers, women, men, elders, and youth. Ultimately, my ethnographic research of Bontok and Kalinga women's corporeal confrontations did not provide a definitive account of their genealogy, practice, or significance. Instead, what emerges is a rich collection of multiple, at times competing, accounts. Some of these accounts complicate and multiply the meanings of the women's mode of embodiment. Others, however, reduce the complexity of this tactic by providing a single explanation of its causality. I argue that the women's tactic is an assertion of political autonomy and territorial control that bears an indeterminate genealogy. The origin of the tactic, however, is not critically important for contemporary Cordillera indigenous activists. Rather, memories of Bontok and Kalinga women's bodily display are important because they vitalize the battles that indigenous peoples are fighting today to protect their ancestral lands from seizure by the state and corporations, for the purposes of extractive development.

According to one activist account:

> Stripping naked [has] been used as a common weapon by women. The act was believed to divert the enemy's attention which would then give the women a chance to attack and strike upon the unsuspecting foes. It is equally believed to neutralize danger of any form. (Tauli-Corpuz 1994, 11)

But besides functioning as a diversionary tactic, how does women's display of sex organs neutralize danger? Another activist emphasized that this is due to a gendered visual prohibition. Gendered visual prohibition strictly disciplines males who look at the unclothed bodies of older generations of female kin. In this account, violations of the visual prohibition trigger unmitigated, unspecifiable misfortune: "Behind this action is the traditional belief that it is taboo for men to see their mothers and grandmothers unclothed, and if they do, they will incur an endless round of bad luck" (Cordillera People's Alliance 2009, 5–6).

Petra Macli-ing, a Bontok woman elder from Mainit *ili* who participated in the opposition against the Chico IV project, has actively opposed
open-pit mining in Bontok territory. She echoes the explanation above for
women's display of their sex organs:

> Being naked as a way to show protest . . . in my own experience,
> some were laughing at us when we did this. But in our culture, to
> look at women's sex organs, to look at where you came from, as well
> as the breast, which feeds people, will bring *bwisit* or extreme mis-
> fortune to anyone. It's a bad omen; something bad will happen to
> you when you look at the female sex organ. So [with Bontok and
> Kalinga] men it worked because you can tell that when they saw us
> naked, they looked too embarrassed and didn't pursue.[2]

Because some of the soldiers and police officers whom Bontok and Kalinga
women confronted were also Bontok and Kalinga, these men were able to
interpret what the women were doing. They understood that women's display of sex organs constituted what we might call a vulval curse. To be subjected to a vulval curse requires a particular male response—a looking away,
a hasty retreat—or the consequences could be catastrophic. The conditions
under which sexed feminine body parts are exhibited for masculine view
are precise. Women subject their reproductive body parts, specifically, to
male visuality under conditions of confrontation. This is how the vulva, in
particular, becomes "a bad omen." This orchestration of visuality is intended
to elicit *bwisit*, extreme misfortune, upon the one who looks. To be subject
to *bwisit* is disruptive because one cannot know what form misfortune will
take or when it will occur. Among those I interviewed, commonly mentioned
forms of misfortune ranged from varieties of illness and all manner of in-
jurious accidents to death.

Women elders in their sixties and seventies, from the Bontok *ili* of Betwagan, recounted a confrontation with prospectors working for a company
identified as Austral Mining. The women were teenagers in the 1950s
and 1960s, when the confrontation was to have occurred. According to Tumrangi Luisa Kanisi and Toy-a Francisca Polon, approximately forty women
from the *ili* of Betwagan and Sadanga—including the mothers and aun-
ties of Kanisi and Polon—confronted a group of perhaps two dozen prospectors and support staff in a loosely planned action. The men of Betwagan and Sadanga villages observed the incident from a higher vantage on
the mountain, "guarding" the women, ready to intervene if the women were
threatened with harm.

Kanisi and Polon stated that women approached the miners where they had begun digging in Sadanga *ili*. According to Kanisi, the women "removed their *tapis* (traditional woven skirt)," while Polon added that they "used their *tapis* to hit the miners."[3] Kanisi and Polon demonstrated this movement by lifting both their arms above their shoulders, their hands positioned as if holding the edge of a *tapis*, and then jerking their arms quickly up and down as if waving or shaking the cloth. Kanisi stated, "there were no pants before and no underwear, so the women's pubic hair and private part was exposed." Polon and Kanisi added that while the women were striking members of the mining team with their *tapis*, they taunted the miners, shouting, "Come mine us! If you don't want to stop mining the land, come mine us!" Kanisi, Polon, and other villagers assert that this action successfully drove away the Austral Mining prospecting team without violent incident. Kanisi and Polon also noted that in this confrontation, the women who removed their *tapis* were strictly women elders of their mothers' and grandmothers' generation, well past childbearing age. Polon explained that this was because younger women could potentially be subjected to violence more easily than older women in such a confrontation.

Bontok anthropologist June Prill-Brett, however, adds that women elders are the ones who exposed themselves in these confrontations because their age affords them greater moral authority than younger women possess. According to Prill-Brett's research, "Male and female elders are given the highest prestige due to their closeness to the ancestors, and their rich experiences in life. Old women, particularly, are known for their ability to communicate with the spirits of the dead as medians (*mensip-ok*) during public rituals" (Prill-Brett 2004, 17). She takes issue though with the explanation that women's exposure of their reproductive organs was effective because of a cultural taboo. She argues that there is no gendered visual prohibition that strictly disciplines men from seeing the unclothed bodies of older generations of female kin. She stated to me,

> It's very misleading to [describe this act as] as disrobing, because women have always been disrobed, especially when they work! And men cannot help but see the bodies of their women, their children, any kind of womenfolk. [Those who argue] that it is *inayan* or taboo to look at your mother's or grandmother's body, this is misleading. Because when women cross the river—and indeed, you have to cross rivers whether you are in Kalinga or Bontok—they remove all their clothes so they don't get them wet. And I've seen when we are going or coming from the fields, during a harvest, and it's so

hot, when we pass by a waterfall or a spring, the men are there carrying the baskets full of the harvest, and the women will just go and
start washing, washing their [vaginas]![4]

Prill-Brett thus takes exception to activist accounts of the vulval curse that
locate its power in a prohibitive visuality; that is, belief that it is taboo for
men to see their mothers and grandmothers unclothed. For her, there is
no generalized prohibition on looking at women's exposed *bodies,* but on
looking at women's *vulvas,* specifically, when these are exposed under conditions of confrontation. For Prill-Brett, as for others I interviewed, *lascivious*
looking at bodies is prohibited as a general rule.

In Kalinga oral literature and ethnographies, however, there is documentation of the kind of *tapis*-waving and exposure of sex organs described
by Kanisi and Polon above. Francisco Billiet has written extensively on the
Kalinga *ullálim. Ullálim* are epic chants that recount events—including jour-
neys, battles, head-taking raids, and romances—featuring southern Kalinga
gods and ancestors. They are performed during feasts, particularly those
celebrating the successful negotiation or reaffirmation of trade and peace
agreements. In chants, accounts of Kalinga women cursing their enemies
by removing and waving their *tapis* refer to this practice as *ikallakallay-abna.*
Billiet and Lambrecht observe, however, that *ikallakallay-abna* do not appear exclusively in *ullálim,* but are a common practice in situations in which
Kalinga villagers have been killed and vengeance is required. According to
them, "in such instances, many women of the village go to the house of the
person who was killed and from the window wave and swing their skirt in
the direction of the killer's village, while they utter [various] cursing formu-
las" (Billiet and Lambrecht 1970, 118).

While I do not want to suggest that the practice of *ikallakallay-abna* is
strictly synonymous with the vulval curse as practiced in the 1970s and 1980s,
one thing both practices have in common is the power accorded to women
in exposing their sexual organs under conditions of confrontation. Bontok
and Kalinga women's embodied form of confrontation with hydropower,
mine workers, and soldiers has only been effective in conflicts that have not
been heavily militarized. Nonetheless, in an era in which Filipino women's
bodies are increasingly instrumentalized for their labor as care workers (nan-
nies and maids) or as sex workers, the deployment of their bodies offers us
another way of understanding the potential power of the Filipino feminine
body—in particular, the femininity of women elders. The women's tactic
mobilizes the feminine body as a weapon to assert political autonomy and

defend territory. They do not expose their bodies to be commodified for domestic or sexual labor.

This is in part why Bontok and Kalinga women's stories are important to contemporary Cordillera indigenous activists, as well as to Philippine feminists who are not indigenous. The stories of women, such as those memorialized in *Dumaloy ang Ilog Chico*, are used to advance Philippine feminism more broadly, by narrating a triumph in which all the nation's children can take pride. These stories vitalize contemporary struggles of Bontok, Kalinga, and other Cordillera peoples to protect their lands from expropriation by the state and private capital for the purposes of geothermal, hydropower, and commercial mining projects today.

Notes

1. The village, or *ili*, constitutes the largest political unit within Bontok and Kalinga modes of governance. "*Ili* citizenship" is established by birth, marriage, and permanent residence. *Ili* range in size from six hundred to three thousand people (Prill-Brett 1987).
2. Petra Macli-ing, interview by author, April 26, 2009.
3. Tumrangi Luisa Kanisi, interview by author with translation by Judith Banga-an and Joanne Panay, January 23, 2010.
4. June Prill-Brett, interview by author, March 1, 2010.

Digitalizing the *Wantok* System in West Papua

JAMES STIEFVATER

FIELDWORK IS AN IMPORTANT, and often required, component of social science research. But what, then, is to become of the researcher who is unable to make it to the field? For various reasons fieldwork is sometimes not an option, due to budget and time restraints. Real or perceived dangers to health and well-being also can discourage one from fieldwork. In the face of such challenges, "digital ethnography" (see Miller and Horst 2012; Underberg and Zorn 2013) is reshaping the way one can undertake research by detaching the field from a specific physical location and bringing it to the researcher via new technologies. As indigenous communities throughout the world, and especially those in the Pacific Islands region, become more engaged with digital communication technologies, traditional social networks like the *wantok* system are simultaneously digitalizing into transnational networks. This has increased connective capacity between rural, urban, and diasporic populations. It has also enabled those engaged in political resistance to circumvent media censorship in order to share their political struggles with the rest of the world, as is the case of the people of West Papua. The digital expansion of the *wantok* system has created a matrix for doing ethnographic and other forms of fieldwork ex situ.

Anyone wanting to do fieldwork in the Southwest Pacific (New Guinea, Solomon Islands, and Vanuatu) should be familiar with the concept of the *wantok* system. Literally translated from Neo-Melanesian Pidgin, *wantok* means "one talk" and refers to one's ability to speak the same language as another. The *wantok* system is described as having "five significant recurrent characteristics," which are, "(a) a common language, (b) common kinship group, (c) common geographical area, (d) common social associations or religious groups, (e) common belief based on the principle of mutual reciprocity" (Mannan 1978, 200). In contemporary times, *wantok* includes speakers of three major forms of Neo-Melanesian Creole: Tok Pisin (Papua New Guinea), Pijin (Solomon Islands), and Bislama (Vanuatu). These connections are important at the individual level as they allow one to gain and use "social capital" (de Renzio 2000, 22), but are also vital to personal, family, and group security both in rural and urban areas. The *wantok* system has been denigrated as a social structure that allows for nepotism, tribalism, and "petty corruption" like "bribery, tax evasion, fraud and forgery, and . . . the use of public facilities for private business by *wantoks*" (Bui 1999, 3). While it may be seen to hinder the implementation of Western modes of government or the efficiency of Weberian bureaucracy, the system is not merely a means of getting favors or free passes and can be useful to one who is trying to meet new people or find out information. It allows one to make connections with others through a common acquaintance or relative. As digital and communications technologies expand across the globe, the *wantok* system itself is undergoing a process of digitalization.

I became passionate about issues in West Papua, many of which are inherently political, as I learned more about my wife's homeland of Papua New Guinea (PNG). I have always been interested in maps and was struck by the number of maps of the Pacific Region that represented the political border between Papua New Guinea and West Papua as a natural cultural divide between Asia and the Pacific. I became aware that hidden within these maps was a violent cartography (see Shapiro 2007) that masked several decades of human rights abuses committed against the West Papuan peoples since they were taken over by Indonesia in 1963. It has been recognized as a place of colonialism, environmental exploitation, and genocide (see Ondawame 1996), and associated with a regional "Arc of Instability" in Melanesia (see Reilly 2000).

The history of West Papua is complex, but conflict and resistance in West Papua are generally centered on the dispute over Indonesia's claim to sovereignty and its denial of the right of indigenous peoples to a fair referendum of self-determination.[1] Indonesia declared independence in 1945, just after the end of World War II. After four more years of war to assert its independence, this declaration was acknowledged by their colonizer—the Netherlands—in 1949; however, the Dutch wanted to retain their New Guinea Territory and prepare it to be an independent state of its own (Chauvel 2005, 61). After continued disputes over West New Guinea, the United Nations intervened with a plan that would allow for Indonesia to administer the area as well as guarantee the indigenous population a chance to vote on whether to become independent or to join Indonesia. That referendum finally occurred in 1969. While it was referred to as the Act of Free Choice, it was anything but free. One thousand men were handpicked by the Indonesian leadership to vote on behalf of all West Papuans, a population which was probably more than eight hundred thousand. Even though violence and coercion during the vote was noted by UN observers, the Act of Free Choice, now often referred to as the Act of No Choice, was accepted by the United Nations General Assembly on November 19, 1969.[2]

Violence has been the Indonesian policy of choice when dealing with indigenous West Papuans who question the sovereignty of the Jakarta-based government over their lands or the Act of Free Choice. Estimates of the number of West Papuans killed vary, but many sources state that as many as five hundred thousand people have been killed there since 1969 (Robinson 2012). Lucrative natural resource extraction projects (most notably the American-owned Freeport-McMoRan Copper and Gold mine), environmental degradation, and the continuation of transmigration (the uncontrolled and often government-sponsored migration of Indonesians to West New Guinea) have also become points of contention between West Papuans and the government of the Republic of Indonesia. The international community has usually opted not to get involved in what Indonesia deems its internal affairs, and many Western states, including the United States, have entered into agreements for military training and arms sales. There is little doubt that the presence of natural resources such as gold, copper, timber, and oil greatly influence such decisions.

My own experience in working with West Papuans developed through the virtual *wantok* communities I joined through digital ethnography of Internet resources on West Papua and friendships I gained in Hawai'i through my connection to New Guinea. For example, on MySpace, the precursor to Facebook, I met and befriended Kathy, a West Papuan who was living on O'ahu in Hawai'i. She had recently relocated to the island from Port Moresby and was looking for *wantoks*. She saw that I had posted images supporting the West Papuan movement, contacted me, and our families quickly became friends. Our common interest and beliefs in West Papuan freedom, my marriage to a Papua New Guinean, and our shared ability to speak Tok Pisin created a new connection within the *wantok* system, which allowed me to gain new insights. As a West Papuan refugee who had been born and raised in PNG, she was able to give me a sense of the feelings of the refugee community and opened the door for me to be able to continue learning about their plight: first through e-mails to her family, then by meeting them in their refugee camp in Port Moresby.

Kathy's experiences and views were very helpful in my work, but equally important were the connections I was able to make through her. She agreed to arrange an opportunity for me to meet her family and the rest of the people in a West Papuan refugee camp in Port Moresby, Papua New Guinea. This connection was especially important in allowing me to meet with the group, as they are sensitive to visitors. As migrants to PNG, West Papuan refugees tread carefully. The time of my visit in 2008 was particularly trying for them as they had just been evicted from their previous campsite, where they had lived for many years, by the PNG landowners, and had also run into serious problems at another site, leading them to resettle yet again near the neighborhood of Gerehu. Further complicating their settlement in PNG is the fact that West Papuan refugees are restricted by the PNG government from participating in political activism and receive very few, if any, government services.

Kathy's sister picked up my wife and me and drove us to the camp, which happened to be nearby. They were expecting me and were displaying the West Papuan flag, called the Bintang Kejora[3] or Morning Star, which has been banned in their homeland. Many of them had been in PNG for as long as thirty years, yet they were still living in canvas tents with blue tarpaulin extensions. For the group of 148 people, there was one water faucet, located at ankle level on the back wall of a government-owned building. From this building, they also had a single outlet with an extension cord, into which was plugged a Macintosh computer, sitting on a table with young people crowded around. There was no Internet connection, but the computer was used to listen to music, watch DVDs, and play games. The youth of the camp had also used it to produce a short video detailing their situation. They gave me a copy.

I did not know what to expect, but the leaders of the group invited me to sit down and we had a discussion lasting several hours. I was able to ask them questions about how they had arrived, why they left, and how they lived. I listened as they spoke in Tok Pisin and English about what they desired for their homelands and their thoughts on Special Autonomy. I asked about relations within the camp, because fighting between groups (or tribal fights, as they are often referred to) can be found at various times in PNG. The refugees told me that traditional affiliations were not a cause of conflict within their group, because their belief in freedom for their homeland united them, despite the difficulties of their situation.[4]

Just as I was curious about their lives, they too were curious about me and asked me some questions. One question was poignant and still stands out. One young man identified himself as a member of the Organisasi Papua Merdeka (OPM)—West Papuan Liberation Organization—the armed wing of the independence movement. He said he was willing to lay down his life for his country and was interested to know what tactics would best bring the plight of West Papua to the attention of the world. We discussed the dangers of being labeled a terrorist and the power of sharing information and images by means of digital technology. Images of the Dili Massacre in what is now East Timor had a major influence in changing international support of Indonesia's claim to that territory. I told him that I imagine significant potential for change if peaceful protestors and citizens armed with cameras are able to capture and disseminate the abuses experienced in their homeland to the world through file-sharing sites and their *wantok* networks. Interestingly, over time many videos documenting such incidents have been made public.

While I was privileged to be able to meet with one group of refugees in Port Moresby, significant groups of refugees also reside in other parts of PNG, as well as in Vanuatu, Australia, the Netherlands, and the United Kingdom. As I explored the Internet for more resources, I found a very active and strong digital presence supporting the West Papuan cause. Benny Wenda is a chief, activist, and musician and he also heads the Free West Papua Campaign, based in England. Despite objections from the Indonesian government, the Free West Papua Campaign opened offices in both Oxford, England, and in the Dutch city of The Hague in 2013. These offices allow them to organize protests and awareness campaigns as well as to maintain an almost constant presence on the Internet via Facebook, their Web site, and other social media and news outlets. Posts highlight speeches and concerts given by Wenda, events such as regular protests at the Indonesian Embassy in London, links to news stories, as well as original news pieces. Some of those pieces are obtained through e-mail from ad hoc correspondents in West Papua and often contain graphic photographs of tortured individuals.

Numerous other groups exist on Facebook and most have resources and contacts that are at least conversant in the English language—a major bonus to one who is unable to learn through language immersion that would take place in a field setting. I personally maintain a Facebook group called the West Papua Association of the Americas. This group is dedicated to the peaceful resolution of decolonization issues in West Papua and seeks to disseminate information and news, mostly garnered from Internet sources, to interested people residing throughout the Americas or territories claimed by any American state. After researching West Papua issues using the Internet and social media sources, I realized that there were currently no online efforts to bring these issues to the knowledge of the peoples living in the Americas. At the time of publication the group has just over one hundred members; many who have joined have expressed increased levels of interest and concern as they see posts in their newsfeeds. Friends—especially Pacific Islanders, academics, and university students—have taken notice and have become more aware and active in human rights organizations as a result of this and other groups.

Digital technology, especially social media, is changing the way West Papuans resist, and may be the key to helping them realize the goal of political independence. The adoption of communication technologies now allows for researchers to get access to information and interlocutors that would be much more difficult if they were to try to physically enter West Papua. Furthermore, to do physical fieldwork would give the researcher only a limited view of the struggle. Fieldwork from afar allows one to digitalize the *wantok* system and communicate with transnational resistance groups and virtual communities both inside and outside of West Papua, allowing one to gain a broader, more nuanced perspective.

It is in the field that theories, be they anthropological, political, or sociological, are developed and empirically challenged, refuted, and remade. Interestingly, the globalization of postmodern communication technologies is reshaping the way one can engage the field. It is decentering the field and enabling postgeographic fieldwork. This has certainly been the case in my own experiences as I have researched political events and resistance in West Papua. Ironically, in many ways, fieldwork can be increasingly accomplished outside of the field.

Notes

1. For more detailed descriptions, see Scott and Tebay (2005), Ondawame (1996), King (2004), and Elmslie (2002).
2. For a detailed chronology of events in West Papua's history, see http://www.papuaweb.org/chrono/files/kp.html.
3. The Morning Star flag can also be referred to as Bintang Fajar in the Bahasa Indonesia language.
4. For more on the creation of Pan-West Papuan nationalism, see Chauvel (2005).

Embattled Stories of Occupied Hawai'i

Ty P. Kāwika Tengan

On March 11, 2010, I was a part of a panel titled "Occupied Hawai'i: Issues of Nationhood and Colonialism" held at the Kamakakūokalani Center for Hawaiian Studies. It was an evening talk at the center's open-air auditorium that blends Hawaiian architectural designs, anticolonial artwork, and modernist building materials. Both the panel and the center were products of the Hawaiian sovereignty and decolonization movements that had dramatically reshaped political, cultural, and academic discourse in Hawai'i since the 1970s. Whereas the transnational tourism industry sells an image of happy natives and white sandy beaches, cultural nationalist discourse foregrounds Kānaka 'Ōiwi (Indigenous Hawaiian) resistance to the illegal occupation of the Hawaiian Kingdom (Trask 1999; Sai 2008). Indeed, the title of the larger symposium of which our panel was a part was "The Place of Hawai'i in American Studies," which was really more a question than a statement. Most of the audience was well aware of the contested status of Hawai'i as a U.S. state. As the organizers wanted to reach a broader audience, they also arranged for 'ŌLELO, the local cable-access station, to record the event.

For my part, I spoke of my early research on Native Hawaiian soldiering and U.S. Empire. My previous research had examined the rearticulation of Hawaiian masculinity in the Hale Mua, a Native Hawaiian men's group (Tengan 2008). I argued that assertions of Hawaiian male warriorhood reflected the gendered dimensions of settler colonialism and Indigenous decolonization. As a Kānaka 'Ōiwi anthropologist who was both a member and scholar of the Hale Mua, my kuleana (rights and responsibilities) led me to strive for an ethnographic research and writing practice that would serve the Lāhui Hawaiʻi (Hawaiian Nation) (Tengan 2005). In my new project, however, I was conducting a different kind of "homework," since I did not serve in the U.S. military like the Hawaiian men I was now interviewing. How would their notions of "service" and "nation" differ from mine? Did they perceive any contradictions in taking up the same arms that were used to overthrow our Queen in 1893?

With a capacity crowd of 150 students, faculty, and community members of all ages and genders, a lively question-and-answer period followed our panel. At its conclusion, a late-middle-aged Hawaiian man approached the microphone and stated, "Tengan, I goin' ask you about the military." After a long pause, he asked, "In the war right now, the stupid war in Iraq—another Vietnam, right—who's watching our boys in the combat zone? Who's watching over them, making sure they got the right weapon, and the weapon work?" He described how he, as a "D-minus" graduate of the Waiʻanae High School on Leeward Oʻahu, was arrested for vagrancy and given the choice of either going to jail or going to war. He entered the Marines and went to Vietnam. There he found himself on the front lines with other "minorities" and with malfunctioning rifles. Years later, he entered college to obtain his bachelor's and master's degrees in Hawaiian language. On the latter degree, he reflected on the dual meaning of the term: "What is that word 'master'—'white man'? Plantation name?" He bemoaned his "indoctrination in the American system" that led him to be willing to "die for that [American] flag," which he later discovered "was da flag that occupied my [Hawaiian] country."

Significantly, he pointed his critique at us and charged, "You guys lied to us from the time we were in kindergarten. . . . Start teaching truth, yeah." He went on to call us all draft dodgers who went to college to escape the horrors of war, including the posttraumatic stress disorder (PTSD) that he now suffers. Finally he returned to his original question, "So who's takin' care of da Hawaiians over dea in Iraq? You guys makin' sure da guys, you guys—are you doing your research so dat somebody can go ovah deah and make sure dat their weapon work?" You could hear a pin drop as no one dared move. I slowly reached for the microphone in front of me and responded, "Uncle, I want to acknowledge everything you said here. You asked me why I'm doing my research. It's so that we don't have any more guns put into our young Hawaiians' hands."

I spoke briefly with Kānehailua after the panel to introduce myself and gauge his interest in further talking story. Though we had an engaging discussion, we did not have that follow-up until seven months later. In

October 2010, I was sitting in my office preparing for my introductory cultural anthropology class at the University of Hawai'i at Mānoa. We were reading Karen Ito's *Lady Friends* (1999), and that day we were covering her chapter that discussed the four emotional complexes she argues are central to Hawaiian definitions of self and other: the cultural ideal of aloha (generosity, love, sympathy); its failing as exhibited in lili (retention, jealousy, stinginess); an internally directed failing manifest in shame-guilt; and an externally directed failing exhibited in hurt-anger (Ito 1999, 81). Just then, as if to electronically manifest an example of all four, I received an e-mail from Kānehailua that read:

> Aloha Kāwika,
>
> I'd like to apologize for my off the wall comments I made at the panel discussion in March of this year at Center for Hawaiian Studies. It was not directed at you or any of the members of the panel but I was indirectly talking to anybody in the audience who represented the present colonizers. In that talk, I was trying to tell of my bad and shocking experience in the U.S. military and how I feel about our people who like me are ignorantly becoming victims to the American military propaganda. I know that . . . some of our people who are presently in the U.S. military enlisted with no idea of what they were getting into. I think if they are knowledgeable of their place in this present system, they would probably take another route in life, like mea Hawai'i [Hawaiian things], instead of making a sacrifice to the wrong government. Thank you for your comment after my unpolished talk and my lack of composure. Please understand that my intention was to support what the panel was saying especially the subject that you covered. Forgive and kala mai ia'u. No'u ka hewa. Na'u Na Charles Kānehailua.

We had not spoken since I went up to him after the panel to introduce myself and talk story more. His e-mail to me was the first I had heard from him since, and as soon as I was done reading it, my phone rang. When I answered, the voice said, "Kāwika, this is Charles Kānehailua." He then started to share what he was feeling—a kaumaha (heaviness, burden) after seeing himself for the first time on the program that was aired on the 'ŌLELO cable channel just the other day. He felt shame and anger at himself and needed to apologize to me, to the panel, and to everyone. I told him that an apology was not needed for anything. I emphasized that I knew he was not really talking to us, but rather to the "system" and the state that put him in harm's way and in the situation that he had found himself.

I also acknowledged that his voice was the one that people in Nānākuli and Wai'anae, predominantly working-class and Native Hawaiian, would listen to—not mine. For that reason, he should not want to change what he said or be sorry for it. Kānehailua shared with me that, in fact, one of his cousins had come up to him a few days after that program was aired and said, "Eh, Chucky, I seen you on TV last night!" His cousin went on to say that he was so moved that he broke down and cried. He said he did not know what that panel was about before, but he wanted to watch it now.

Kānehailua said he wanted to learn from me and wanted my help in preparing him to speak in public. He said he had a hard time with the words, and with the PTSD. He explained that one of the main reasons he came back to school to earn his BA and now pursue his MA in Hawaiian language was so that he could tell his stories as a Hawaiian and as a Vietnam veteran. After the war, he worked at the post office before coming back to school with his daughter who was also pursuing an MA in Hawaiian language. In fact he had two daughters who were pursuing higher education, both graduates of the private college-preparatory Kamehameha Schools for Native Hawaiians. He and his brother had an opportunity to go to Kamehameha in the 1960s, and he regretted his decision not to attend. At the time, the school implemented a military education for the boys. He recalled that when he got the letter of admission, he turned it down, telling his mother that "they wear uniforms and they give you demerits." She said, "Demerits, what is that?" He replied, "I don't know, but it don't sound good! I no like demerits!" He now thought that had he gone, perhaps he might have been "officer material."

When Kānehailua finally went off to boot camp in San Diego in 1968, he was part of an all-Hawai'i platoon of recruits. He recalled that he was an excellent marksman, shooting "high expert" the entire week. On qualification day though, a "big hand" came out of the sky in the form of a gust of wind and "slapped" a mix of dust and bugs into his eyes, messing up his shot. He said it was a good thing that happened; otherwise, he would have made it "personal" if he went to war as a sniper.

Kānehailua spent ten months in Vietnam and was hit three times in combat. Yet even deeper than those wounds were the injuries he suffered at the hands of his fellow Americans. In one story he recalled suffering discrimination when visiting a base camp for an engineer unit. He and his fellow infantrymen (most of whom were also minorities) were forced to eat out of their helmets, because they were denied plates when they came out of the jungle dirty and stinking. Later that same base was bombed while his unit was out in the field. Payback—he thought. He laughed and said how crazy it seems that he could find that funny, but that was the survivor in him—that was how he had to operate in survival mode.

Yet one of the greatest challenges he faced in the jungle was a spiritual and cultural one. While in Vietnam, he said there was a Native American scout in his unit who made them stop at one point because he thought something was going to happen. He started "dancing" like "powwow," and so Kānehailua jumped in behind him. He turned around and said, "Charlie, what are you doing?" "I saw you doing the powwow, and ever since I was a little boy watching cowboys and Indians I wanted to do powwow," he replied. His companion said, "I'm Indian, this is my religion. What are you?" "I'm Catholic," Charlie replied. "I thought you were Hawaiian," was the response. Kānehailua said that this was the worst thing his friend could have said; it was worse than a bullet, and it went right through his heart. When he thought about it later, he said he wanted to kill him. The scout then said, "That's all right, I forgive you. They did something to you guys. But I'm Indian and I know my religion." That memory still stung when he recalled it over the phone.

Kānehailua said that today he is active in his church, but since they do not recognize Hawaiians or their situation of colonization, it is a struggle for him. He is always looking somewhere for the answer—in church, in school, in the language, and in the culture—to who he is and what his way forward is. He represents many Hawaiian men who ended up in the military and are looking to find their way. That is why he appreciated my work and my book on Hawaiian men (Tengan 2008). He said that when he came back, he was asking, where are the men? God told him, "You da man." He said he was not ready, but that was God's plan. He struggles with school but persists. Now he is being asked to give motivational talks to the students at Nānākuli where he is from. He says he tries to discourage boys from going into the military, but knows that a lot do, so he just tries to prepare them. But he agrees with my political and intellectual project, and he would like to share more of his experiences and get others like him who might want to talk to do so. He even mentioned that he just convinced a Tengan that he served with (who like me is Hawaiian-Okinawan from Maui, though I do not know if we are related) to come home from Guam and get help for his PTSD and claim the veteran's benefits that are due to him for his disability.

We spoke for nearly an hour before hanging up. I sat in my office overwhelmed by a complex of emotions that ranged from sadness and anger to joy and sympathy. In light of the fact that I was reading about those very emotions in Ito (1999) and preparing to lecture on them in class, I could not see his e-mail and call at that time as a "coincidence." I decided that I needed to show the video of the panel discussion and his response in my anthropology class and talk about the exchange that I had just had. I called him back and asked for his permission to do so, and I also invited him to come to my ethnic studies class on Hawai'i and the Pacific in a couple of days when, as fate would also have it, I was planning to talk about my research on Native Hawaiian veterans. He allowed me to use his video in class and agreed to come up to visit my students. He said that it was good to get people to know his story. In fact, that was one of the more moving statements he made in our earlier conversation. He wanted to go back so he could tell his story. He said it with tears, and explained how he had been writing these short stories on his own. His family and Hawaiian language teachers like No'eau Warner had all encouraged him to continue his higher education, which he did. We also got to speaking ma ka 'ōlelo makuahine (in our mother tongue), and we made connections through our shared membership in the Hawaiian language community. At the end of this second conversation, he gave me permission to use the film in my class and agreed to come to my ethnic studies class later that week.

Since then we have continued to talk story and work together to find ways of telling his mo'olelo (story). The perfect opportunity for collaboration came in 2011 with the visit to Hawai'i of StoryCorps, a national nonprofit oral-history project that allows regular people to sit down and record interviews to be archived at the American Folklife Center at the Library of Congress. Kānehailua and I recorded some of his stories, which now have the potential of reaching an audience even broader than the 'ŌLELO program. He has also continued to visit my classes to share his stories, which he sometimes struggles tremendously with as the memories of pain and anguish threaten to overtake him. In these battles, humor is usually his most effective weapon for disarming his demons.

This brief synopsis of our relationship points to the fraught political and ethical terrain of doing ethnographic research with at least one Native Hawaiian veteran. For him, the process of coming to consciousness and awareness of his indigenous history—one characterized by dispossession and betrayal—is at odds with a U.S. military ideology of self-sacrifice for country and meritorious advancement through the ranks. And just as clear distinctions separate the enlisted men and women from the officers, so too do class and educational differences set apart professors and scholars from military personnel. Yet none are completely separated by these histories and social relations. On that count, shared stories—those that are produced in dialogue and for the purpose of not only conveying information but also nurturing relationships and creating mutual understandings—play a particularly important role in both enacting and transforming indigenous and anthropological (and indigenous anthropological) identities.

Ta'aroa Is Great, Good and Mā'ohi

Nationalism and Spiritual Identity in Contemporary Tahiti

Lorenz Gonschor

IN 2001, I started documenting and analyzing the contemporary movement to revitalize ancient Tahitian religion and its relations and conflicts
with Christianity within the framework of a political independence movement. My studies focus on Te Hivarereata, a religious organization based
in Hamuta Valley, Tahiti,[1] founded by Sunny Moana'ura Walker—a former
French Navy officer and deputy leader of a Tahitian proindependence
political party, in 2000.[2]

Tahiti has been inhabited for more than a thousand years by Polyne-
sians who call themselves Mā'ohi. It is a landscape filled with spiritual
reference points, including various natural features imbued with *mana*
(spiritual power) as well as numerous places of worship constructed of dry
stone masonry called *marae*. Worshipped entities included the supreme
God Ta'aroa and several other major deities, as well as *tāura* (totemic family
guardians) and deified ancestors. *Tahu'a* (priests) led the *marae* rituals and
gave spiritual advice to the *ari'i* (chiefs) (Henry 1928). In 1815 Pomare II, an
ari'i converted by missionaries of the London Missionary Society (LMS),
defeated his traditionalist rival Opuhara, and the whole population of Tahiti
formally converted to Protestantism.

Interestingly, Protestant Christianity eventually became not only an
element but a central pillar of Mā'ohi identity. When from 1842 Tahiti gradually came under the rule of initially Catholic, and later secular and largely
agnostic France, Protestant Christianity became a place of refuge for the
Mā'ohi. It was a context in which they kept their language alive and resisted
French cultural assimilation. Distribution of the Tahitian Bible to virtually

every household and Sunday schools at the mission stations were central in preserving the Tahitian language.

With the emergence of a modern anticolonial nationalist movement after World War II, Christianity consequently became a central factor therein. Proceeding in this logic, it is not surprising that the largest present-day proindependence party, Tāvini Huira'atira Nō Te Ao Mā'ohi (Serving the People of the Mā'ohi World), headed by former French Polynesia president Oscar Temaru, uses a cross and the motto *Te Atua Tā'u Fatu* (God Is My Lord) as its party emblem. The successor to the LMS mission, which is still the largest denomination in the country, has itself incorporated Polynesian nationalism into its theology over the past several decades. It was even renamed from 'Ētārētia 'Evaneria nō Porinetia Farāni (Evangelical Church of French Polynesia) to 'Ētārētia Porotetani Mā'ohi (Mā'ohi Protestant Church) in 2004 (*Tahitipresse*, August 16, 2004).

The new trend of the Protestant Church to identify itself explicitly as a Mā'ohi institution is most prominently represented by the theological writings of the late linguist and theologian Turo a Raapoto (1948–2014). Contrary to earlier, more directly missionary-influenced native theologians who saw the process of conversion as a change from "pagan darkness" to "Christian enlightenment," for Raapoto there is no longer an antagonism between the traditional religion and Christianity. Instead, he has developed what Tahiti-based French anthropologist Bruno Saura (1998) sees as a syncretistic and millenarian liberation theology. It identifies the Mā'ohi as one of God's chosen people and equates the God of the Bible with the ancient supreme God Ta'aroa. In his 1989 tract *Poroì i te nūnaa māìtihia e te Atua* (Message to the People Chosen by God), Raapoto states:

> *'Ua fa'a'ite te Atua, te Tumu Nui iāna i te Mā'ohi i te i'oa ra o Ta'aroa, mai iāna i fa'a'ite iāna i te 'Īterā'era i te i'oa ra o 'Iehova. Teie 'Iehova tā te mau mitionare i 'āfa'i mai, 'o Ta'aroa ia i fafau i te Mā'ohi i tāna faufa'a, 'oia te aroha 'e te here ei niu nō te fenua.*
>
> God, the Great Origin, has revealed himself to the Mā'ohi in the name of Ta'aroa, while he revealed himself to the Israelites in the name of Jehovah. This Jehovah, whom the missionaries brought here, is Ta'aroa who promised the Mā'ohi his good deeds, which are love and compassion as a foundation for the land. (Raapoto 1989, 45–46)

What Raapoto thus attempts is to reconcile his faith as a Christian with his cultural identification as a Mā'ohi and his commitment to an anticolonial liberation struggle. Since they are the chosen people, to whom God spoke in the form of Ta'aroa, he urges the Mā'ohi to return to the original ways of worshipping Ta'aroa in order to achieve salvation, since *"hou te mau mitionare, 'ua tae 'ē mai na te 'Evaneria a te Atua iō te Mā'ohi"* (before the Missionaries, God's Gospel had already arrived amongst the Mā'ohi) (Raapoto 1989, 45).

Until around the time of my initial fieldwork, some forms of syncretistic Christianity similar to that promoted by Raapoto were common among most Mā'ohi identifying themselves as traditional practitioners. Around the turn of the millennium, however, a movement arose that articulates Mā'ohi cultural identity through a complete break with the religion of the missionaries. The first organization to systematically pursue this agenda, called Te Hivarereata (the clan flying into the clouds), was founded in the year 2000 by Sunny Moana'ura Walker.

Walker was born in 1955 on his mother's home island of Rurutu.[3] Among his ancestors on his father's side is the high-ranking chiefly family Ma'i of the island of Huahine, some lesser *ari'i* families, and, somewhat ironically, also the LMS missionary John M. Orsmond. His mother descends from Polynesian missionaries serving in Vanuatu. Moana'ura Walker's great-grandfather William F. Walker was a Scottish settler who acquired large tracts of land in Hamuta Valley. Raised in the Protestant Church, Walker's interest increasingly extended toward non-Christian religions during the 1990s. Initially turning toward Eastern philosophies, especially Taoism, he soon realized the similarities with the traditional religion of his ancestors and began studying the latter (*La Dépêche* 2012). Concurrently involved in politics, he began to question the prevailing logic of Tahitian nationalism. It seemed a paradox to him that a movement to liberate a colonized people from Western domination identifies with Christianity, one of the central elements of Western culture.

An anticolonial movement, he began to argue, could not at the same time refuse the political colonization by France in the 1840s but accept the radical cultural changes brought about by the missionaries only about twenty-five years earlier as a given fact. Instead, a true nationalist Mā'ohi movement should be consistent and resist all forms of colonization, be they political or cultural. In contrast to Raapoto, who identifies his brand of Mā'ohi-Christian syncretism as *te fa'aro'o mā'ohi mau* (the true Mā'ohi religion) (Raapoto 1989, 45), Walker defines Mā'ohi culture as distinct and holistic:

> *Tā mātou hi'ora'a, mea tano a'e, 'iā ora 'oe i tō 'oe hīro'a tumu ma te fa'atura ato'a, 'e te fa'aro'o ato'a, o te mau tupuna. E reira ia, i ni'a i te*

parau no te hīroʻa, e tāʻatoʻa ai. . . . Faʻaoti tō anaʻe tau nō te parau nō te faʻaroʻo o te mau tupuna, ʻua tāʻatoʻa ia te parau nō te hīroʻa.

Our view is, it is right to live your original culture while also practicing the worship and belief of the ancestors. This way, the talk of culture becomes total. . . . Go all the way about the talk of the belief of the ancestors; this is how the talk of culture becomes total. (Walker 2000b)

Walker thus emphasizes that in order to practice genuine Māʻohi culture, one should practice the religion of one's ancestors. That religion, *te faʻaroʻo o te mau tupuna,* is seen as being fundamentally different from *te mau faʻaroʻo ʻeʻē* (foreign religions) like Christianity:

I te tau mātāmua ra e tiʻaturi te mau tupuna e rave rahi mau atua parauhia e "Nuʻu Atua," ʻaita e fifi nō rātou ʻia tāuiui ahere i tō rātou mau atua, nō reira ia i ʻōhie ai te faʻaroʻo teretitiāno i te faʻariʻihia e te nūnaʻa māʻohi. ʻĀreʻa i teie faʻaroʻo teretitiāno ʻaita ʻōna e faʻariʻi ʻia haʻamurihia te tahi atua e atu; ua faʻahepo ʻōna i te nūnaʻa māʻohi e tāpeʻa noa i te faʻaroʻo teretitiāno ʻe tōna "atua mau."

In the olden times, the ancestors believed in many gods, called a "Multitude of Gods," that is polytheism; there was no problem for them in changing their gods, this way it was easy for the Christian religion to be embraced by the Māʻohi people. But, in this Christian religion, it does not embrace that another god is being admitted, that is monotheism. It obliges the Māʻohi people to maintain only the Christian religion and its one and only "true god."[4]

By emphasizing this difference, and not attempting to cover it up, as Raapoto and other Christian liberation theologians have done, Walker represents a radical innovation in contemporary Tahitian discourse. In the words of Tahiti-based French anthropologist and philosopher Bernard Rigo:

It is through the denial of a polytheistic logic that the defenders of Polynesian culture believed to find a dignity equivalent to that of the European cultures. This is no longer the case. The association in Hamuta valley pursues the quest for identity in its most logical consequences: One cannot pretend to live and love one's culture while denying its most fundamental aspect. (Rigo 2004, 333)

When defining the relation between Māʻohi religion and Christianity, Walker stresses his tolerance for other beliefs, but makes it equally clear that each place has a religion most suited for its particular circumstances, and urges foreign religions to acknowledge the native religion of the host society. A manifesto of Te Hivarereata by Walker published in the Tahiti daily *La Dépêche* in mid-2000 thus starts and concludes as follows:

> Allah est Grand, Jéhovah est bon! Taʻaroa est grand, bon et maʻohi.
> [. . .] Te Moana nui o Hiva est l'œuvre de Taʻaroa Tahitumu. Si
> généreux, il accorda son hospitalité à Jéhovah, Allah, Bouddha et
> les autres . . . Lui seront-ils reconnaissants?
>
> Allah is great! Jehovah is good! Taʻaroa is great, good and
> Māʻohi. [. . .] Te Moana nui o Hiva [that is the Pacific Ocean] is the
> work of Taʻaroa Tahitumu. So generous, he even extends his hos-
> pitality to Jehovah, Allah, Buddha and the others. . . . Will they be
> grateful to him? (Walker 2000a)

On December 26, 2000, Walker and other members of Te Hivarereata re-consecrated a *marae* on family land in Hamuta. The *marae*, its ancient name being lost, received the name Tupuhaea (occurrence of sacrifice), revealed to Walker in a dream. Apart from conducting religious ceremonies on this *marae*, the association advocates the revival of other traditional cultural practices that had been abandoned after Christian conversion, such as kava drinking. Corresponding to Walker's above-mentioned concept of hīroʻa tāʻatoʻa (holistic culture), members of the association live as self-sufficiently as possible, and one of their goals is the restoration of Hamuta valley as a self-sufficient agricultural site, as it had been under Walker's father until the early 1960s.

Even though a large majority of Māʻohi are still identifying as Christians, and even though French anthropologists have charged Walker's theology with being reinventive rather than strictly restorative (Rigo 2004, 333–337; Saura 2008, 418–420), the wider social effect of Te Hivarereata's project of Māʻohi spiritual revival cannot be underestimated. Within the past decade, I have witnessed the rise of Te Hivarereata from a shunned fringe group to a nonnegligible actor in Tahitian society. While in 2001 I observed very negative reactions by some Christian independence activists,[5] and shortly thereafter a Tahitian anthropologist with anti-independence political leanings expressed her worries about a possible Christian theocracy in case of independence (Grand 2002), the overall amount of tolerance by

Christian Mā'ohi toward Te Hivarereata appears to have since increased. Most noteworthy, in 2006, the new proindependence local government under President Oscar Temaru's strongly Christian-oriented Tāvini Huira'atira party not only decided to make Matari'i I Ni'a (the rising of the Pleiades in late November, marking the beginning of the most fertile season in the pre-Christian calendar) the new local holiday, but invited Te Hivarereata to lead the opening procedures for the celebration (*Tahitipresse*, November 19, 2006). When in February 2011 Jean-Marc Tera'ituatini Pambrun, an anthropologist, key figure of the Tahitian cultural renaissance and director of the territorial museum, passed away, Walker was invited by the family to conduct the funerary rituals in a strictly traditional, non-Christian, way. Most recently, Walker was a leading crew member of the *Fa'afaite* (Reconciliation), the first neotraditional Tahitian canoe to sail to Hawai'i, and, as the "soul of the expedition" (*La Dépêche* 2012), lead the religious protocol when the crew was received by Hawaiian dignitaries in Hilo Harbor in June 2011. Not directly involving Te Hivarereata, but nevertheless important in the same respect, a monument honoring Opuhara (the leader of the traditionalist party who was slain in the decisive 1815 battle between Christians and traditionalists) was inaugurated in front of the town hall of Pāpara on Tahiti's South Coast by a group of political leaders including practicing Christians and descendants of Pomare II (*Tahitipresse*, November 12, 2011), a symbolic gesture of reconciliation that would have been unthinkable only a few years ago.

My research on contemporary religious revival in Tahiti shows that an identity problem exists among many contemporary Mā'ohi. Although recent Christian theologians have attempted to reconcile this problem by simply equating Christianity with the traditional Tahitian religion, Walker's analysis of the two religions shows they are fundamentally different. Reconciling the two belief systems is thus more likely to be achieved if the two acknowledge each other's difference and respect each other's right to exist as equals within a pluralistic society. As the thoughts and actions of Moana'ura Walker and his association Te Hivarereata have shown, traditional Mā'ohi religion has no problem acknowledging other religions. Christianity and other belief systems that perceive themselves as world religions, on the other hand, have historically shown little inclination to respect indigenous religions as equals, but have rather attempted to eliminate them. While there are indications that this is currently changing among progressive Christian theologians, it is now more urgent than ever to engage in such a dialogue, as Hawai'i-based scholar of Polynesian religion John Charlot already suggested more than twenty years ago (1986).

Notes

1. Tahiti is the largest of the Society Islands, located near the center of the Polynesian triangle. Today it is the principal island of French Polynesia, a French colonial possession with a partially autonomous local government formally known as an "Overseas Country" (Pays d'Outre-mer). Hamuta Valley is located in the municipality of Pīra'e, a suburb of the capital Pape'ete. The lower part of the valley is completely urbanized, but it reaches up into a rural zone (owned by the Walker family) and farther into heavily forested uplands.

2. Biographical information about Walker as well as his thoughts and opinions cited in this chapter are based on personal communications with him in April and May 2001, unless indicated otherwise. All translations from Tahitian and French to English are mine.

3. The small island of Rurutu is located about 550 kilometers south of Tahiti and has about two thousand inhabitants. It is known as a stronghold of Protestantism and was one of the two last islands of present French Polynesia to be annexed by France (only in 1900).

4. Sunny Moana'ura Walker, interview by author, March 11, 2012.

5. One of them, a member of the Seventh Day Adventist Church, considered Walker and his followers "crazy people who pray to stones instead of the true God" (Interview with a church member, April 2001).

PART 9

Deep Encounters

Worldview, Religion, Spiritual Practices

(*overleaf photo*) A woman squats down to burn her candles, incense, and paper money offerings at the elephant in the Wenshu Buddhist temple, Chengdu (Sichuan Province). The gray elephant scorched by flame and smoke and sheathed with layers of ash in its belly and around its feet from continuous burning signifies the common desire for worldly fortune and rebirth. Photo by C. Fred Blake.

Introduction

GUIDO CARLO PIGLIASCO

WORLDVIEW REFERS to the general conceptual principles and practices that peoples and social groups use to find meaning in life and make sense of reality. While all aspects of a cultural system may derive from or be linked to worldview, "religion," "spiritual practices," and "worldview" are not synonymous. Religion is a set of institutionalized beliefs and behaviors pertaining to those forces and powers outside the known laws of nature. Spiritual practices consist of specific actions and beliefs intended to allow people to understand and interact with the range of visible and invisible powers and forces they perceive. Religious and spiritual practices influence our construction of reality, but they are just one aspect of our cultural system. Every society varies greatly in how the people interact with these powers and forces. The case studies outlined in this section explore particular collective interpretations and responses to both our natural and cultural worlds.

This section opens with Gaia Cottino's examination of her journey among bodies of knowledge and knowledge of bodies in the Kingdom of Tonga to gauge the obesity phenomenon in an archipelago that ranks fifth in the worldwide World Health Organization obesity classification. Her research contrasts Western and Tongan worldviews of human bodies, revealing Western norms of "thinness" to be cultural constructs. Toru Yamada swims across the channel between Goto and Nagasaki in the middle of the night, reflecting on his both physical and ethnographic encounter with a particular concept of time—tidal time—during his fieldwork in Japan's island communities. Focusing on the efficacy of Buddhist spiritual practices for Westerners attending a Buddhist meditation retreat in Southern

Thailand, Geoff Ashton shows how the introspective self-study involved in Buddhist meditation enacts a form of ethnographic research. This section, and the volume, concludes with C. Fred Blake's masterful exploration of the nature of value in ancient Chinese spiritual practices of burning paper replicas of valuable things—most often money—for the spirits of deceased family ancestors.

Tiptoeing among the Knowledge of the Bodies and the Bodies of Knowledge in Tonga

Gaia Cottino

"Oh, Gaia! You grew fat!" said Lina when I got off the plane, inaugurating my stay in Tonga. It was a compliment meant to remark on my beauty and healthy condition more than my actual size, a compliment that clashed with the Western obsession with thinness. In the Pacific Islands, and specifically in Tonga, references to bigness are, indeed, constant. "We are known for our big thighs," "Tongans are big people," and "Culturally, Tongans tend to bigness" are just some of the assertions I have heard. Physical size was, for example, mentioned by a young Tongan woman born and raised in Hawai'i, after one year back in Nuku'alofa, as a matter of constant concern. In Hawai'i, where the ideal body size is influenced by the Japanese and Filipino communities, she had had the strong desire to be "small and thin," feeling physically out of place, and would engage in unhealthy actions, such as starving herself, to match such ideals. In Tonga, in contrast, she felt "more proportioned," and therefore abandoned the desire to be thin.

The Western worldview, as a matter of fact, demonizes fat, and considers excess weight as repulsive, unhealthy, and a sign of social uselessness. In the West, "being in shape" and controlling one's body weight implies saving oneself from moral degradation. As Sander Gilman (2008) explains, the demonization of fatness is as old as humankind. What changes across time and space are the preferred weights and sizes, meaning that the thresholds of what is acceptable are not fixed. In the Western history of the body, we can highlight some moments, such as during the Middle Ages and the Renaissance, in which big bodies were valued as symbols of richness, power, prestige, and therefore beauty. Today, bodies have entered the jurisdiction of the biomedical sphere (Foucault 2003) and big bodies are considered sick (Vineis and Satolli 2009). Ideal weight is now derived from the algorithm of a normalization process that shapes the body and formats the soul. Hence, I agree with Patricia Cassidy (1991) when she argues that we should probably rethink the global "obesity epidemic" and consider it as a Western social phenomenon. As anthropologists, we know that body sizes and beauty ideals are relative to the context; therefore, when I heard Lina's compliment, rather than being surprised, I thought it sounded very interesting.

During my first month in Tonga, I was introduced to the extended family of the owners of the guesthouse at which I was staying. Their uncle offered me a place to sleep and, while time passed, I slowly realized how this process was like an adoption. I shared the house, in Mau'fanga village, with seven people regularly—and a dozen coming and going—who included me in all activities and even responsibilities, such as trusting me to keep an eye on the children and a newborn baby. They changed my name to "Mele" ("Mary" vs. "to marry") as a comment on my marital condition, single at the tender age of twenty-eight, and spent long hours with me, patiently explaining everything I could not quite understand, laughing loudly at my mistakes and cultural inappropriateness, sharing all my things, and interviewing me on my home country, as comparing places could help me to better understand Tonga. Here it became evident to me how reductive it was to look for answers—"Tongans think that . . ."—and how important it was, instead, to ask the right questions. Women—my neighbors and my family of sisters and nieces—were my main interlocutors: women of every age, social status, and profession. Women who were, as one of them told me once, "carrying around a whole world in their bodies." Women indeed have strong *mana,* and their bodies show it, again, through their size.[1]

In the Tongan worldview, both male and female physical abundance is valued as a sign of beauty, healthiness, strength, high social status, and power. This view is connected to a past in which chiefs, controlling resources, were physically bigger than the rest of the population and represented the ideals of beauty and body size. On the contrary, a small size, and more specifically skinny legs, is a sign of unhealthiness, reproductive incapacity, and scarcity of resources. For this reason, the most evident signs of beauty are two: a nice pair of *fo'i va'e* (big legs) and a *fo'i mui* (big bottom). As Siaosi once told me: "Thin legs are a no-no! Even according to new generations. Once I used to wear shorts, and I don't have nice legs, and people would look at me and tell me 'Jees, put on some jeans!' If someone wears shorts it is because he has good legs, which from a Western point of view is a lot of meat!" It is not an accident that such signs of beauty are associated with different status foods: the expressions *va'e kapa pulu* (*va'e*, "legs," and *kapa pulu*, "tin meat") and *va'e kapa ika* (where *kapa ika* is "tin fish") represent two different aesthetic forms. Since tinned meat is a higher-status food than tinned fish—which is cheaper and considered poor food—big legs can be called *va'e kapa pulu* and thin ones *va'e kapa ika*.

Such a cultural accent on bigness, which certainly results in the glorification of big body sizes, from a Western view is unacceptable. Statistics seem to confirm widespread obesity among Pacific Island populations, raising much concern among international health organizations.[2] The six countries recorded as having the highest weights worldwide are indeed all located in Oceania, with Tonga ranking fifth (WHO 2011). However, ready to find what has been called an "obesogenic milieu" (Neel 1998)—meaning an environment populated by a high percentage of overweight people—I instead found myself among big people—tall, stout, bulky, strong, muscular—only a few of whom were visibly overweight. Furthermore, I never glimpsed the Western profound detachment between the "optimal size" and what people perceive as the "right body." Leaving aside the problems with the expression "obesity epidemic," as if obesity were not only a disease but also viral, one of the biggest criticisms I raise has to do with the index meant to measure body fat (the body mass index, or BMI), which does not take into consideration bulkiness, bone density, or the proportion between lean mass and fat. As an interlocutor pointed out, such an index depicts as sick any people who live in a context where thinness is not the norm. She commented, "when I look at this BMI thing, I think it is impossible to lose so much weight, I would disappear! They say my ideal weight should be eighty-seven kilograms, but have they ever seen me at ninety?! Everybody was asking me what was wrong with me!" The "obesity epidemic" alarm has raised concern not only within medical institutions but also, from a different perspective, among the population. As one of my interlocutors said, "Growing up they tell you to eat to become big and healthy, and when you are an adult they tell you to lose weight. It is disorienting."

The Tongan bodyscape has obviously changed with time, in particular with wider access to food, the result of which has been what I call a "democratization" of big body sizes. There is a growing middle class that has resources and full access to food. As Siosane said to me, "You can't really tell anymore from the body size who belongs to a higher class and who is a commoner." Today in Tonga, the slim body sizes valued by the Western world meet the bigger ideal body sizes still valued as part of the grand-mothers' worldview, creating a differentiated bodyscape in which two ide-als coexist and are constantly negotiated, influenced not only by older gen-erations' and Western views but also by the growing biomedical concern about obesity. Nevertheless, if big bodies are valued in Tonga, fat ones are not. As Moana once told me, "My mother has always said that beauty is bigness, but the point is to define bigness. You can be big and obese, big and firm, big and lean." The differences between such physical conditions, all of which clearly define thresholds, represent the social distinction of taste (Bourdieu 1984), created and resulting from the different genders, social statuses, ages, and life histories of the population. As my neighbor told me once, during one of our conversations under the wooden porch of my Tongan family's house: "When I got married, I started to gain weight and my husband's family would tell me not to gain too much weight, otherwise my husband could look for someone else. They didn't want me to be fat."

Big body size is, though, mainly a characteristic of female adults, since, with due exceptions, young nubile girls are more slender. Women, once they marry and give birth to their first child, seem to embody their new social status by gaining weight and differentiating themselves physically from their previous nubile physical condition, generally slender.[3] The birth of a child is an important social status change, and therefore, it is not a surprise that the time after childbirth, when women are cared for and fed while they stay in the shade, is when women are considered to be most beautiful: pale, soft, and chubby (Morton 1996). If locally everybody explains such acquired big-ness with the term *fakapikopiko* (lazy), I believe that the following story gives a better explanation: "I know this girl, very beautiful, who got married a while ago and incredibly didn't put on weight, and she remained exactly the same after marrying and having a child! While I think she was good to keep her body, my mom and many people think that she is selfish, thinking more about herself than her family." An old lady wearing makeup and dressing herself beautifully also is considered to be selfish, because her beauty is in her children and grandchildren, not in her individual characteristics. So, beauty and bigness, often superimposed, are a synecdoche of a wider body, the family, and are passed down to the offspring, with a descending movement.

The term "beauty" has challenged my work, since I took it for granted that, anywhere, such a term would have an aesthetic connotation. Instead, after receiving answers that defined beauty as an interior characteristic of the person—"beauty is inside"—I realized that, to investigate the physical characteristics of a beautiful body, I had to reformulate my questions to directly address the body.[4] Only then was I able to discover the whole set of characteristics that made an old choreographer affirm: "Tongan beauty is detailed: from the top of the head to the tip of the toe." Those precise characteristics draw a complex bodyscape that I can here only mention, in which are discernible two bodily conditions, the *sino fakatonga* (the Tongan body: a well-proportioned body with big legs, big thighs, and a big bottom) and the *sino lelei* (the beautiful body). These two bodily conditions are interchangeable among the older generations and separate among the younger ones. If both older and younger generations describe the *sino fakatonga* the same way, agreeing on the fact that such a body is the only body suited to dance the traditional *tau'olunga,* when it comes to the *sino lelei* the new generations do not recognize it as matching the *sino fakatonga,* as the elders do, but describe a hybrid set of characteristics, partly Tongan and partly Western. Beyoncé's and Jennifer Lopez's Western full bodies represent the new beauty ideals; far from the anorexic models of the Western catwalks, Tongan body ideals seem a mediation between the West and the local. But no bodyscape is given once and for all. The Tongan beauty contest, the Miss Heilala Pageant—of which even the crowned Miss Heilala is said to be "not representative of the local beauty"—has a growing influence on the younger generations' collective imagery. The many beauty messages entering Tonga through the media (not always screened by the family), through the beauty pageants, and through the international health task forces who are worried about the high BMI of the population, contribute, with no doubt, to creating a new self that contrasts with the "fundamentally interpersonal" self typical of the Pacific Islands (Becker 1995).[5] As Becker highlighted in the Fijian context, eating disorders can be the consequence of detachment from the experience of the interpersonal self and the traditional Fijian body and progressive exposure to Western values and lifestyles through media and tourism. The situation in Tonga has not led yet, in my observation, to visible eating disorders, but needs to be monitored.

My observations in Tonga lead me to take a critical position toward the Western worldview, and its power to name and define. As Nancy Pollock, writing of Nauru, explains, "Love of food and admiration of large body size are as much part of the new scene as they were of the old. What have changed are many of the material surroundings and negative values associated with large body size that have been superimposed on the society"

(1995, 106). It is exactly this negative value that the West has introduced in Tonga: the idea that a big body, obese or just overweight, is a sick body.

Notes

1. As Kerry James (1988) has explained, the equilibrium between genders can be understood through the distinction between *mana* and *pule*, the first a spiritual power representing the continuity between the skies and the human world, and the second the inalienable secular political power of the title system. This distinction, never clear within a gender, is determinant in the gender distinction: *mana* in fact belongs to both male and female, just like *pule*, James writes, but the sister's *mana* encompasses its contrary, the brother's *pule*. Sisters were in the past and still are in the present of a higher social position than their brothers, but in the past, sisters, in particular the oldest sisters, the *mehekitanga*, were surrounded with many more taboos than at present. As some of my interlocutors recall, they had in their brother's house their own furnishings, dish, and spoon, which could not be touched by others, because such objects were loaded with spiritual powers and could be dangerous to others. It is not the case that relationships between brothers and sisters are full of *tapu*, and brothers fear the sisters' retaliation. Sisters do, indeed, have power in regard to the fertility of their sisters-in-law, are treated with a high form of respect, and are the ones who can cut their brother's progenies' hair at their father's death. As Elisabeth Bott (1981) recalls, when there is a dispute regarding matters pertaining to the male sphere, such as land (to which only males are entitled), it is the eldest sister who makes the final decision.

2. When obesity became a disease, in 1996, body weight became the main indicator for so-called noncommunicable diseases (NCDs), widespread in the Kingdom of Tonga and in the Pacific in general. Nevertheless, as many have argued (Gard and Wright 2005; Gilman 2008) and as I could myself observe, such diseases are the result of multifactorial causes. The emphasis that is given to body weight ignores the many other elements, foremost among which is food, that cause NCDs.

3. Physical activity has been discouraged for years, with the exception of the 1990s, when King George Taufa'ahau Tupou IV launched a "stay active campaign." Today, female physical activity is less discouraged, but it is still considered generally inconvenient for women, with the exception of the more westernized middle-class women and young girls in schools, for whom specific double-layer uniforms for physical activity classes are created.

4. It was indeed through the formulation of contextually influenced questions that this research took shape. My direct questions, for example, "What is obesity?" or "When is a body big?" had to be reformulated in local terms, often with recourse to indirect speech—in the third person—or with

recourse to my own body as a "neutral" basis of comparison, meaning outside of the taboo and social respect rules. Through such bodily wisdom, I learned how to tiptoe in the field.

5. Such an expression refers to a collective view of the self. In Tonga, a person perceives himself or herself as part of a wider network of selves, corresponding to the extended family.

Being and Time in Nagasaki, Japan

Toru Yamada

On June 7, 2010, I was walking around a small fishing village on Nagasaki's Hisaka Island doing a brief preliminary cultural landscape survey.[1] This was the first time that I intended to conduct nonprearranged interviews in a fishing community, and almost as soon as I arrived, I sensed that something was amiss. There was nobody in sight. The reason, I was to find out, was related to time. Coming from Japan, I assumed that something as fundamental as time would be understood in the same way in this fishing village as it was in suburban Tokyo.

This particular fishing village was rapidly depopulating as remaining residents aged. The village was located opposite a small bay that contained the island's only commuter pier. Agricultural plots had been abandoned and reforested, and the wooden building of the only local grade school had not been in use in more than twenty years. Still, it was far from a ghost town. Individual houses were in good condition. Most of the fishing boats not only looked well maintained but were docked in an orderly fashion at community piers. Yet I could not find anybody on the streets; it was as if all of the residents had been abducted to another world. It took me more than an hour to find a single local resident. Even though I was able to conduct my initial geographic survey on the land use patterns of this community, it seemed that it would not be possible to conduct any interviews or ethnographic observations that day. Eventually I left.

I went to other communities on Hisaka, but I knew I would eventually have to return and find a way to talk to the people from this village. It was easier for me to find farmers because, as it was June, it was their active working season on the island. As I interviewed local farmers and other residents on Hisaka, one of them laughed at me and kindly explained why I had not found anybody from the local fishing communities. She told me, "It's low-tide hour now, young man. They are out fishing. Some of them might be on other islands shopping. If you want to talk to them, you have to avoid low-tide hours." She suggested I check the tidal calendar or the moon phases to design a better research plan if I wanted to meet local fishermen. Her suggestion was probably one of the most helpful and critical suggestions I received while conducting my research on Hisaka. I urgently needed to incorporate the tidal calendar into my research considerations. I wondered why I had made such an elementary mistake in forgetting to consider the significance of tidal time to the residents of fishing communities.

On the same day that I received this advice, I checked the upcoming tidal schedule to improve my fieldwork strategy. I wrote down both the low-tide and high-tide hours in my agenda book to remind myself when to avoid visiting fishing communities. This approach led me to do more effective research and allowed me to more precisely locate local residents.

One aspect of a worldview reflects how humans adapt to their living environment. Ecological anthropologists, such as Julian Steward, developed the field of cultural ecology by analyzing the ways that humans adapt to different environments (Steward 1972), and such adaptation processes have fascinated social scientists for decades. In the Pacific, for example, the Polynesian Voyaging Society revived traditional navigation techniques by carefully examining the seasonal tidal and wind changes around the Pacific Ocean (Finney 1991, 2001; Kyselka 1987). Likewise, on Hisaka I started to see how important it was to acquire local residents' worldview to precisely understand the particular and specific cultural and geographical context of the field. I found out that my dependency on what I thought of as a *regular* calendar turned out to be an obstacle to acquiring a proper understanding of local communities around the Goto archipelago.

The Goto archipelago is located at the western edge of Japan, and is one of the least convenient places to travel to from Tokyo, Japan's national capital. Surrounded by the ocean, Goto seems isolated from the rest of Japan. Maritime transportation is necessary for every aspect of local lives. Residents have to use boats not only to commute to Japan's main islands but also for inter-island travel and for commodity logistics. Travelers have to arrange and to pay for their maritime transportation. With the advent and improvement of roads and vehicular motorization, Goto's dependency on boats has led many to conclude that the archipelago is an inconvenient and disadvantaged place. Those without a solid knowledge of ocean tides or maritime direction perceive Goto as isolated, rather than connected to Japan's major islands via an ocean highway.[2]

Prior to my visit in the summer of 2010, I had visited Hisaka several times. However, while I was conducting my initial fieldwork, I could always find someone to talk to without prior arrangements. I had never encountered a situation in which all of the residents were completely absent. Most of my informants were government officials who kept regular office hours, and they scheduled most meetings based on "clock time." Also, all local maritime transportation systems in Goto followed strict preset schedules (with accommodation for possible delays depending on weather and sailing conditions). Therefore, even though I had lived in this island community for over a year, I had not needed to pay much attention to tidal time.

I needed to adjust my scheduling habits as soon as I started working for the local government and as I made more progress with my research. Even after the shift to motorized boats in the 1970s, the ocean and its tides still play an integral role in the everyday cycles of local residents in the Goto archipelago. Boats are the essential mode of transportation in inter-island logistic networks. Residents initially settled and still live in places accessible by sea. Fishermen in particular must know the ocean currents and the correct tidal time not only to plan effective fishing strategies but also to conserve fuel and energy. Divers can get to deeper underwater zones to conduct effective hunting during low-tide hours, and boat captains can reduce the chance of getting caught in strong head currents by knowing the general tidal schedule. Due to the constant increase of crude oil prices throughout the 2000s, it was of pressing importance for those in maritime industries in Goto to properly understand tidal time to minimize the financial burden of buying fuel. Moreover, as Hisaka's population was graying, it was especially important to them to plan their diving schedules based on tidal time to make diving more physically efficient. As in other fishing communities around the world, the residents on Hisaka juggled and often hybridized two different calendar systems for different purposes.

It had not been easy for me to gain that initial knowledge that the residents of Hisaka's fishing communities depended on tidal time. This was due to a limitation of my own, formed not only by my upbringing but also by my work schedule as a cultural landscape surveyor. As a government surveyor, I initially tried to follow standard administrative work hours. For six weeks in the summer of 2010, I went to a small local pier at 9:00 a.m. to take an inter-island boat (kaijō takushī, or ocean taxi) from Fukue Island to Hisaka every morning, and I conducted my survey until 3:00 p.m. every afternoon. After I got back to my apartment, I usually spent time processing my ethnographic report and geographic information system (GIS) data. The inter-island boat was motorized, and the company provided their service wherever and whenever their customers needed it. In other words, since I could call the boat company whenever I needed them, I did not pay much attention to tidal time, even as I was traveling across the ocean every day.

As my governmental work and my follow-up fieldwork were winding down in July 2010, I learned much more about how ocean tides formulated not only local residents' sense of time but also their spatial orientation. Again, this realization happened in an unexpected way; I swam the channel between Goto and Nagasaki (approximately seventy miles) in a relay with local triathletes from Nagasaki prefecture. The group of triathletes approached me and convinced me to be a part of their team. This group had done the same swim in the summer of 2009, and informed me that it had taken them twenty-six hours. Personally, this was the last thing I wanted to commit to, because I easily get seasick. I thought it would be unbearable to be continuously on the ocean for that long a time.

The swim turned out to be one of the most useful experiences for me in learning, physically and ethnographically, how the ocean tide works around the Goto archipelago. Spending over twenty-five hours on the ocean, I could physically sense how the tide worked by literally swimming in the water (and occasionally in the debris). It was extremely helpful to spend so many hours with experienced local fishermen and local ocean taxi conductors. Since the average speed of our swimmers was much slower than that of the commuter ferry, the fishermen and the conductors of accompanying boats chose a route that went through the calmest waters possible. Instead of taking a direct route, as most of the local commuter boats do, we took a bow-shaped route in a counterclockwise direction. The longer route with calmer tides was also more energy-efficient both for the swimmers and the accompanying boats. As we were swimming across the ocean in the middle of the night, I could see the lights from the fishing villages surrounding the ocean. Many of these villages do not have convenient road access and seem hidden from the perspective of those who depend on ground transportation. In fact, some Nagasaki prefectural government members had attempted to promote these fishing villages by emphasizing that they seemed to be located in hidden and secret places (Yamada 2014). However, local residents did not see the villages this way. Most of the fishing villages were neatly located around the core maritime route of low-speed boats. The spatial arrangement of the fishing villages is systematic with respect to the fact that they are accessible from what was previously understood as the most efficient maritime route. Now, with the development of high-speed boats such as hydrofoils, short-term travelers—including myself—cannot intuit the maritime knowledge of local residents in Goto.

Anthropological fieldwork is a constant process of finding out the anthropologists' own limitations. However, some of those limitations often go unrealized for the duration of our fieldwork, as shared advanced technologies, such as ferries, cars, and digital devices (for example, smartphones), lead us to false assumptions that residents in the field share our sense of spatial and temporal orientations, or more generally, of ecological orientations. My dependency on clock time and on the latest technologies initially helped me to conduct my research among the officials in the local public administration around the Goto archipelago, as their meetings were scheduled on clock time. However, as my research extended outside of the circle of bureaucrats and outside of the governmental environment, I started realizing that my own worldview was a major obstacle to properly understanding the orientation in time and space of the maritime residents.

I was accustomed to clock time and to strictly scheduled maritime and ground transportation. In addition to clock time, however, knowledge of ocean tides was integral to the everyday cycle of island residents, from scheduling the most efficient fishing time to knowing the most effective maritime logistics. The calendar became more than just a taken-for-granted tool for fieldwork scheduling as I learned how important it was for me to acquire local residents' concepts of time.

Ethnographers, depending on where they conduct their fieldwork, have to take into consideration multiple systems of time. In some parts of Asia, this means taking lunar and/or religious calendars into consideration to map out time, place, and distance for more effective fieldwork strategies. When I conducted my fieldwork, clock time initially seemed to be the most dependable and effective medium for the scheduling of my research because many of my informants used it, most local public transportation schedules were based on it, and local bureaucrats depended on it for their administrative scheduling. Initially, I relied heavily on an agenda book to schedule interviews and to remind myself of key local events.

Temporal and spatial orientation is often held at the subconscious level, and also is understood as common sense among those who engage in the same daily activities. However, it is not common sense for those who are outside of the shared network, and we are often puzzled by subtle differences when we face the presence of multiple concepts of time and space. I felt displaced in a deserted fishing community on Hisaka Island. As we often design our fieldwork schedules based on our own cultural logic, we risk limiting our ability to understand local cultural logic. To get beyond our own limitations, it is important to put ourselves in the unpredictable contexts of the field.

Notes

1. Goto Archipelago, of which Hisaka Island is a part, is located approximately 670 miles west of Tokyo, and 110 miles southeast of South Korea's Jeju Island. As of 2012, approximately five hundred islanders reside on Hisaka Island, which is nine square miles (twenty-five square kilometers).
2. See Hauʻofa (1993) for a conception of the ocean as connecting, rather than isolating, island worlds.

Losing My Mind and Loving Mosquitoes, Crickets, and Other Jungle Inhabitants

Reflections on Field Research and Its Frustrations at a Buddhist Meditation Retreat in Southern Thailand

GEOFF ASHTON

ON SEPTEMBER 29, 2007, I boarded a train at Hualamphong Station in Bangkok, Thailand, and traveled overnight to the town of Chaiya in the southern Thai province of Surat Thani.[1] The purpose of this trip was to conduct ethnographic fieldwork at the nearby Wat Suan Mokh, or the Temple of the Garden of Release.[2] Established in 1932 by the late Buddhadasa, Thailand's most influential Buddhist philosopher of the twentieth century, Suan Mokh has been a vital center of Buddhism for the Thai people.[3] It has also helped to promote Buddhist beliefs and practices abroad: Suan Mokh has hosted over twenty thousand foreigners for meditation retreats in English since 1989.

Buddhism centers around the teachings (*dhamma*) of Siddhartha Gautama, or the Buddha (literally, the Enlightened One), who lived in the fifth century BCE. These teachings address themes of suffering (*dukkha*), impermanence (*anicca*), and no-self (*anatta*), and are encapsulated in four "noble truths" disclosed by the Buddha shortly after his enlightenment. According to these truths, life experience is characterized by suffering (*dukkha*), the cause of suffering is craving, the cure for suffering is the elimination of craving, and the extinction of craving (*nibbana*) occurs by means of an eightfold path. Three main aspects constitute this eightfold path: ethical conduct, mental discipline or meditation (*samadhi*), and wisdom. Buddhist wisdom involves realization of the transient, fluid, and empty nature of things; everything is in constant flux (*anicca*), while the identities that we associate with seemingly persistent entities are nothing more than mental fabrications enacted by the ego in order to create a sense of security. This holds for the self as well: there is no permanent, unchanging "self" or "soul." Our ignorance concerning "the way things are" stokes our craving (for control and self-preservation), thus working in tandem with it in perpetuating our suffering (Gombrich 1984). The Buddha's teachings provide a practical remedy for life's suffering by enabling us to let go of our self-made fictions and the afflictions of craving.

Strong parallels exist between Buddhism and Western religions, particularly Christianity. Most notably, both religions propose salvation.[4] However, the Buddha's teachings provide no consolation for the inevitable passing away of things, such as eternal repose in heaven with an "all-embracing spiritual essence" (De Marquette 1965, 24).[5] They simply make the realistic assessment that suffering is a fact that transcends value judgments, and they counter the first noble truth ("life is suffering") with a path that empowers the individual to eliminate suffering through mental discipline, not ritual worship or prayer to a supernatural being.

This is evident at Buddhist monasteries such as Suan Mokh. Many Westerners are drawn to Suan Mokh because, in spite of the differences between Buddhist and Western worldviews, Buddhist spiritual practices (for example, meditation) purport to transcend cultural differences: through progression along the eightfold path, any individual with the right attitude and devoted effort can gain firsthand insight into the way things are. As a forty-four-year-old male participant from the Netherlands later told me, "What better way to understand Buddhist liberation than to *do* Buddhist meditation?" But is Buddhist salvation equally available to all, particularly those whose religious sensibility is considerably foreign to the Buddhist worldview? And how exactly does Buddhist meditation bring about liberating realization? To examine these questions, I initially planned to conduct daily interviews and organize collective discussions with the foreigners participating in the October 2007 retreat at Suan Mokh. However, upon arrival at the center I quickly realized that I would be unable to apply these research methods. The gentleman behind the registration desk avoided all of my questions, pointed to the instructions on the retreat sign-up sheet, and told me to return the form to him only after I had read it thoroughly. Two details caught my eye: (1) "The use of electronics, and reading or writing anything unrelated to the meditation guide book provided to you, are prohibited"; and (2) "This is a SILENT retreat. Talking is not permitted." Any research writing that I intended to do would have to be done by hand in the privacy of my own room. Moreover, my means of study were limited to direct observation, participation in the life of the group, and self-analysis. In order to appreciate the participants' experiences and evaluate the efficacy of

Buddhist spiritual practices, I had to "walk in the moccasins of the (aspiring) faithful," as it were.

After signing in, I was led to the male dormitories. The accommodations were very basic: concrete walls, a straw mat on a concrete shelf for a bed (with a mosquito net draped over it), and a wooden pillow. Shortly after this, a bell summoned the participants to an open-air meditation hall, where the schedule for the upcoming ten days was explained: 4:00 a.m.: Wake-up (to the sound of the monastery bell); 4:30: Morning Reading; 4:45–5:15: Sitting Meditation; 5:15–7:00: Yoga; 7:00–8:00: *Dhamma* Talk/Sitting Meditation; 8:00–9:00: Breakfast; 9:00–10:00: Chores; 10:00–11:00: *Dhamma* Talk; 11:00–11:45: Walking Meditation; 11:45–12:30: Sitting Meditation; 12:30–1:30 p.m.: Lunch; 1:30–2:30: Free Time; 2:30–3:30: Sitting Meditation Instruction; 3:30–4:15: Walking Meditation; 4:15–5:00: Sitting Meditation; 5:00–6:00: Chanting/Loving Kindness Meditation; 6:00–6:30: Tea, Hot Milk; 6:30–7:30: Hot Springs; 7:30–8:00: Sitting Meditation; 8:00–8:30: Group Walking Meditation; 8:30–9:00: Sitting Meditation; 9:30: Lights Out.

The rationale behind this tightly structured program was to quiet the mind and draw attention to the immediacy of each moment. By providing clear instructions for the most simple of events (for example, eating, walking, sitting, breathing, etc.), Buddhist spiritual practices transform daily activities into meditations. Walking meditation aims to bring awareness to the sensations that attend each step and to make each event involved in the act of walking more deliberate and natural. One walking meditation learned by the participants was the "three step" method, which includes three distinct events: lifting the foot, moving the foot forward, and placing the foot on the ground. Participants also learned the "five step" approach, which includes two additional events: an initial tilting of the foot and a lowering of the foot prior to placing it. But the main practice was a form of sitting meditation known as *anapanasati,* or "mindfulness of breathing." The directions for this technique are simple: sit directly on the floor and cross the legs so that your weight is evenly balanced, lay the hands in the lap (one hand on top of the other), maintain an upright posture, and, fixing the outer end point of your attention upon the tip of the nose (with eyes open) and the inner end point of your awareness upon the navel, follow the breath as it moves back and forth between these two points. Next, gradually relax the breathing and the body, increasing your attention to the movement of the breath. After this stage, stop chasing the breath, rest quietly, and turn your awareness to the tip of the nose, where the breath makes contact as it moves in and out. Little by little, your attention to the body's movements should become subtle, gentle, and natural, leading to deeper states of concentration (*samadhi*).

This method was successfully taken up by at least a few participants. During the train ride back to Bangkok, one participant (a German man in his early twenties) described his experience as follows: "At the beginning of the retreat my mind felt like a bag of popcorn that was popping away in a microwave. But towards the end, it felt more like the less frequent popping of oatmeal that was barely simmering." Other participants, however, became more frustrated as the retreat continued, with nearly one-third of the original participants (twenty-three out of seventy-one) leaving Suan Mokh by the end of the eighth day. I was able to covertly speak with an American female in her mid-twenties just before her departure on Day 7. "This whole experience just was not what I had in mind," she said. "I'm having trouble controlling my thoughts and feel like I'm not getting anywhere. I thought meditation was supposed to be comforting."

Buddhadasa himself observes that the first week of meditation tends to be the most challenging period, particularly for Westerners who are unfamiliar with the Buddhist worldview, its practices, and the humidity and countless inhabitants of Suan Mokh's jungle setting. Buddhadasa explains:

> There is a power which seems to have already taken away all of your will when you begin to realize that you will be alone in a place without any protection [that is, the jungle environs of Suan Mokh]. But as your will becomes stronger, your mindfulness quicker, your familiarization better, such incidents will gradually become a normality. Therefore, you must give at least seven days to this first lesson so that you can practice until you get a satisfactory result. (Buddhadasa 1990, 8)

In addition to humans, Suan Mokh's residents include monkeys, gibbons, bats, a variety of reptiles (for example, giant geckos, the poisonous pit viper snake, and the more lethal king cobra), and a whole range of insects, including giant wasps, biting red ants, scorpions, centipedes, mosquitoes, and hand-sized cane spiders. Though harmless, the cane spiders presented a significant problem for those suffering from arachnophobia, and the open-air meditation hall was by no means off limits to them. By the second day, participants had learned the importance of checking beneath their meditation pillows before each sitting meditation (apparently the spiders also enjoy meditating in the main hall, albeit by sitting in the shadow of participants' meditation pillows!).

By contrast, the monks at Suan Mokh use the jungle as a teacher, whether for its natural quietness or the terror that tests their willpower, mindfulness, and loving kindness (*metta*). This was evident in the daily "loving kindness meditation," which was led by a young Thai monk. If and when one's attention strays from the breath to a thought, memory, feeling, or external occurrence, he told us, recognize that phenomenon and then let it go. Of course, this is particularly challenging in a place where mosquitoes abound and regularly fly into one's field of vision or hearing (and sometimes dive straight into your eyes!). To prevent this, the vast majority of participants used mosquito repellent. But the monks generally refrained from doing so in order to free their minds from false psychological reassurances. As Buddhadasa himself writes, "We may rely on some kind of protection such as a fence or a *klot* (an umbrella hung around with a mosquito net) to lessen our anxiety . . . [but] you should not use it, for you will not get a new mind which is completely free" (Buddhadasa 1990, 9–10). The same monk who instructed us in the loving kindness meditation also explained as follows: "When mosquito try land on you, very important not to kill mosquito. Don't try kill mosquito when he try bite you. He is your friend. Better to send loving kindness to mosquito, think of yourself as tree that give the life. If mosquito distract your mind and you have to push it away, gently brush it away without anger."

Despite initial setbacks, then, I was still able to conduct ethnographic research through direct observation and limited interviews. Moreover, I employed a methodology to which Buddhist mindfulness training is particularly amenable through its emphasis upon introspective awareness: self-analysis. As a retreat participant, I endured my own psychological struggles. This all came to a head during the night of Day 8. Frustrated by the fact that I was unable to carry out my original plan of research or even just relax in the midst of a jungle teeming with intrusive life forms, I lay in bed that night counting the days and hours until the end of the retreat. But even this was interrupted—by a cricket. And not just any cricket—it was the same cricket that I had removed from the dormitory area the night before! For the previous four nights a cricket had robbed me of hours of sleep by chirping up a storm from a small crack in the cement wall of my room. I had tried to coax him out by using a variety of methods—poking at him with a stick, spraying mosquito repellent into his hiding place—but he withstood them all. Finally, during the late hours of the previous night, I noticed that the cricket had vacated his hiding place and was chirping from the wall behind my head. After a long chase, I trapped him under a cup and gently escorted him from the dormitory area. But somehow he had found his way back to my room. Needless to say, I slept very little that night.

The next morning I felt defeated, and I resigned myself to being unable to change the conditions surrounding me. During the morning meditation, I even let the mosquitoes feed on me, the ants wander over my skin, and the flies tickle my neck. But in the midst of this surrender I experienced an opening outward: thoughts and feelings arose and released, passing over the landscape and then receding into the distance, not unlike the sound vibrations of the bell that awakened us each morning. Through a simple act of letting go, fears and aversions no longer had power over me, and experiences became clear. Thoughts of self vanished as I relinquished control over my worldly involvements and no longer sought escape from them. But it is important to emphasize that this letting go was not an act of disengagement. To the contrary, it occurred with increased mindfulness of the subtle movements within both the outer environment and my mind. In short, the exercises of the retreat enacted a form of ethnographic research whereby I attended to my own inner experiences as a means to its own end, namely, practicing mindfulness. This quasi-liberating self-study enabled me to conduct participant observation with respect to another major theme of my project: examining the difficulties for a largely Christianized Westerner (me) of engaging in Buddhist spiritual practices.

As for my vociferous roommate, he once again began to chirp just as I was drifting off to sleep that night. After ten minutes of sleeplessness, I came out from behind my mosquito net, scanned the floor and walls for spiders and scorpions, and shined my flashlight on the grasshopper, who was boldly tormenting me (or so it seemed) from outside of his hiding place. I promptly grabbed my sandal and was ready to silence him once and for all. But then something came over me that gave me pause, a feeling that was neither guilt nor shame, but something close to compassion. I crawled back under my mosquito net, gave the grasshopper five minutes to sing his heart out, and then silently said to him, "Okay, grasshopper, enough already. I'll send you some loving kindness, and you'll please send me some silence." A minute later, he stopped chirping, and I was able to sleep.

Notes

1. Geographically the largest province of southern Thailand, Surat Thani has forested limestone mountains in the west, mostly grassland plains along its eastern mainland coast, and various islands in the Gulf of Thailand,

which make up the farthest eastern part of the province. The majority of its approximately 966,000-person population is Thai and Buddhist, while up to 30 percent of its inhabitants are Muslim, most of whom are Malay in origin. Tourism and agriculture constitute much of the local economy, with salted red eggs, oysters, rambutan, and silk representing some of the region's most well-known products.

2. Fieldwork has made significant contributions to the study of religion. In contrast to lab research (also known as the "armchair" method), which often makes dangerously speculative claims, field research uses direct participant observation and requires the researcher to live in close proximity with the group of individuals being studied. This approach, which is typically not available to students of religion who have not received training in anthropology, helps the researcher to gain intimate familiarity with the practices of the group, thereby bringing into focus the religious experience of the group members. It also provides more detailed and accurate information concerning the values, beliefs, and ideals associated with the religious practices of the population under study. In many ways, my approach here has been influenced by what has been called "The New Ethnography." For more on this topic, see Saliba (1974).

3. While Thailand is host to Muslims, Christians, Jews, and Hindus, the national religion is Buddhism: nearly 95 percent of the population is Buddhist. Muslims make up close to 4 percent of the population, Christians almost 1 percent, while Jews and Hindus are few in number. Many historians hold that Buddhism first arrived in Thailand in 228 BCE through the efforts of a royal monk sent by Ashoka, then the emperor of India. The Sukhothai Kingdom of the thirteenth century made Buddhism the first state religion in Thailand, a status it retains to the present day. The Surat Thani region (and Chaiya district, in particular) has been an important center of Buddhism since at least the seventh century CE.

4. In addition, both Christianity and Buddhism center around the teachings of a historical figure who challenged the authority of the social and religious status quo; councils were organized following the deaths of Jesus and the Buddha in order to organize their teachings into unified texts—the Bible and the Tripitaka (lit., "three baskets"), respectively; and both religions recognize the existence of heaven, hell, and the ordinary human world (Morris 2006, 48–49).

5. Contrary to Edward Tylor's thesis (Tylor 1871), not all religions require belief in supernatural beings, and Buddhism represents a clear example of a religion that does not fit into a theistic definition. Many Buddhists (particularly in Thailand) recognize gods, demons, spirits, and the like, but Buddhism's pursuit of salvation does not depend upon the grace of a creator-spirit or faith in some transcendent, other-worldly divinity (Morris 2006, 54–74).

"Papa! What's Money?"

An Enduring Question Finds Answers in Burning
It for the Spirits of the Dead in China

C. Fred Blake

In Charles Dickens' *Dombey and Son* (1974, 93–94), little Paul and his father, Mr. Dombey, were sitting by the fireside, each absorbed in his own reverie, when little Paul suddenly asked: "Papa! What's money?" This dumbfounded his father, who as a merchant knew a great deal about money but labored to put it into simple words:

"Gold, and silver, and copper. Guineas, shillings, half-pence. You know
 what they are?"

"Oh yes, I know what they are," said Paul. "I don't mean that, Papa. I
 mean, what's money after all . . . I mean, Papa, what can it do?" . . .

"Money, Paul, can do anything." . . .

But Paul . . . looking at the fire again, as though the fire had been his
 adviser and prompter—repeated, after a short pause:

"Anything, Papa?" . . . "Why didn't money save me my Mama?" . . . "It isn't
 cruel, is it?"

"Cruel!" said Mr. Dombey . . . seeming to resent the idea. "No. A good
 thing can't be cruel."

"If it's a good thing, and can do anything," said the little fellow, thoughtfully, as he looked back at the fire, "I wonder why it didn't save me my
 Mama."

He didn't ask the question of his father this time. Perhaps he had
seen, with a child's quickness, that it had already made his father

uncomfortable. But he repeated the thought aloud, as if it were quite an old one to him, and had troubled him very much; and sat with his chin resting on his hand, still cogitating and looking for an explanation in the fire.

Over a century later and on the other side of the world in China, we find Jingjing whose innocent questions about money vexed his father. The setting in this short story by Chen Dahao (1997) is the death anniversary of Jingjing's grandpa. Jingjing's father and mother were burning stacks and stacks of paper money in the courtyard. When six-year-old Jingjing asked his mother what she was burning, she answered, "We are just burning paper money (*zhǐqián*) for your grandpa; your grandpa in the otherworld also needs to use money, so we burn it once every year; it is like sending him money once a year."

Jingjing kept asking naive questions, which prompted his father to interject: "Little kid, why are you asking so many questions?" Jingjing stopped asking and realized that "Papa and Mama were doing things that cheat people, again," but now the person being cheated was his grandpa who had loved him most dearly. When Jingjing's parents finished burning the paper money, his mother took real money from the bedroom dresser and she and Jingjing's father repaired to the second floor to play mahjong with guests who had just arrived. Left alone, Jingjing decided to burn some real money so his grandpa could avoid having to use fake money to buy things in the otherworld and being caught and sent to the police station. From his mother's dresser, Jingjing took a thick stack of real money and carried it to the courtyard. From the kitchen he took a match, then imitating his parents' way just a moment ago, piece by piece, he burned it up.

The two stories, widely separated in time and space, pose "childish" questions about the mystery of money. Had the two lads been able to meet through some international time warp, Jingjing might have assured little Paul that even if money could not prolong his mama's stay in this world, it could keep her spirit vital in the other world, although Jingjing did not realize that the money has to take a different form in order to be used by spirits.

This is why the money that Jingjing's parents were burning is called *zhǐqián* (paper money). In Chinese, the term is unambiguous. It refers to paper replicas of things that take the form of money plus all the things that money can buy. Monetary forms include strings of copper, cash, silver, and gold ingots. The cash is replicated by perforating sheets of coarse paper made from the straw of grasses, while silver is replicated by bleaching paper or pasting tinfoil on squares of paper, and gold by dyeing paper yellow or daubing yellow pigment on the shiny foil. The things that money buys, virtually every material effect of Chinese civilization old and new, are variously replicated in paper cutouts (for example, clothes), papier-mâché and pasteboard (for example, servants), or paper tied to bamboo frames (for example, refrigerators and houses). In the past century, another money form has become popular; these are simulated modern treasury bills, some of which bear a striking resemblance to Chinese or U.S. treasury bills—it is these that Jingjing's parents were burning for his grandpa.

To understand this thousand-year-old custom in its medieval and modern garbs, I crisscrossed China intermittently over a number of years, traveling from place to place by foot, bicycle, bus, boat, and train, often depending on my wife, friends, colleagues, students, and, everywhere, the kindness of strangers; and in every place I came to I found paper money to be an integral part of local customs and ritual services. One of those places was Yu County with its long and storied past, a rich agricultural basin hemmed in by mountains, about two hundred kilometers west of Beijing. To augment their income from agriculture, the peasants of Yu County traditionally engage in the paper-cutting craft, which Wang Li, my wife, studied over a period of years. Many of the paper cuttings depict dramatic scenes from the local folk opera. The novelty of the paper craft extends to the local paper money practices. One such novelty is a family guardian that goes by the name *shénshén;* the duplication of *shén* connotes an endearing and familiar spirit and is perhaps best rendered as "family divine." *Shénshén* is invisible but its aura becomes apparent when the family enjoys prosperous times; and to give its aura tangible form, a piece of paper money is pasted to a wall inside the house; they call it *chángqián,* "perpuating money." The paper money connects with other domestic crafts including a regionwide tradition of replicating all kinds of things in flour dough, and steaming or frying them for festive gifts and ritual offerings alongside paper monies. Here is a traditional lifeworld, a material world, a world of tangible, textured forms that exists in virtue of its aura and spirit. I call it a material spirit because its axiom is that everything is related to everything; in itself, a thing is finite, dead, and irrelevant; things only exist for other things—only the *relationship* counts because it transcends the finitude of things.

For the peasants of Yu County, this material spirit begins with the mixtures of windblown deposits of loess soil and generations of decayed flesh and bone that nourish the current tillers of those soils. The peasants bury their dead in the same ground that grows their staple crops (millet, corn, wheat, sorghum, and hemp), and at some point in time, they plow over the top of the burial mounds. The spirit of the flesh and bones interred in that earth is nonetheless as much a part of the family as are its living members. And again, it is not just spirit, as the flesh and bones provide organic sustenance for the living: "The loess contains an apparently inexhaustible store of chemicals (from decayed organic matter), which works its way to the surface by capillary attraction when water soaks down from the surface and is then drawn back again by evaporation. Because of this natural mechanism, loess soil retains its fertility over centuries, even without the application of manure" (Lattimore 1947, 29).

In China, the spirits of the dead are thought of as sentient and thus subject to cold and hunger. The pathos of the spirit world is vividly conveyed through "entrusted dreams" (spirits of deceased family members contact the living through dreams to request things like food and clothes). The pathos of the spirit is synonymous with a "piety of the flesh" (parents and children literally feel each other's pain). An entrusted dream is thought to be a portent indicating one's negligence toward the deceased and the immediate need to offer what is requested along with paper money. And if the apparition in the dream is not a sufficient warning, in Yu County at least, the furniture in the home begins to move, weird sounds are heard, the children act in bizarre ways, or there is a sudden onset of illness.

Cold and hunger are presumably felt most keenly in the wintertime; so the Winter Sacrifice is geared to preparing winter clothes for deceased spirits. The typical outfit is a set of dark blue padded jacket, pants, and shoes scaled to the size of a doll about forty-five centimeters tall. For the spirits of the recently deceased (the new tombs), this set of clothes is ideally hand stitched from real cloth, often silk. For spirits of the old tombs, in the ground for more than three years, the clothes are made from paper. The offering may also be an unfinished bolt of cloth signified by a role of blue paper held fast by a rubber band or a length of thread holding a needle, and if bought from a vendor in town, with a wad of cotton stuffed in one end. The rationale here is "let the spirits make their own clothes." This tube of paper may be offered by people who do not take the trouble to make or buy the finished (paper) clothes or it may be offered to more remote ancestral spirits, whose bones, now part of the tilled soil, are only a vague memory or a notion. The rule of thumb seems to be that as the persona of the deceased recedes from the living memory, the offerings become more generic and cater less to the personal tastes of the recipient.

To observe the Winter Sacrifice firsthand, and specifically the role of paper money in it, Wang Li and I set off by bus for Yu County in December 2007. Our host, who we addressed as Lao Tian, was widely recognized for his studies of Yu County opera and paper-cutting trades. Arriving in the county seat late in the evening, we set off for Tian's cottage, built against the outer side of the city wall. Threading our way through the maze of brick-walled lanes, we had only the moonlight to keep us from stumbling over a stray brick or falling into a hole. The thought of losing our way or not finding our host at home only quickened the cold that was already working its way through the pads of my coat. Just as I began thinking that we had better try something else, Wang Li came to the familiar gate, and with a shared frisson of relief, we pounded on it. A light went on and we were invited inside, where we were given a drink of hot water and some warm quilts. In the following days, Tian vouched for our presence in the county and introduced us to a member of the Zhang family from an outlying village, who kindly agreed to let us accompany his extended family on their *shàngfén* (pilgrimage to the family burial mounds) on old tombs day.

If the Yu County ballads that tell of the pathos of *shàngfén* are any measure, then we could anticipate the emotional importance of the pending pilgrimage. On the morning of old tombs, the Zhang family gathered in one of their cottages to prepare their *shàngfén*. For our little assembly of seven adults and a child, the way to the mounds took a half-hour walk through gullies and ravines flanked by terraces of yellow earth with its stubble of the autumn harvest. The four men (each representing a branch of the extended family) walked ahead carrying a cooler and plastic bag of paper offerings plus dried cornstalks from the harvest, and the three women (wives) followed some little distance behind with baskets of steamed wheat buns. The little boy with a stocking cap, just about the age of Jingjing and little Paul, ran ahead of the men. The day was cold; only the late morning sun shining in a clear blue sky gave me a feeling of warmth inside my padded coat. Everyone was dressed in dark winter clothes with padded coats; the somber color was somewhat offset by the red decor on the women's coats. Ascending the ridge, we came to the cluster of Zhang family burial mounds rising one or two meters above the surrounding surface. The six unmarked, more or less eroded mounds retained a vague semblance of their original conical shape, representing several generations back to a common great-grandfather. Since people forget whose bones are in which mound, some Yu County families paste a big picture on the wall over their family altar depicting the names and locations of the tombs and their genealogical connections. The first thing the men did was to point to each mound and remind each other of the genealogical relationship of each of the interred to the men assembled there.

When the women arrived, everyone went about the business at hand, with which I had become familiar in other parts of China. Some of the men went to each mound, placing and lighting a pair of candles to illuminate a space in the shadowy world where each spirit could receive a share of the food and paper money. Another man planted three locally made incense sticks on each mound to alert the spirit to the presence of the offerings. The central offering was food, a plate holding a steamed wheat bun with chopsticks plus another bowl of festive food, which one of the women went about placing in the luminous space at the foot of each mound. The fare seemed simple and sparse to me, but this was winter, when things are spare.

Meanwhile, some of the men took the various paper monies out of their plastic bags—again, as with the food, nothing extravagant—and with no particular procedure and rather nonchalantly, placed a share of the papers at the foot of each mound. I was able to note the papers in front of the main mound; they included home-folded gold and silver ingots known around China as *yuánbǎo* (first treasures), a few of the traditional Yu County–style folded *báizhǐ* (white paper) signifying "silver," and a stack of "ghost bills"—this is the term Yu County folks use for simulated treasury notes—with face values of ¥50 and ¥100. These were unceremoniously peeled off in small bunches. The men then placed the dried cornstalks over the bottom edge of the papers as "fire starters." And within a matter of minutes, the cornstalks were turned into torches gobbling up the paper clothes and valuables. While one of the men stirred the fire with a stick to make sure the whole treasure was delivered to the other side, the little boy came by with a small fistful of ghost bills—these were the same kind of money that Jingjing's parents burned—which he was urged to throw on the fire. He threw some on, then ran off to another fire to feed it in like manner, with none of Jingjing's qualms; he delighted in darting about burning the paper money—he went from mound to mound with his little fistful of ghost bills, feeding each little fire. At about the same time, the women took the remaining wheat buns from their baskets, pulled off pieces and tossed them on each mound as if tossing food to birds. The same fragrance that alerts family spirits to the presence of returning sustenance also attracts other ghosts from around the vicinity, and they also need to be fed, lest they take from the family members.

My task was, first, trying to physically keep out of the way while remaining attuned to the local norms of sociability, and, second, keeping a peripheral view of all the concurrent happenings and making mental notes of them all. My only participation in the ceremony was to observe it with as much informed and intuitive empathy as I could muster. I was not going about inspecting, much less recording every detail of every offering. From what I gathered, each old tomb received somewhat different paper monies, but based on the manner in which the papers were placed, I surmised that the differences were more fortuitous than planned and that each of the interred got an equitable share of the pie. If it was otherwise, then I missed it.

Of course, the more often we see these kinds of ceremonies, the easier it is to make such inferences. Having seen hundreds of common services, I could anticipate each part and then notice what was different about this particular one. In this case, there were (with the exception of firecrackers) the usual categories of offerings in proper sequence, although each member of the group followed the sequence according to his or her own sense of task and timing, with little formal attempt at coordination.[1] Everyone knew the order of things and what had to be done and went about doing it. The participants seemed casual and low key in their actions, continuing in subdued tones the small talk that had been going on during the walk to the mounds. But on the whole, taken in its totality, the sequence of offerings was noticeable to anyone who cared to notice it, and from long experience, one understands that there was nothing arbitrary about it (Blake 2011a).

The essential message to the spirits was conveyed in the sequence of burning things. This obviates but does not exclude the spoken word. Words are often muttered: "Mama, come here, take these winter clothes; Papa, come take the money . . ." But words are not necessary, and our hosts addressed no words of which I was aware, either spoken or written, to the assembled spirits. The unspoken gestures and sequence of material offerings, each a different kind of fire, conveyed the message.

To my knowledge, there is no common exegesis that explains the reasoning behind the common ritual service, but a little reflection discloses an implicit reasoning, which I base on the axiom of the material spirit mentioned earlier. It goes something like this: The whole service has as its purpose to separate space from time, to create a "time out of time" in order to commune with the spirits and recreate the cosmic vitality between the deceased and the living. This is the Chinese notion of immortality. Second, this purpose is accomplished by the alchemy of fire. Each material in the offering sequence (candle, fragrant wood, food, paper, and thatch) helps to recreate cosmic vitality with its unique way of burning (or aural fire). It begins with the slow burning of candles (glowing) and incense (smoldering). It ends in the rapid burning of thatch and paper money (popping and crackling). In between the slow burning and the rapid burning, which is visible, there is the invisible heat that food gives off in its metabolic phase. Thus, through the fire of candlelight, which lights up the "mind's eye" in imagination, reverie, and insight, we experience a suspension in the blooming, buzzing confusion of the here and now. This suspension is as if stepping through the veil of mundane time into timeless space, a Wordsworthian sort of "intimation of immortality." This aural luminescence of candlelight is further animated by the fragrance of burning wood; for nothing seems to trigger intimations of immortality as acutely as the scent of burning wood. It is the fragrant smoke that alerts the sentient spirits, and the spirits of the flesh, to each other's presence.[2] Chinese say "burning fragrance is the food of the spirits." Having awakened the sentience of the spirits, the offering of worldly sustenance (steamed wheat buns and other dishes) vivifies the gathering of embodied and disembodied spirits around the act of eating food together.[3] Commensality (eating together) is the ultimate "social metabolism," perhaps because it is a metonym for the food that is being consumed and metabolized—the aural fire par excellence. The metabolic fire is manifest in the inner feeling of fullness and warmth, the essence of life. In both the social and the physiological metabolic phases, distinctions between spirit and flesh are suspended and unapparent to the world of mundane objects (that is, the metabolic phase of aural fire is not visible to the mundane gaze). Spirit becomes sentient and sentience (flesh) becomes spirit. After the food service comes the offering of paper money (and thatch). The aural fire is relit, but now it flares, pops, and crackles, producing exterior heat and sound, animating sensations of tactility and hearing that are consonant with return to the blooming, buzzing confusion of the *temporal* ordering of space, discreet *objects of value*, and the *mortal* souls of individual beings.

Asked how they explain the reasoning behind this or that part of the service, local folks can offer other mystifications to explain this one or come up with less interesting utilitarian reasons, or refer you to a spirit master, but generally they seem satisfied in answering that "it's our tradition." For the ethnographer, "it's our tradition" sounds trite and comes across as dismissive. That is, until we come to realize that for our hosts, the notion of tradition is entirely adequate as a motive, a reason, and an explanation. For it not only preserves a mysterious truth, *a truth that by its very nature is ineluctable,* but it invokes what is more to the point—the way things have always been and will always be. This point of view finds little or no resonance among inmates of the modern or postmodern world of interests, utilities, and relativities. Those of us who take up the challenge of ethnography must preserve our hosts' sense of tradition, their mysteries, and their auras of authenticities. At the same time, we must wear our ethnologist hat, which calls us to the task of disclosing the deeper, often implicit meaning that links this particular tradition to other traditions and to bigger questions, such as the ones little Paul and Jingjing asked their papas. To the extent that we can disclose some of the reasoning implicit in the ritual of indemnifying spirits by burning money, we can also show that it is not the hodgepodge of superstitious nonsense that many outsiders, including many Chinese, think it is (Blake 2011b), but a rather sophisticated alchemy of the material spirit wherein aural fire makes becoming human possible. Certainly, the Chinese service is not to be disparaged by those who prefer their mysteries in the Judeo-Christian and Islamic Book of Genesis (1:3) where "God said, let there be light, and there was light."

Notes

1. The coordination came with the finale of the offering service when every member of this little assembly got down on hands and knees and in perfect unison kowtowed to each mound in turn. This is described in the longer version of this essay.
2. The notion that fragrance animates spiritual being(s) is known to many peoples; it is pervasive among Native Americans who burn fragrant leaves (tobacco) and also among religious devotees in other parts of the world who burn a variety of fragrant woods (incense).
3. The food offering is a shared feast between the live donors and the spirit recipients. The spirits ingest the "life" or spiritual aspect of the animal or plant offering (or sacrifice) while the living donors ingest the "flesh" or material remains of the offering. They may eat it picnic style at the tomb, or take it home to eat, or leave it for scavengers or the ants. In the present case, the material remains of the food offering were simply left at the tomb.

Epilogue

Fieldwork Today

Geoffrey White

Disciplines thrive on crisis. Area studies thrive on crisis. Not the kinds of crises associated with economic distress or political violence, but crises of the episteme, of the bases for knowledge that underpin our assumptions about what we do and the institutional structures that support them. It may seem clichéd to begin this epilogue with an invocation of the value of Kuhnian moments of change, but reviewing the issues taken up in these contributions offers a snapshot of the shifting terrain for fieldwork-style research. If we require evidence for today's instabilities, we need only reflect on the fragile nature of all the terms of the project: "field," "ethnography," "Asia," "Pacific"—all in motion and contested. Yet all in some way validated by the on-the-ground work taken up in these essays.

Consider, for example, the terms "Asia" and "Pacific"—terms ingrained in our geopolitical vocabulary but also subjects of critical scrutiny examining their contingent historical and political character. Even as scholars now see terms such as "Asia" or "the Pacific" as always to some degree arbitrary and political, they continue to guide programmatic and institutional identities in Asian and Pacific studies. The University of Hawai'i, for instance, prides itself as an "Asia Pacific" university, acknowledging the importance of the region in its School of Pacific and Asian Studies with its many area studies centers and strengths featured in departments throughout the campus. And just across the street the East-West Center (where cultural "east" is geographically "west" and cultural "west" "east") inhabits a genealogy of research "on" Asia that has long been associated with formations of U.S. empire.

In the 1990s, in response to the recognition that the idea of "culture area" and the traditions of study that go with it were increasingly destabilized by the forces of globalization, the Ford Foundation launched a major initiative called "Crossing Borders: Revitalizing Area Studies." Under this rubric, the foundation gave out a significant number of institutional grants, including to the University of Hawaiʻi, to support innovative projects designed to stimulate new approaches to area study. Far from launching a new era of "global studies," however, the Crossing Borders projects for the most part demonstrated that insight into the social significance of globalization requires research strategies capable of *both* depth (ability to "thicken" descriptions of context) and breadth (ability to trace global connections and flows).

Despite our inclination to deconstruct the "areas" of area studies, these concepts remain valuable and even necessary among scholars whose research takes culture and local knowledge seriously. The kind of attention to local(ized) realities typical of area scholarship not only fosters a certain methodological sophistication capable of reading local subjectivities but also fosters awareness of the political and ethical dimensions of research itself. Granted a heightened awareness of the global forces that traverse localities everywhere, the intensely human and interpersonal dimensions of fieldwork reported in this volume draw these scholars into close engagements with the communities they study.

In a variety of ways, then, the conversations that emerge from today's fieldwork projects demonstrate the continuing value of the geopolitical fictions that have long facilitated dialogue in the sociocultural disciplines. Thus, for example, the authors reporting on work in the Pacific Islands region, including most of those in Hawaiʻi, are concerned in some measure with formations of indigeneity—formations that concern not only the valorization of ancestry, land, and oral traditions but also, importantly, awareness of the need to recreate and indigenize research practices that have often been bound up with colonial histories. Having said this, it is also important to note that "indigeneity" today is not what indigeneity may have been in earlier generations; we see here a set of ideologies and practices in motion, moving in concert with political histories and movements that articulate with global developments in the form of political changes, new international legal regimes, and global alliances among indigenous groups.

Consider, also, another key term in this volume's title: "the field." The field for the majority of authors in this collection is still "out there," a place distant from personal and academic homes. Yet, for a number, the field *is* home. The figure of the native researcher (whether indigenous or simply working at home) now complicates much of the discourse about insiders and outsiders doing fieldwork. The conventional paradigms of fieldwork are built on narratives of travel and boundary crossing. But as the number of ethnographers working "at home" has expanded, the category of native ethnographer has itself become more complex and internally varied. Like more traditional sorts of boundary crossing, the voices of native scholars now speak of negotiating all sorts of boundaries to validate their identities as community members and as researchers. One of the important lessons to emerge from the mix of field situations presented here is the insight that the most significant elements of our concept of "the field" may have nothing to do with travel. Whether fieldworkers travel outside their own homelands or reestablish themselves in familiar communities, each confronts the need to (re)define himself or herself in ways that elucidate and validate research as social action.

Certainly, the studies gathered here tell us about border crossing. The titles are replete with spatial metaphors of location (". . . Placing Rapa Nui Language," "Entering Moloka'i . . . ," ". . . Locating Marriage Partners . . ."), travel (". . . A Navigator's Journey," "Fieldwork on Two Wheels . . . ," "They Came for Nature . . ."), and positionality, especially the predicament of in-betweenness (". . . Home Court (Dis)Advantage . . . ," "When the Field Is Your Home . . ."). Reading these authors' personal accounts, it quickly becomes apparent that spatial metaphors are not so much about movement and place as morality. Again and again these fieldworkers discover that being "in-between" is fraught with moral risks and rewards to be negotiated in the experience-near encounters of fieldwork.

These authors describe a stunning variety of problems and predicaments confronted in the course of carrying out their research. Their accounts show, first, that even knowing what counts as a relevant problem or meaningful question requires communicative competence, knowledge of local issues, and a measure of trust and cooperation. Whereas these exigencies have always been part of successful fieldwork, today's fieldworkers deal with these issues in an environment that is always already structured by global flows of information and capital.

The contributions to this volume, all intensely embedded in the particularities of cultural contexts, local histories, and political practices, also document the extent to which new technologies have accelerated the pace of flows of culture and capital. Far from erasing difference or dissolving boundaries, however, the new technologies that appear in these studies are just as likely to be put to use in the intensification of the local. Whereas these effects may be empowering, they may also have a darker side. After a brief period in which the new possibilities introduced by the Internet and cellular networks led to speculation that a world made smaller by interconnection would also be a world of enhanced mutual understanding, we now know that exactly the opposite has occurred. It is now apparent that although the Internet and social media afford wildly expanded connectedness, today's hyperaccelerated connections are driven by the same desires and tastes that have always driven efforts to create and validate existing identities. Longstanding boundary-making and "othering" practices are now elaborated with untold new possibilities through the consumption of likeminded "news," blogs, feeds, and tweets. These developments should not surprise anyone who understands that it is not technology as brute fact but technology as used, as social practice, that most affects our lives.

The updates that we are privy to in this volume make it clear that even (or especially?) in the era of the Internet, cellular networks, social media, and so forth, the success of international and intercultural study has as much to do with the ethical and political dimensions of research as new modes of data collection and analysis (although those modalities, too, have a strong presence in these essays). The stories from the field that unfold here provide a kind of map of the moral terrain for twenty-first century fieldwork. We should not be surprised, then, to find that many of the titles of these essays reflect the personal and affective dimensions of fieldwork: "An Anthropologist Behaving Badly . . . ," "Head Candy/Gut Connection . . . ," "Manning Up . . . ," "Embattled Stories . . . ," ". . . Inspiring the Future in Hawai'i," ". . . Transformative Experience . . . ," ". . . Negotiating Sentiment . . ."

The valuable thread that ties these studies together is their shared concern to confront these issues and articulate the shifting ethics of fieldwork in an era when globalization is intensifying the politics of the local at the same time it expands the reach of global connectivity. Among the useful lessons emerging from these pages is that just as the challenges of fieldwork today are radically different than they were just two or three decades ago, so they will be, also, in the decades to follow. As we ponder the possibilities for the future when "the field" may be unrecognizable in ways we cannot yet imagine, it is also useful to hear in these stories echoes of a longer history of fieldwork as a space for (re)defining research itself.

Bibliography

Abo, T., B. Bender, A. Capelle, and T. DeBrum. 1976. *Marshallese-English Dictionary*. Honolulu: University of Hawai'i Press.

Akutagawa, M. 2014. "Restoring 'Āina Momona and Sust 'ĀINA bility to the Earth/Sust 'āina ble Molokai." http://sustainablemolokai.org/restoring -aina-momona-and-sust-aina-bility-to-the-earth/.

American Anthropological Association (AAA). 2012. "Code of Ethics of the American Anthropological Association, Approved February 2009." http://www.aaanet.org/issues/policy-advocacy/Code-of-Ethics.cfm.

Amos, J. 2012. "Path of Tsunami Debris Mapped Out. BBC." http://earthquake.usgs.gov/earthquakes/recenteqsww/Quakes/usc0001xgp.php#summary.

Anderson, B. 1983. *Imagined Communities: Reflections on the Origin and Spread of Nationalism*. London: Verso.

Arno, A. 2005. "*Cobo* and *Tabua* in Fiji: Two Forms of Cultural Currency in an Economy of Sentiment." *American Ethnologist* 32 (1): 46–62.

Ascher, M. 1995. "Models and Maps from the Marshall Islands: A Case in Ethnomathematics." *Historia Mathematica* 22: 347–370.

Bacdayan, A. S. 1967. *The Peace Pact System of the Kalingas in the Modern World*. Ithaca, NY: Cornell University Press.

Bakhtin, M. M. 2002. *The Dialogic Imagination: Four Essays*. Austin: University of Texas Press.

Barker, H. 2013. *Bravo for the Marshallese: Regaining Control in a Post-Nuclear, Post-Colonial World*. Belmont, CA: Wadsworth Cengage Learning.

Barnard, H. R. 2006. *Research Methods in Anthropology: Qualitative and Quantitative Approaches*. 4th ed. Lanham, MD: Alta Mira Press.

Beasley, I. L., H. Marsh, T. A. Jefferson, and P. Arnold. 2010. "Conserving Dolphins in the Mekong River: The Complex Challenge of Competing Interests." In *The Biology and Ecology of the Mekong River,* edited by I. Campbell, 365–388. Amsterdam: Academic Press.

Becker, A. 1995. *Body, Self and Society: The View from Fiji.* Philadelphia: University of Pennsylvania Press.

Berkes, F. 2008. *Sacred Ecology.* New York: Routledge.

Besnier, N. 2009. "Modernity, Consumption, and the Emergence of Middle Classes in Tonga." *Contemporary Pacific* 21 (2): 215–262.

———. 2011. *On the Edge of the Global: Modern Anxieties in a Pacific Island Nation.* Palo Alto, CA: Stanford University Press.

Billiet, F., and F. Lambrecht. 1970. *Studies on Kalinga Ullálim and Ifugaw Orthography.* Baguio City, Philippines: Catholic School Press.

Blake, C. F. 2011a. *Burning Money: The Material Spirit of the Chinese Lifeworld.* Honolulu: University of Hawai'i Press.

———. 2011b. "Lampooning the Paper Money Custom in Contemporary China." *Journal of Asian Studies* 70 (2): 449–469.

Boas, F. 1911. "Introduction." In *Handbook of American Indian Languages.* Bulletin 40, Part 1, edited by Boas, 1–83. Bureau of American Ethnology. Washington, DC: Government Printing Office.

Bolton, L. 2003. *Unfolding the Moon: Enacting Women's Kastom in Vanuatu.* Honolulu: University of Hawai'i Press.

Bott, E. 1981. "Power and Rank on the Kingdom of Tonga." *Journal of the Polynesian Society* 90(1): 7–81.

Bourdieu, P. 1984. *Distinction: A Social Critique of the Judgment of Taste.* Translated by R. Nice. Cambridge, MA: Harvard University Press.

Briggs, C. L. 1986. *Learning How to Ask: A Sociolinguistic Appraisal of the Role of the Interview in Social Science Research.* Cambridge: Cambridge University Press.

Brosius, J. P., A. L. Tsing, and C. Zerner. 1998. "Representing Communities: Histories and Politics of Community-Based Natural Resource Management." *Society and Natural Resources* 11 (2). doi: 10.1080/08941929809381069.

Buddhadasa Bhikhu. 1990. *The First Ten Years of Suan Mokh.* Chaiya, Thailand: Dhammadana Foundation.

Bui, M. 1999. "An Anti-Corruption Strategy for Provincial Government in Papua New Guinea." *Asia Pacific School of Economics and Management Working Papers.* Asia Pacific Press at the Australian National University. https://digitalcollections.anu.edu.au/handle/1885/41606 (accessed 9 August 2013).

Campbell, I. C. 2009. *The Mekong: Biophysical Environment of an International River Basin.* Amsterdam: Academic Press.

Carino, J., and R. Villanueva. 1995. *Dumaloy ang Ilog Chico (And so the Chico River Flows)*. Manila: GABRIELA National Alliance of Women's Organizations.

Carino, J., J. Carino, and G. Nettleton. 1979. "The Chico River Basin Development Project: A Situation Report." *Agham-Tao* 2.

Carson, M. T. 2002. "*Ti* Ovens in Polynesia: Ethnological and Archaeological Perspectives." *Journal of the Polynesian Society* 4: 339–370.

Cassidy, P. 1991. "The Good Body: When Big Is Better." *American Anthropologist* 13: 181–213.

Chandra, R., and K. Mason, eds. 1998. *An Atlas of Fiji*. Suva: University of the South Pacific.

Chappell, D. 1995. "Active Agents versus Passive Victims: Decolonized Historiography or Problematic Paradigm?" *Contemporary Pacific* 7 (2): 303–326.

Charlot, J. 1986. "Towards a Dialogue between Christianity and Polynesian Religions." *Sciences Religieuses/Studies in Religion* 15 (4) (Fall): 443–450.

Chauvel, R. 2005. *Constructing Papuan Nationalism: History, Ethnicity, and Adaptation*. Washington, DC: East-West Center.

Chen, D. 1997. *Zhiqian (xiaoxiaoshuo)* [Paper money (short story)], *Renmin Ribao* (Overseas edition), July 21, 7.

Clifford, J. 1986. "Introduction: Partial Truths." In *Writing Culture: The Poetics and Politics of Ethnography*, edited by J. Clifford and G. Marcus, 1–26. Berkeley: University of California Press.

———. 1988. *The Predicament of Culture: Twentieth Century Ethnography, Literature, and Art*. Cambridge, MA: Harvard University Press.

———. 1996. "Spatial Practices: Fieldwork, Travel, and the Disciplining of Anthropology." In *Anthropological Locations: Boundaries and Grounds of a Field Science*, edited by Akhil Gupta and James Ferguson, 185–222. Berkeley: University of California Press.

Clifford, J., and G. E. Marcus, eds. 1986. *Writing Culture: The Poetics and Politics of Ethnography*. Berkeley: University of California Press.

Cohen, E. 2007. "The 'Postmodernization' of a Mythical Event: Naga Fireballs on the Mekong River." *Tourism, Culture, and Communication* 7 (3): 169–181.

Collins, E. F. 2002. "Indonesia: A Violent Culture?" *Asian Survey* 42 (4): 582–605.

Cookson, M. 2013. "Chronology of Papua (Irian Jaya, West Papua, . . .)." http://www.papuaweb.org/chrono/files/kp.html.

Cordillera People's Alliance. 2009. "Mother Petra 'Tannaw' Macliing: A Shining Light in the Rural Landscape of Northern Philippines." *Hapit* 17 (3): 5–6.

Costa, L. M., and A. Matzner. 2007. *Male Bodies, Women's Souls: Personal Narratives of Thailand's Transgendered Youth*. New York: Routledge/Haworth.

Cumings, B. 2011. *The Korean War: A History.* New York: Modern Library.

Davidson, J. W. 1966. "Problems of Pacific History." *Journal of Pacific History* 1: 5–21.

de Blij, H. 2009. *The Power of Place: Geography, Destiny, and Globalization's Rough Landscape.* Oxford: Oxford University Press.

De Marquette, J. 1965. *Introduction to Comparative Mysticism.* Bombay: Bharatiya Vidya Bhavan.

de Renzio, P. 2000. "Bigmen and Wantoks: Social Capital and Group Behaviour in Papua New Guinea." *QEH* Working Paper no. 27. http://citeseerx.ist.psu.edu/viewdoc/download?doi=10.1.1.199.2663&rep=rep1&type=pdf, January 2000.

Dickens, C. 1974. *Dombey and Son,* edited by E. A. Horsman. Oxford: Clarendon Press.

Digicel Vanuatu. 2012. "Prepaid Digicel." http://www.digicelvanuatu.com/en /plans/digiflex.

Di Luca, J. 2012. "Adriano Favole, Oceania. Isole Di Creivitá Culturale." *Antropologia e Teatro* 3: 347–348.

Doi, T. 1986. *The Anatomy of Self: The Individual vs. Society.* Tokyo: Kodansha.

Dozier, E. P. 1964. "The Kalinga Peace-Pact Institution." Des Actes du VI Congress International des Sciences Anthropologiques et Ethnologiques, Paris, 1960, Tome II (Volume 2), 315–319.

Duranti, A. 2003. "Language as Culture in U.S. Anthropology." *Current Anthropology* 44 (3): 323–347.

Duranti, A., and C. Goodwin. 1992. *Rethinking Context: Language as an Interactive Phenomenon.* Cambridge: Cambridge University Press.

Elmslie, J. 2002. *Irian Jaya Under the Gun: Indonesian Economic Development Versus West Papuan Nationalism.* Honolulu: University of Hawai'i Press.

Erickson, K. A. 2007. "Tight Spaces and Salsa-stained Aprons: Bodies at Work in American Restaurants." In *Restaurants Book: Ethnographies of Where We Eat,* edited by D. Beriss and D. Sutton, 17–23. Oxford: Berg.

Eriksen, A. 2008. *Gender, Christianity and change in Vanuatu: An Analysis of Social Movements in North Ambrym.* Burlington: Ashgate.

Ernest-Jenks, A. 1905. "The Bontoc Igorot, Ethnological Survey Publications." Vol. 1. Manila: Bureau of Public Printing.

Faubion, J. D., and G. Marcus. 2009. *Fieldwork Is Not What It Used to Be: Learning Anthropology's Method in a Time of Transition.* Ithaca, NY: Cornell University Press.

Feld, S., and K. H. Basso. 1996. *Senses of Place.* Santa Fe: School of American Research Press.

Finin, G. A. 2008. *The Making of the Igorot: Contours of Cordillera Consciousness.* Manila: Ateneo de Manila University Press.

Finney, B. R. 1979. *Hokule'a: The Way to Tahiti.* New York: Dodd, Mead.

———. 1991. "Myth, Experiment, and the Reinvention of Polynesian Voyaging." *American Anthropologist* 93 (2): 383–404.

———. 1994. *Voyage of Rediscovery*. Berkeley: University of California Press.

———. 1998. "Traditional Navigation and Nautical Cartography in Oceania." In *The History of Cartography, Vol.3, part 2: Cartography in the Traditional African, American, Arctic, Australian, and Pacific Societies*, edited by D. Woodward and G. M. Lewis, 443–492. Chicago and London: University of Chicago Press.

———. 2001. "Voyage to Polynesia's Land's End." *Antiquity* 75: 172–181.

———. 2003. *Sailing in the Wake of the Ancestors: Reviving Polynesian Voyaging*. Honolulu: Bishop Museum Press.

Finney, S. S., and M. W. Graves. 2002. *Site Identification and Documentation of a Civil War Shipwreck Thought to Be Sunk by the C.S.S. Shenandoah in April 1865*. Prepared for the American Battlefield Protection Program, National Park Service, Washington, DC.

Forsyth, M. 2004. "Beyond Case Law: Kastom and Courts in Vanuatu." *University of Wellington Law Review* 35: 427–446.

Foucault, M. 1972. "The Discourse on Language." In *The Archaeology of Knowledge*, 215–237. New York: Pantheon Books.

———. 1981. "The Order of Discourse." In *Untying the Text: A Post-Structuralist Reader*, edited by R. Young, 48–78. Boston: Routledge and Kegan Paul.

———. 1990 [1978]. *The History of Sexuality, Volume 1: An Introduction*. R. Hurley, trans. New York: Vintage.

———. 2003. *"Society Must Be Defended": Lectures at the College de France 1975–1976*. New York: Picador.

Fujikane, C., and J. Y. Okamura. 2008. *Asian Settler Colonialism: From Local Governance to the Habits of Everyday Life in Hawai'i*. Honolulu: University of Hawai'i Press.

Gard, M., and J. Wright. 2005. *The Obesity Epidemic: Science, Morality, and Ideology*. London: Routledge.

Gaudes, R. 1993. "Kaundinya, Preah Thaong Kauṇḍinya, Preah Thaong, and the 'Nāgī Somā': Some Aspects of a Cambodian Legend." *Asian Folklore Studies* 52 (2): 333–358.

Geertz, C. 1973a. "Deep Play: Notes on the Balinese Cockfight." In *The Interpretation of Cultures*, 412–453. New York: Basic Books.

———. 1973b. *The Interpretation of Cultures: Selected Essays*. New York: Basic Books.

———. 1983. *Local Knowledge: Further Essays in Interpretative Anthropology*. New York: Basic Books.

Gegeo, D. W., and K. A. Watson-Gegeo. 2001. "'How We Know': Kwara'ae Rural Villagers Doing Indigenous Epistemology." *Contemporary Pacific* 13: 55–88.

Genz, J. 2011. "Navigating the Revival of Voyaging in the Marshall Islands: Predicaments of Preservation and Possibilities of Collaboration." *Contemporary Pacific* 23 (1): 1–34.

Genz, J., J. Aucan, M. Merrifield, B. R. Finney, K. Joel, and A. Kelen. 2009. "Wave Navigation in the Marshall Islands: Comparing Indigenous and Scientific Knowledge of the Ocean." *Oceanography* 22 (2): 234–245.

Gilman, S. 2008. *Fat: A Cultural History of Obesity.* Cambridge: Polity Press.

Goldman, M. 2004. "Eco-governmentality and Other Transnational Practices of a 'Green' World Bank." *Liberation Ecologies: Environment, Development, Social Movements,* edited by R. Peet and M. Watts, 166–192. New York: Routledge.

Gombrich, R. 1984. "Introduction: The Buddhist Way." In *The World of Buddhism,* edited by H. Bechert and R. Gombrich, 9–14. London: Thames and Hudson.

Goodman, A., T. N. Williams, and K. Maitland. 2003. "Ciguatera Poisoning in Vanuatu." *American Journal of Tropical Medicine and Hygiene* 68 (2): 263–266.

Goodman, D. S. G. 2004. "Qinghai and the Emergence of the West: Nationalities, Communal Interaction and the Emergence of the West." *China Quarterly* 178: 379–399.

Goodyear-Kaopua, N., and M. T. Baker. 2012. "The Great Shift: Moving beyond a Fossil Fuel-Based Economy." *Hūlili: Multidisciplinary Research on Hawaiian Well-Being* 8: 131–164.

Grand, S. 2002. "Dieu serait-il devenu indépendantiste?" *Tahiti-Pacifique* 136 (August): 37.

Grosz, E. 1994. *Volatile Bodies: Toward a Corporeal Feminism.* London: Routledge.

Gumperz, J. J. 1982. *Discourse Strategies.* Cambridge: Cambridge University Press.

Gunson, N. 1963. "Histoire de la Mamaia ou hérésie visionnaire de Tahiti, 1826–1841." *Bulletin de la Société des Etudes Océaniennes* 143–144: 235–294.

Halapua, W. 1998. *Destination Culture: Tourism, Museums, and Heritage.* Berkeley: University of California Press.

———. 2003. *Tradition, Lotu and Militarism in Fiji.* Lautoka: Fiji Institute of Applied Studies.

Hall, T. D. 2009. *Indigenous Peoples and Globalization: Resistance and Revitalization.* Boulder, CO: Paradigm.

Hanks, W. F. 2000. *Intertexts: Writings on Language, Utterance, and Context.* Boulder: Rowman and Littlefield.

Hanlon, D. 2003. "Beyond 'The English Method of Tattooing': Decentering the Practice of History in Oceania." *Contemporary Pacific* 15 (1): 19–40.

Hashimoto, S. 2008. "Spirit Cults and Buddhism in Luang Prabang, Laos: Analyses of Rituals in the Boat Race Festivals." *International Journal of Sport and Health Science* 6: 219–229.

Hatsadong, K., K. Dougansila, and P. Gibson. 2006. "Rice-Based Traditions and Rituals in the Lower Mekong River Valley." In *Rice in Laos,* edited by J. M. Schiller, M. B. Chanphengxay, B. Linquist, and S. Appa Rao, 65–78. Manilla: International Rice Research Institute.

Hau'ofa, E. 1993. "Our Sea of Islands." In *A New Oceania: Rediscovering Our Sea of Islands,* edited by E. Waddell, V. Naidu, and E. Hau'ofa, 2–16. Suva: University of the South Pacific School of Social and Economic Development.

Hawaii Business Research Library. 2007. *Maui County Data Book 2007.* http://www.hbrl-sbdc.org/mcdb.htm.

Hayamizu K. 2011. *Rāmen to aikoku.* Tokyo: Kodhansha.

Hays, I., ed. 2005. *Qualitative Research Methods in Human Geography.* Melbourne: Oxford University Press.

Helman, C. 2000. *Culture, Health and Illness.* 4th ed. New York: Oxford University Press.

Henry, T. 1928. *Ancient Tahiti* (based on material recorded by J. M. Orsmond). Honolulu: Bishop Museum.

Hoang, H. P., and Y. Nishimura. 2000. "The Historical Environment and Housing Conditions in the '36 Old Streets' Quarter of Hanoi." In *Shelter and Living in Hanoi,* edited by Trin Duy Luan, 10–56. Hanoi: Cultural Publishing House.

Holt, J. C. 2009. *Spirits of the Place: Buddhism and Lao Religious Culture.* Honolulu: University of Hawai'i Press.

Horst, H., and D. Miller. 2006. *The Cell Phone: An Anthropology of Communication.* Oxford: Berg.

Howard, A. 2000. "Pacific-Based Virtual Communities: Rotuma on the World Wide Web." In *Voyaging Through the Contemporary Pacific,* edited by D. Hanlon and G. M. White, 403–418. Lanham, MD: Rowman and Littlefield.

Hunt, T. L., and C. P. Lipo. 2012. *The Statues that Walked: Unraveling the Mystery of Easter Island.* New York: Free Press.

Inda, J. X., and R. Rosaldo. 2008. "Tracking Global Flows." In *The Anthropology of Globalization: A Reader,* 2nd ed., edited by J. X. Inda and R. Rosaldo, 1–46. Oxford: Wiley.

International Work Group for Indigenous Affairs (IWGIA). 2012. *Rapa Nui: The Human Rights of the Rapa Nui People on Easter Island.* IWGIA Report 15. Copenhagen: International Work Group for Indigenous Affairs.

Ito, K. L. 1999. *Lady Friends: Hawaiian Ways and the Ties that Define.* Ithaca, NY: Cornell University Press.

Jackson, P. A. 1995. *Dear Uncle Go: Male Homosexuality in Thailand.* Bangkok: Bua Luang Books.

James, K. 1988. "Rank Overrules Everything: Hierarchy, Social Stratification and Gender in Tonga." *Journal of the Polynesian Society* 96: 233–243.

Jiang, H. 2004. "Cooperation, Land Use, and the Environment in Uxin Ju: A Changing Landscape of a Mongolian-Chinese Borderland in China." *Annals of Association of American Geographers* 94 (1): 117–139.

———. 2006. "Poaching State Politics in Socialist China: Uxin Ju's Grassland Campaign during 1958–1966." *Geographical Review* 96 (4): 633–656.

Johnston, B. R., and H. M. Barker. 2008. *Consequential Damages of Nuclear War: The Rongelap Report*. Walnut Creek, CA: Left Coast Press.

Johnstone, B. 2008. *Discourse Analysis*. Malden, MA: Blackwell.

Jolly, M. 1982. "Birds and Banyans of South Pentecost: *Kastom* in Anti-Colonial Struggle." *Mankind* 13 (4): 338–356.

Keesing, R. M. 1982. "*Kastom* in Melanesia: An Overview." *Mankind* 13 (4): 297–301.

———. 1989. "Creating the Past: Custom and Identity in the Contemporary Pacific." *Contemporary Pacific* 1: 19–42.

Keskinen, M. 2006. "The Lake with Floating Villages: Socio-economic Analysis of the Tonle Sap Lake." *International Journal of Water Resources Development* 22 (3): 463–480.

King, P. 2004. *West Papua & Indonesia since Suharto: Independence, Autonomy or Chaos?* Sydney: University of New South Wales Press.

Kirshenblatt-Gimblett, B. 1998. *Destination Culture: Tourism, Museums, and Heritage*. Berkeley: University of California Press.

Kleinman A., V. Das, and M. Lock. 1997. *Social Suffering*. Berkeley: University of California Press.

Kondo, D. K. 1990. *Crafting Selves: Power, Gender, and Discourses of Identity in a Japanese Workplace*. Chicago: University of Chicago Press.

Kulick, D., and M. Wilson, eds. 1995. *Taboo: Sex, Identity and Erotic Subjectivity in Anthropological Fieldwork*. New York: Routledge.

Kummu, M., J. Sarkkula, J. Koponen, and J. Nikula. 2006. "Ecosystem Management of the Tonle Sap Lake: An Integrated Modelling Approach." *International Journal of Water Resources Development* 22 (3): 497–519.

Kyselka, W. 1987. *An Ocean in Mind*. Honolulu: University of Hawai'i Press.

Labov, W. 1972. *Language in the Inner City*. Philadelphia: University of Pennsylvania Press.

Labrador, R. N. 2004. "'We Can Laugh at Ourselves': Hawai'i Ethnic Humor, Local Identity and the Myth of Multiculturalism." *Pragmatics* 14 (2–3): 291–316.

Lal, B. 2002. *Broken Waves: A History of the Fiji Islands in the Twentieth Century*. Honolulu: University of Hawai'i Press.

Larcom, J. 1982. "The Invention of Convention." *Mankind* 13 (4): 330–337.

———. 1990. "Custom by Decree: Legitimation Crisis in Vanuatu." In *Cultural Identity and Ethnicity in the Pacific*, edited by J. Linnekin and L. Poyer, 175–190. Honolulu: University of Hawai'i Press.

Lattimore, O. 1947. "Inner Asian Frontiers: Chinese and Russian Margins of Expansion." *Journal of Economic History* 7 (1) (May): 24–52.

Lauer, M., and S. Aswani. 2009. "Indigenous Ecological Knowledge as Situated Practices: Understanding Fishers' Knowledge in the Western Solomon Islands." *American Anthropologist* 111 (3): 317–329.

Lawson, S. 1997. "The Tyranny of Tradition: Critical Reflections on Nationalist Narratives in the South Pacific." In *Narratives of Nation in the South Pacific,* edited by T. Otto and N. Thomas, 15–31. Amsterdam: Harwood Academic.

Lebra, T. S. 1976. *Japanese Patterns of Behavior.* Honolulu: University of Hawai'i Press.

Lee, H. M. 2003. *Tongans Overseas: Between Two Shores.* Honolulu: University of Hawai'i Press.

Lee, H. M., and S. T. Francis, eds. 2009. *Migration and Transnationalism: Pacific Perspectives.* Canberra: Australian National University.

Lévi-Strauss, C. 1966. *The Savage Mind.* Chicago: University of Chicago Press.

Lévi-Strauss, C., J. Weightman, D. Weightman, and P. Wilcken. 2012. *Tristes Tropiques.* New York: Penguin Books.

Li, T. M. 2007. *The Will to Improve: Governmentality, Development, and the Practice of Politics.* Durham, NC: Duke University Press.

Lindstrom, L. 1997. "Context Contests: Debatable Truth Statements on Tanna (Vanuatu)." In *Rethinking Context: Language as an Interactive Phenomenon,* edited by A. Duranti and C. Goodwin, 101–124. Cambridge: Cambridge University Press.

———. 2008. "Melanesian *Kastom* and Its Transformations." *Anthropological Forum* 18 (2): 161–178.

Lindstrom, L., and G. M. White. 1994. "Cultural Policy: An Introduction." In *Culture, Kastom, and Tradition: Developing Cultural Policy in Melanesia,* edited by L. Lindstrom and G. M. White, 1–20. Suva: Institute of Pacific Island Studies, University of the South Pacific.

Linnekin, J. 1991. "Structural History and Political Economy: The Contact Encounter in Hawai'i and Samoa." *History and Anthropology* 5: 205–232.

Longhurst, R., E. Ho, and L. Johnston. 2008. "Using 'the Body' as an 'Instrument of Research': Kimch'i and Pavlova." *Area* 40 (2): 208–217.

Low, S. M., and D. Lawrence-Zuniga. 2003. *The Anthropology of Space and Place: Locating Culture.* Oxford: Blackwell.

Low, S. M., and S. E. Merry. 2010. "Engaged Anthropology: Diversity and Dilemmas." *Current Anthropology* 51 (52): S203–S226.

Lowie, R. H. 1947 [1920]. *Primitive Society.* New York: Liveright.

Lucy, J. A. 1996. "The Scope of Linguistic Relativity: An Analysis and Review of Empirical Research." In *Rethinking Linguistic Relativity,* edited by J. J. Gumperz and S. C. Levinson, 37–69. Cambridge: Cambridge University Press.

Malinowski, B. 1948. "Myth in Primitive Psychology." In *Magic, Science and Religion, and Other Essays*, 93–148. Long Grove, IL: Waveland Press.

———. 1961. *Argonauts of the Western Pacific: An Account of Native Enterprise and Adventure in the Archipelagoes of Melanesian New Guinea.* New York: Dutton.

———. 1965. *Coral Gardens and Their Magic, Volume II: The Language of Magic and Gardening.* Bloomington: Indiana University Press.

———. 1989. *A Diary in the Strict Sense of the Term.* Stanford, CA: Stanford University Press.

Mannan, M. 1978. "Group Norm and Developmental Change in Papua New Guinea." In *Paradise Postponed: Essays on Research and Development in the South Pacific*, edited by A. Mamak and G. McCall, 198–208. Sydney: Young Nations Conference.

Mansfield, S., and M. Koh. 2008. *Cultures of the World: Laos.* Tarrytown, NY: Marshall Cavendish Benchmark.

Marcus, G. E. 1995. "Ethnography in/of the World System: The Emergence of Multi-Sited Ethnography." *Annual Review of Anthropology* 24: 95–117.

Marcus, G. E., and D. Cushman. 1982. "Ethnographies as Texts." *Annual Review of Anthropology* 11: 25–69.

Marek, S. A. 2010. "Māori Urban Geographies of Whakamanatanga: Empowered Māori Urbanism, Space/Place-Based Social Movements and Practices of Everyday Life in Auckland, New Zealand." PhD diss., University of Hawai'i-Mānoa.

Marx, K., and F. Engels. 1978. *The Marx-Engels Reader.* Edited by Robert C. Tucker. New York: W. W. Norton.

Mascia-Lees, F., ed. 2011. *A Companion to the Anthropology of the Body and Embodiment.* Oxford: Wiley-Blackwell.

Mauss, M. 1990. *The Gift: The Form and Reason for Exchange in Archaic Societies.* New York: Norton.

McGregor, D. P. 2007. *Nā Kua'āina: Living Hawaiian Culture.* Honolulu: University of Hawai'i Press.

McKinnon, S. 2005. *Neo-Liberal Genetics: The Myths and Moral Tales of Evolutionary Psychology.* Chicago: Prickly Paradigm Press.

Mead, M. 2001. *Coming of Age in Samoa: A Psychological Study of Primitive Youth for Western Civilisation.* New York: HarperCollins Perennial Classics.

Meleisea, M. 1987. *The Making of Modern Samoa: Traditional Authority and Colonial Administration in the History of Western Samoa.* Suva: Institute of Pacific Studies of the University of the South Pacific.

Meyer, M. A. 2001. "Our Own Liberation: Reflections on Hawaiian Epistemology." *Contemporary Pacific* 13: 124–148.

Miller, D., and H. A. Horst. 2012. *Digital Anthropology.* New York: Bloomsbury Academic.

Mo'olelo Aloha 'Āina. 2010a. "Kupuna vs. Academic Knowledge: Walter Ritte, Jr." http://moolelo.manainfo.com/2010/11/kupuna-knowledge-versus-academic-knowledge/.

———. 2010b. "The Essence Was Aloha 'Āina: Walter Ritte, Jr." http://moolelo.manainfo.com/category/videos/activist/walter-ritte-jr/.

———. 2011. "Aloha 'Āina Is Survival: Joyce Kainoa." http://moolelo.manainfo.com/category/videos/activist/joyce-kainoa/.

Moore, H. L. 1988. *Feminism and Anthropology*. Minneapolis: University of Minnesota Press.

Morales, R., ed. 1984. *Ho'iho'i Hou: A Tribute to George Helm & Kimo Mitchell*. Honolulu: Bamboo Ridge Press.

Moreno, Eva. 1995. "Rape in the Field: Reflections from a Survivor." In *Taboo: Sex, Identity, and Erotic Subjectivity in Anthropological Fieldwork*, edited by D. Kulick and M. Willson, 219–250. London: Routledge.

Morris, B. 2006. *Religion and Anthropology: A Critical Introduction*. London: Cambridge University Press.

Morton, H. 1996. *Becoming Tongan: An Ethnography of Childhood*. Honolulu: University of Hawai'i Press.

Morton Lee, H. 2002. "Creating Their Own Culture: Diasporic Tongans." In *Pacific Diaspora: Island Peoples in the United States and across the Pacific*, edited by P. Spickard, J. L. Rondilla, and D. Hippolite Wright, 135–149. Honolulu: University of Hawai'i Press.

Nabobo-Baba, U. 2006. *Knowing and Learning: An Indigenous Fijian Approach*. Suva: Institute of Pacific Studies, University of the South Pacific.

Nakane, C. 1970. *Japanese Society*. Berkeley: University of California Press.

Na Mata. 1885. "Ai Vola I Tukutuku Vaka Viti." November 30: 1–3.

Nayacakalou, R. 1978. *Tradition and Change in the Fijian Village*, Suva: University of the South Pacific.

Neel, J. 1998. "The Thrifty Genotype in 1998." *Nutrition Reviews* 57 (5): 2–9.

Newendorp, N. D. 2008. *Uneasy Reunions: Immigration, Citizenship, and Family Life in Post-1997 Hong Kong*. Stanford, CA: Stanford University Press.

Okamura, J. Y. 1998. *Imagining the Filipino American Diaspora: Transnational Relations, Identities and Communities*. New York: Garland Publishing.

Ondawame, J. O. 1996. "West Papua: The Discourse of Cultural Genocide and Conflict Resolution." In *Cultural Genocide and Asian State Peripheries*, edited by B. Sautman, 103–138. New York: Palgrave Macmillan.

Peoples, J., and G. Bailey. 2009. *Humanity: An Introduction to Cultural Anthropology*. Belmont, CA: Wadsworth.

Pigliasco, G. C. 2007. "The Custodians of the Gift: Intangible Cultural Property and Commodification of the Fijian Firewalking Ceremony." PhD diss., University of Hawai'i-Mānoa.

————. 2009. "Na Vilavilairevo: The Fijian Firewalking Ceremony." *Domo-domo, Journal of the Fiji Museum* 22 (1 and 2).

————. 2010. "We Branded Ourselves Long Ago: Intangible Cultural Property and Commodification of Fijian Firewalking." *Oceania* 80 (2): 237–257.

Pigliasco, G. C., and F. Colatanavanua, directors. 2005. *A Ituvatuva Ni Vakadi-dike E Sawau* (The Sawau Project). Suva: Institute of Fijian Language and Culture.

Plath, D. 1964. *The After Hours: Modern Japan and the Search for Enjoyment*. Berkeley: University of California Press.

Pollock, N. J. 1995. "Social Fattening Patterns in the Pacific: The Positive Side of Obesity. A Nauru Case Study." In *Social Aspects of Obesity*, edited by I. De Garine and N. Pollock, 87–109. London: Taylor and Francis.

Prill-Brett, J. 1987. *Pechen, the Bontok Peace Pact Institution, Cordillera Mono-graph 1*. Baguio, Philippines: Cordillera Studies Center, University of the Philippines.

————. 2004. "Gender Relations and Gender Issues on Resource Manage-ment in the Central Cordillera, Northern Philippines." *Review of Women's Studies* 14 (1): 1–29.

Raapoto, T. 1989. *Poroi i te nūnaa māitihia e te Atua*. Papeete: Etārētia Evaneria no Porinetia Farāni.

Rabinow, P. 2007. *Reflections on Fieldwork in Morocco*. Berkeley: University of California Press.

Rabinow, P., and G. E. Marcus, with J. D. Faubion and T. Rees. 2008. *Designs for an Anthropology of the Contemporary*. Durham, NC: Duke University Press.

Radcliffe-Brown, A. R. 1940. "On Joking Relationships." *Africa: Journal of the International African Institute* 13 (3): 195–210.

Ramirez, M. A. 1993. *Los Ehemplus Chamorritus/Chamorro Proverbs*. Hagåtña: Konsehelon Tinaotao Guam.

Ravuvu, A. 1983. *Vaka i Taukei: The Fijian Way of Life*. Suva: University of the South Pacific.

————. 1987. *The Fijian Ethos*. Suva: Institute of Pacific Studies, University of the South Pacific.

Regenvanu, R. 2007. "The Year of the Traditional Economy: What Is It all About?" http://www.vanuatuculture.org/site-bm2/trm/20070207_kastom _ekonomi.shtml.

Reilly, B. 2000. "The Africanisation of the South Pacific." *Australian Journal of International Affairs* 54 (3): 261–268.

Rheingold, H. 1996. "A Slice of My Life in My Virtual Community." In *High Noon on the Electronic Frontier: Conceptual Issues in Cyberspace*, edited by P. Ludlow, 413–436. Cambridge, MA: MIT Press.

Rigo, B. 2004. *Alterité polynésienne, ou les métamorphoses de l'espace-temps*. Paris: CRNS Editions.

Robben, A. C. G. M., and C. Nordstrom. 1995. "The Anthropology and Ethnography of Violence and Sociopolitical Conflict." In *Fieldwork under Fire: Contemporary Studies of Violence and Survival*, edited by C. Nordstrom and A. C. G. M. Robben, 81–103. Berkeley: University of California Press.

Robbins, P. 2004. *Political Ecology: A Critical Introduction*. New York: Blackwell.

Robinson, J. 2012. "The UN's Chequered Record in West Papua." http://www.aljazeera.com/indepth/opinion/2012/03/201232172539145809.html.

Rohlf, G. 2003. "Dreams of Oil and Fertile Fields: The Rush to Qinghai in the 1950s." *Modern China* 29 (4): 455–489.

Rosaldo, R. 1988. "Ideology, Place, and People without Culture." *Cultural Anthropology* 3 (1): 77–87.

———. 1993. *Culture & Truth: The Remaking of Social Analysis*. Boston: Beacon Press.

Sahlins, M. 1988. "Cosmologies of Capitalism: The Trans-Pacific Sector of the World System." *Proceedings of the British Academy* 74: 1–51.

———. 1992. "The Economics of Develop-Man in the Pacific." *Res* 21: 12–25.

———. 2011. "What Kinship Is (part one)." *Journal of the Royal Anthropological Institute* (N.S.) 17: 2–19.

Sai, D. K. 2008. "The American Occupation of the Hawaiian Kingdom: Beginning the Transition from Occupied to Restored State." PhD diss., University of Hawai'i-Mānoa.

Salesa, D. 2003. "'Travel Happy' Samoa: Colonialism, Samoan Migration, and a 'Brown Pacific.'" *New Zealand Journal of History* 37 (2): 171–188.

Saliba, J. 1974. "The New Ethnography and the Study of Religion." *Journal for the Scientific Study of Religion* 13 (2): 145–159.

Samudra, J. K. 2003. "Ethics against Violence in a Chinese-Indonesian Martial Art School." *E-AsPac* (Electronic Journal for Asian Studies on the Pacific Coast). http://mcel.pacificu.edu/easpac/2003/sandra.php3/ (accessed August 10, 2012).

Samuels, M. S. 1978. "Individual and Landscape: Thoughts on China and the Tao of Mao." In *Humanistic Geography: Prospects and Problems*, edited by D. Ley and M. S. Samuels, 283–296. Chicago: Maaroufa Press.

San Buenaventura, S. 1995. "Filipino Immigration to the United States: History and Legacy." In *The Asian American Encyclopedia*, edited by F. Ng, 439–453. New York: Marshall Cavendish.

Sasaki, S. 2002. *Rāmen-o ajiwai tsukusu*. Tokyo: Kobunsha.

Saura, B. 1998. "The Emergence of an Ethnic Millenarian Thinking and the Development of Nationalism in Tahiti." *Pacific Studies* 21 (4): 33–65.

———. 2001. "The Prophetic and Messianic Dimension of Pouvanaa a Oopa (1895–1977), the Father of Tahitian Nationalism." *Canadian Review of Studies in Nationalism* 28: 45–55.

——. 2008. *Tahiti Māʻohi: Culture, indentité, religion et nationalisme en Polynésie française.* Papeete: Au Vent des Iles.

Schiffrin, D. 1986. *Discourse Markers* (Studies in Interactional Sociolinguistics; 5). New York: Cambridge University Press.

Scott, B. 2005. *Re-imagining PNG: Culture, Democracy and Australia's Role.* New South Wales: Lowy Institute for International Policy.

Scott, C., and N. Tebay. 2005. "The West Papua Conflict and Its Consequences for the Island of New Guinea: Root Causes and the Campaign for Papua, Land of Peace." *Round Table* 94 (382): 599–612.

Scott, J. C. 1977. *The Moral Economy of the Peasant: Rebellion and Subsistence in Southeast Asia.* New Haven, CT: Yale University Press.

——. 1985. *Weapons of the Weak: Everyday Forms of Peasant Resistance.* New Haven, CT: Yale University Press.

——. 1990. *Domination and the Arts of Resistance: Hidden Transcripts.* New Haven, CT: Yale University Press.

Shah, A. 2010. "Poverty Facts and Stats." http://www.globalissues.org/article/26/poverty-facts-and-stats/.

Shankman, P. 1976. *Migration and Underdevelopment.* Boulder, CO: Westview Press.

Shapiro, J. 2001. *Mao's War against Nature: Politics and the Environment in Revolutionary China.* Cambridge: Cambridge University Press.

Shapiro, M. J. 2007. "The New Violent Cartography." *Security Dialogue* 38: 291–313.

Shore, B. 1982. *Salaʻilua, a Samoan Mystery.* New York: Columbia University Press.

——. 2005. "Reading Samoans through Tahitians." *Ethos* 33 (4): 487–492.

Sijapati-Basnett, B. 2009. *Social and Economic Impact of Introducing Telecommunications throughout Vanuatu.* Port Vila: Pacific Institute of Public Policy.

Silva, N. K. 2004. *Aloha Betrayed: Native Hawaiian Resistance to American Colonialism.* Durham, NC: Duke University Press.

Sinnott, M. J. 2004. *Toms and Dees: Transgender Identity and Female Same-Sex Relationships in Thailand.* Honolulu: University of Hawaiʻi Press.

Small, C. 1997. *Voyages: From Tongan Villages to American Suburbs.* Ithaca, NY: Cornell University Press.

Smith, L. T. 1999. *Decolonizing Methodologies: Research and Indigenous Peoples.* London: Zed Books.

Smith, N. 2010. "Remapping Area Knowledge: Beyond Global/Local." In *Remaking Area Studies: Teaching and Learning Across Asia and the Pacific,* edited by T. Wesley-Smith and J. Cross, 24–40. Honolulu: University of Hawaiʻi Press.

Spickard, P., J. L. Rondilla, and D. H. Wright, ed. 2002. *Pacific Diaspora: Island Peoples in the United States and across the Pacific.* Honolulu: University of Hawaiʻi Press.

Sponsel, L. E. 2012. *Spiritual Ecology: A Quiet Revolution*. Oxford: Praeger.

Steward, J. H. 1972. *Theory of Culture Change: The Methodology of Multilinear Evolution*. Ann Arbor, MI: University Microfilms.

Stocking, G. W. 1992. "The Boas Plan for the Study of American Indian Languages." In *The Ethnographer's Magic and Other Essays in the History of Anthropology*, 60–91. Madison: University of Wisconsin Press.

Strathern, M. 2005. *Kinship, Law and the Unexpected: Relatives Are Always a Surprise*. Cambridge: Cambridge University Press.

Stuart, K. 1999. "Introduction." *Asian Folklore Studies* 58: 1–3.

Sutton, D. E. 2007. "Tipping: An Anthropological Meditation." In *The Restaurants Book: Ethnographies of Where We Eat*, edited by D. Beriss and D. E. Sutton, 191–204. Oxford: Berg.

Tamahori, L. (director) & Scholes, R. (producer). 1994. *Once Were Warriors* (Motion picture). New Zealand: Fine Line Features; a Communicado film in association with the New Zealand Film Commission, Avalon Studios, and New Zealand on Air.

Tauli-Corpuz, V. 1994. *The Cordillera Women in the Struggle for Self-Determination, Change*. Baguio City: Cordillera Women's Education and Resource Center.

Taylor, J. P. 2007. *The Other Side: Ways of Being and Place in Vanuatu*. Honolulu: University of Hawai'i Press.

Tcherkézoff, S. 2000. "Are the *Matai* Out of Time? Tradition and Democracy: Contemporary Ambiguities and Historical Transformations of the Concept of Chief." In *Governance in Samoa*, edited by E. Huffer and A. So'o, 113–132. Canberra: Asia Pacific Press.

Teaiwa, K. M. 2004. "Multi-sited Methodologies: 'Homework' in Australia, Fiji, and Kiribati." In *Anthropologists in the Field: Cases in Participant Observation*, edited by L. Hume and J. Mulcock, 216–233. New York: Columbia University Press.

Tengan, T. P. K. 2005. "Unsettling Ethnography: Tales of an 'Ōiwi in the Anthropological Slot." *Anthropological Forum* 15 (3): 247–256.

———. 2008. *Native Men Remade: Gender and Nation in Contemporary Hawai'i*. Durham, NC: Duke University Press.

Tengan, T. P. K., T. O. Ka'ili, and R. T. Fonoti. 2010. "Genealogies: Articulating Indigenous Anthropology in/of Oceania." *Pacific Studies* 33 (2/3): 139–166.

Thomson, B. 1894. "The Fiery Furnace." In *South Sea Yarns*, 194–207. Papakura, NZ: R. McMillan.

Toganivalu, D. 1914. "The Fire-Walkers (A Vilavilairevo)." *Transactions of the Fijian Society*, translated and read by G. A. F. W. Beauclerc. March 9: 1–3.

Tomlinson, M. 2009. *In God's Image: The Metaculture of Fijian Christianity*. Berkeley: University of California Press.

Tonkinson, R. 1982. "National Identity and the Problem of *Kastom* in Vanuatu." *Mankind* 13 (4): 306–315.

Torres-Kitamura. 1993. "A Generation Lost?" *Fil-Am Courier,* October 1993: 6–7.

Trask, H. 1999. *From a Native Daughter: Colonialism and Sovereignty in Hawai'i,* rev. ed. Honolulu: University of Hawai'i Press.

Tsing, A. L. 2005. *Friction: An Ethnography of Global Connection.* Princeton, NJ: Princeton University Press.

Twemlow, S. W., and F. C. Sacco. 1998. "The Application of Traditional Martial Arts Practice and Theory to the Treatment of Violent Adolescents." *Adolescence* 33 (131): 505–518.

Tylor, E. 1871. *Primitive Culture.* London: Murray.

Underberg, N. M., and E. Zorn. 2013. *Digital Anthropology: Anthropology, Narrative, and New Media.* Austin: University of Texas Press.

United States Geological Survey (USGS). 2012. "Magnitude 9.0 Near the East Coast of Honshu, Japan." http://earthquake.usgs.gov/earthquakes/recent eqsww/Quakes/usc0001xgp.php#summary.

Uperesa, F. L. 2010. "A Different Weight: Tension and Promise in Indigenous Anthropology." *Journal of Pacific Studies* 33 (2/3): 280–300.

Uxin Ju documents. 1959–1972. Unpublished material in the author's field collection.

Vergara, B. M., Jr. 2008. *Pinoy Capital: The Filipino Nation in Daly City.* Philadelphia: Temple University Press.

Vineis, P., and R. Satolli. 2009. *I due dogmi: Oggettività Della Scienza e Integralismo Etico.* Milan: Feltrinelli.

Visweswaran, K. 1994. *Fictions of Feminist Ethnography.* Minneapolis: University of Minnesota Press.

Viveiros de Castro, E. 2009. "The Gift and the Given: Three Nano-Essays on Kinship and Magic." In *Kinship and Beyond: The Genealogical Model Reconsidered,* edited by S. C. Bamford and J. Leach, 237–268. New York: Berghahn Books.

Walker, S. M. 2000a. "La lettre de l'association Te Hiva Rereata." *La Dépêche de Tahiti,* August 13: 8.

———. 2000b. Radio interview, broadcast by Radio Fara, Tahiti (Fall 2000). Audio file in possession of the author, obtained from personal archives of Sunny Moana'ura Walker in May 2001.

Walsh, J. M. 2003. "Imagining the Marshalls: Chiefs, Tradition, and the State on the Fringe of US Empire." PhD diss., University of Hawai'i.

Weber, M. 1946. *From Max Weber: Essays in Sociology.* Edited by H. H. Gerth and C. Wright Mills. New York: Oxford University Press.

Weiner, A. 1992. *Inalienable Possessions: The Paradox of Keeping-While-Giving.* Berkeley: University of California Press.

West, P. 2006. *Conservation Is Our Government Now: The Politics of Ecology in Papua New Guinea.* Durham, NC: Duke University Press.

White, M. 2012. *Coffee Life in Japan.* Berkeley: University of California Press.

Whorf, B. L. 2000. "The Relation of Habitual Thought and Behavior to Language." In *Language, Thought and Reality: Selected Writings of Benjamin Lee Whorf,* edited by J. B. Carroll, 134–159. Cambridge, MA: Technology Press of Massachusetts Institute of Technology.

Williams, R. 1989. *The Politics of Modernism.* London and New York: Verso.

Winduo, S. 2000. "Unwriting Oceania: The Repositioning of the Pacific Writer Scholars within a Folk Narrative Space." *New Literary History* 31 (3): 599–613.

———. 2013. "Steven's Window." *National.* http://stevenswindow.blogspot.com/2013/05/publication-culture-at-upng-alive-em-tv.html

World Health Organization (WHO). 2011. *Global Status Report on Noncommunicable Diseases 2010.* Geneva.

Yamada, Toru. 2014. "Maritime Crossroads of Geopolitics in East Asia: A Reexamination of Historic Ocean Perspectives in Japan." *Education About Asia,* 19(2): 1–6 (online).

Yamanaka, L.-A. 1993. *Saturday Night at the Pahala Theatre.* Honolulu: Bamboo Ridge Press.

———. 1998. *Blu's Hanging.* New York: Farrar, Strauss and Giroux.

Yamashita, M. 2007. "Save La'au Point, Molokai." http://www.youtube.com/watch?v=ceQQAZvtyds&feature=youtube_gdata/.

———. 2008. "Molokai—Return to Pono." http://www.youtube.com/watch?v=KclJtYFawyw&feature=youtube_gdata_player.

Young, F. W. 2012a. "'I Hē Koe? Placing Rapa Nui." *Contemporary Pacific* 24 (1): 1–30.

———. 2012b. "Rapa Nui. Polynesia in Review: Issues and Events, 1 July 2010 to June 2011." *Contemporary Pacific* 24 (2): 190–199.

———. 2013. "Rapa Nui: Political Review of Polynesia July 2011–June 2012." *Contemporary Pacific* 25 (1): 172–183.

Zivin, G., N. R. Hassan, G. F. DePaula, D. A. Monti, C. Harlan, K. D. Hossain, and K. Patterson. 2001. "An Effective Approach to Violence Prevention: Traditional Martial Arts in Middle School." *Adolescence* 36 (143): 443–459.

LIST OF CONTRIBUTORS

Hokulani K. Aikau is Kanaka 'Ōiwi and an associate professor in the Department of Political Science at the University of Hawai'i-Mānoa. She received her PhD from the Department of American Studies at the University of Minnesota at Minneapolis.

Geoff Ashton is an assistant professor in the Department of Philosophy at the University of Colorado, Colorado Springs. He received his PhD from the Department of Philosophy at the University of Hawai'i-Mānoa.

Mary Tuti Baker is a PhD candidate in the Department of Political Science at the University of Hawai'i-Mānoa.

Keith Andrew Bettinger is a lecturer in Geography at Kapi'olani and Leeward Community Colleges in Hawai'i. He received his PhD from the Department of Geography at the University of Hawai'i-Mānoa.

C. Fred Blake is a professor in the Department of Anthropology at the University of Hawai'i-Mānoa. He received his PhD from the Department of Anthropology at the University of Illinois at Urbana-Champaign.

Margaret Barnhill Bodemer is a lecturer in Asian Studies and Cultural Anthropology at California State Polytechnic University in San Luis Obispo, California. She received her PhD from the Department of Anthropology at the University of Hawai'i-Mānoa.

Melisa Casumbal-Salazar is an assistant professor of Politics at Whitman College. She received her PhD from the Department of Political Science at the University of Hawai'i-Mānoa.

LeeRay M. Costa is a professor of Gender and Women's Studies and Anthropology at Hollins University. She received her PhD from the Department of Anthropology at the University of Hawai'i-Mānoa.

Gaia Cottino is an independent researcher based in Italy. She received her PhD from the Department of Anthropology at the Università La Sapienza di Roma, Italy. She completed graduate studies in the Department of Anthropology at the University of Hawai'i-Mānoa.

Lynette Hi'ilani Cruz is an assistant professor and Kupuna-in-Residence in the Department of Anthropology at Hawai'i Pacific University. She received her PhD from the Department of Anthropology at the University of Hawai'i-Mānoa.

Suzanne S. Finney is president of the Maritime Archaeology and History of the Hawaiian Islands Foundation (MAHHI). She received her PhD from the Department of Anthropology at the University of Hawai'i-Mānoa.

Satomi Fukutomi is on the adjunct faculty at the Center for International Studies at the University of St. Thomas in Houston, Texas. She received her PhD from the Department of Anthropology at the University of Hawai'i-Mānoa.

Joseph H. Genz is an assistant professor of Anthropology at the University of Hawai'i-Hilo. He earned his PhD from the Department of Anthropology at the University of Hawai'i-Mānoa.

Lorenz Gonschor is a Ph.D. candidate in the Department of Political Science at the University of Hawai'i-Mānoa.

Carl J. Hefner is the chair of the Social Sciences Division at Kapi'olani Community College. He received his PhD from the Department of Anthropology at the University of Hawai'i-Mānoa.

Lisa Humphrey is a researcher and writer at Cultural Surveys Hawai'i in Waimanalo. She earned her PhD from the Department of Anthropology at the University of Hawai'i-Mānoa.

Hong Jiang is an associate professor and chair of the Department of Geography at the University of Hawai'i-Mānoa. She received her PhD from the Department of Geography at Clark University.

Nahaku Kalei is a Nature Conservancy Marine Fellow. She received her BS in Biological Engineering from the University of Hawai'i-Mānoa.

Hirofumi Katsuno is an associate professor in the Department of Human Sciences at Osaka University of Economics, Japan. He received his PhD in Anthropology from the University of Hawai'i-Mānoa.

Roderick N. Labrador is an assistant professor of Ethnic Studies at the University of Hawai'i-Mānoa. He received his PhD from the Department of Anthropology at the University of California, Los Angeles.

Hyeon Ju Lee is an adjunct professor at the University of Kochi, Japan. She received her PhD from the Department of Anthropology at the University of Hawai'i-Mānoa.

Serge A. Marek is an assistant professor in the Department of Geography at Hawai'i Pacific University. He received his PhD from the Department of Geography at the University of Hawai'i-Mānoa.

Alexander Mawyer is an assistant professor at the Center for Pacific Islands Studies, University of Hawai'i-Mānoa. He received his MA in Pacific Islands Studies at the University of Hawai'i-Mānoa and his PhD from the Department of Anthropology at the University of Chicago.

Mary Mostafanezhad is an assistant professor in the Department of Geography at the University of Hawai'i-Mānoa. She earned her PhD from the Department of Anthropology at the University of Hawai'i-Mānoa.

Emerson Lopez Odango is a PhD candidate (ABD) in the Department of Linguistics at the University of Hawai'i-Mānoa and a Student Affiliate with the East-West Center.

Jonathan Y. Okamura is a professor in the Department of Ethnic Studies at the University of Hawai'i-Mānoa. He received his PhD in Social Anthropology from the University of London.

Guido Carlo Pigliasco is an adjunct assistant professor of Anthropology at the University of Hawai'i and a Foreign Law Consultant in the State of Hawai'i. He holds a JD from the University of Milan, Italy, and a PhD from the Department of Anthropology at the University of Hawai'i-Mānoa.

Pamela L. Runestad is a lecturer in Anthropology and Global Health at Elon University in North Carolina. She earned her PhD in Anthropology from the University of Hawai'i-Mānoa.

Jaida Kim Samudra is an independent researcher in medical anthropology and managing editor of the archaeological journal *Asian Perspectives*. She earned her PhD from the Department of Anthropology at the University of Hawai'i-Mānoa.

James Stiefvater is an adjunct professor in the Political Science Department at BYU-Hawai'i. He earned an MA from the Center for Pacific Islands Studies at the University of Hawai'i-Mānoa.

Ty P. Kāwika Tengan is chair of the Department of Ethnic Studies and associate professor of Anthropology at the University of Hawai'i-Mānoa. He received his PhD from the Department of Anthropology at the University of Hawai'i-Mānoa.

Fa'anofo Lisaclaire Uperesa is assistant professor of Ethnic Studies and Sociology at the University of Hawai'i-Mānoa. She received her PhD from the Department of Anthropology at Columbia University.

Ashley Vaughan is a lecturer in Anthropology at the University of Hawai'i-Mānoa. She received her PhD from the Department of Anthropology at the University of Hawai'i-Mānoa.

James Perez Viernes is a lecturer in the History and Chamorro Studies programs at the University of Guam. He graduated with an MA in Pacific Islands Studies from the University of Hawai'i-Mānoa, where he is currently a PhD candidate in the Department of History.

Geoffrey White is a professor in the Department of Anthropology at the University of Hawai'i-Mānoa. He received his PhD from the Department of Anthropology at the University of California, San Diego.

Steven Edmund Winduo is the director of Melanesian and Pacific Studies at the University of Papua New Guinea. He received his PhD in English and Cultural Studies from the University of Minnesota. In 2011, he visited the University of Hawai'i-Mānoa as the Arthur Lynn Andrews Chair in Pacific and Asian Studies.

Bradley Wong is a Nature Conservancy Program associate. He received his bachelor's degree in Marine Biology from California State University, Long Beach.

Naomi C. F. Yamada is a visiting assistant professor in the Department of Policy Studies at Chuo University in Tokyo. She earned her PhD in Anthropology at the University of Hawai'i-Mānoa.

Toru Yamada is an assistant professor at the University of Tsukuba. He received his PhD from the Department of Anthropology at the University of Hawai'i-Mānoa.

Christine R. Yano is a professor and chair of the Department of Anthropology at the University of Hawai'i-Mānoa. She received her PhD from the Department of Anthropology at the University of Hawai'i-Mānoa.

Forrest Wade Young is a lecturer in Anthropology and Pacific Island Studies at the University of Hawai'i-Mānoa. He received his PhD from the Department of Anthropology at the University of Hawai'i-Mānoa.

Index

Page numbers in boldface type refer to illustrations.

Production Notes for Finney | *At Home and in the Field*
Jacket and cover design by Julie Matsuo-Chun
Composition by Westchester Publishing Services, with display type
   in Christiana Medium and text type in Scala Pro.
Printing and binding by Maple Press
Printed on 60 lb. House White, 444 ppi.